AF328678

Foucault and Philosophy

Foucault and Philosophy

Edited by
Timothy O'Leary & Christopher Falzon

A John Wiley & Sons, Ltd., Publication

This edition first published 2010
© 2010 Blackwell Publishing Ltd

Blackwell Publishing was acquired by John Wiley & Sons in February 2007. Blackwell's publishing program has been merged with Wiley's global Scientific, Technical, and Medical business to form Wiley-Blackwell.

Registered Office
John Wiley & Sons Ltd, The Atrium, Southern Gate, Chichester, West Sussex, PO19 8SQ, United Kingdom

Editorial Offices
350 Main Street, Malden, MA 02148-5020, USA
9600 Garsington Road, Oxford, OX4 2DQ, UK
The Atrium, Southern Gate, Chichester, West Sussex, PO19 8SQ, UK

For details of our global editorial offices, for customer services, and for information about how to apply for permission to reuse the copyright material in this book please see our website at www.wiley.com/wiley-blackwell.

The right of Timothy O'Leary and Christopher Falzon to be identified as the authors of the editorial material in this work has been asserted in accordance with the UK Copyright, Designs and Patents Act 1988.

Library of Congress Cataloging-in-Publication Data

Foucault and philosophy/edited by Timothy O'Leary & Christopher Falzon.
   p.   cm.
   Includes bibliographical references and index.
   ISBN 978-1-4051-8960-6 (hardcover : alk. paper)
   1. Foucault, Michel, 1926–1984. I. O'Leary, Timothy, 1966– II. Falzon, Christopher, 1957–
   B2430.F724F6835 2010
   194–dc22

                                    2009033122

ISBN HB: 9781405189606

A catalogue record for this book is available from the British Library.

Set in 10.3/13pt Minion by SPI Publisher Services, Pondicherry, India
Printed in Malaysia

1   2010

Contents

List of Contributors   vii
Acknowledgments   x

Introduction: Foucault's Philosophy   1
Christopher Falzon & Timothy O'Leary

1   Foucault, Hegel, and Philosophy   17
Gary Gutting

2   "I am Simply a Nietzschean"   36
Hans Sluga

3   Foucault, Heidegger, and the History of Truth   60
Timothy Rayner

4   The Entanglement of Power and Validity:
Foucault and Critical Theory   78
Amy Allen

5   Foucault, Davidson, and Interpretation   99
C. G. Prado

6   The "Death of Man": Foucault and Anti-Humanism   118
Béatrice Han-Pile

7   Foucault's Theory of Knowledge   143
Barry Allen

8   Rethinking Experience with Foucault   162
Timothy O'Leary

9   Foucault, Queer Theory, and the Discourse of Desire   185
Jana Sawicki

 Contents

10 Foucault and Normative Political Philosophy 204
Paul Patton

11 Foucault, Philosopher of Dialogue 222
Christopher Falzon

Index 246

Contributors

Amy Allen is the Parents Distinguished Research Professor in the Humanities and Professor of Philosophy at Dartmouth College. She is the author of *The Power of Feminist Theory: Domination, Resistance, Solidarity* (2000) and *The Politics of Our Selves: Power, Autonomy, and Gender in Contemporary Critical Theory* (2007).

Barry Allen is Professor of Philosophy at McMaster University (Ontario, Canada). He is an associate editor of the interdisciplinary journal *Common Knowledge*, and author of *Truth in Philosophy* (1993), *Knowledge and Civilization* (2004), and *Artifice and Design: Art and Technology in Human Experience* (2008).

Christopher Falzon teaches philosophy at the University of Newcastle, Australia. He is the author of *Foucault and Social Dialogue* (1998), and *Philosophy Goes to the Movies* (2002 and 2007). He is also co-editing, with Jana Sawicki and Timothy O'Leary, *A Companion to Foucault* (Blackwell).

Gary Gutting teaches at the University of Notre Dame, where he holds the Notre Dame Endowed Chair in Philosophy. He is the author of six books: *Religious Belief and Religious Skepticism* (1982), *Michel Foucault's Archaeology of Scientific Reason* (1989), *Pragmatic Liberalism and the Critique of Modernity* (1999), *French Philosophy in the Twentieth Century* (2001), *Michel Foucault: A Very Short Introduction* (2005), and *What Philosophers Know: Case Studies in Recent Analytic Philosophy* (2009). He has co-authored or edited another six volumes.

Béatrice Han-Pile studied philosophy, classics, and literature at the École normale supérieure (Paris) before obtaining a PhD from the University of

Paris XII. She is now a philosophy professor at the University of Essex (UK) and the author of *Foucault's Critical Project: Between the Transcendental and the Historical* (2001). She has contributed to the *Cambridge Companion to Foucault* (2nd edn., 2005) and has written a number of journal articles and chapters in books on Foucault, Heidegger, Schopenhauer, and Nietzsche.

Timothy O'Leary teaches philosophy at the University of Hong Kong. He has published widely on Foucault, ethics, and the philosophy of literature. He has written *Foucault and the Art of Ethics* (2002 and 2006), and *Foucault and Fiction: The Experience Book* (2009). He is also editing, with Jana Sawicki and Christopher Falzon, *A Companion to Foucault* (Blackwell).

Paul Patton is Professor of Philosophy at The University of New South Wales in Sydney, Australia. He is the author of *Deleuze and the Political* (2000) and *Deleuzian Concepts: Philosophy, Colonization, Politics* (2009). He has published widely on the work of Foucault and related issues in political philosophy.

C. G. Prado, BA, MA (University of California, Berkeley), PhD (Queen's University), is Professor Emeritus of Philosophy at Queen's University, Kingston, Ontario. He is the author of ten books, the most recent being *Choosing to Die* (2008) and *Searle and Foucault on Truth* (2006), co-author of two, the most recent being *The Best Laid Plans* (2002), editor of three, the latest being *Foucault's Legacy* (2009), and author of more than 30 anthology and journal articles.

Timothy Rayner has taught philosophy at the University of Sydney and the University of New South Wales, Australia. He is the author of *Foucault's Heidegger: Philosophy and Transformative Experience* (2007).

Jana Sawicki is the Carl W. Vogt '58 Professor of Philosophy at Williams College. She is the author of *Disciplining Foucault: Feminism, Power and the Body* (1991) and many articles on Foucault, feminism, and queer theory. She is currently working on a collection of essays on the reception of Foucault by queer theorists and is co-editing *A Companion to Foucault* (Blackwell) with Timothy O'Leary and Christopher Falzon.

Hans Sluga is the William and Trudy Ausfahl Professor of Philosophy at the University of California at Berkeley. He is the author of *Gottlob*

Frege, on the origins of analytic philosophy (1980) and of *Heidegger's Crisis*, on German philosophy and National Socialism (1993). He has also edited four volumes on the philosophy of Frege and (together with David Stern) *The Cambridge Companion to Wittgenstein*. In addition, he is the author of essays on Frege, Wittgenstein, Heidegger, Foucault, and political philosophy.

Acknowledgments

The editors would like to thank Bill Herfel for his expert editorial assistance. Christopher Falzon would like to acknowledge a research grant in 2008 from the School of Humanities and Social Science at the University of Newcastle, Australia, which made this editorial support possible.

Introduction: Foucault's Philosophy

Christopher Falzon & Timothy O'Leary

There is a sense in which every philosopher both constructs and confronts the philosophical universe in which their work takes form and has its effect. Plato's thought unfolds within the gravitational pull of the Greek city-state, the wandering sophists, the agonistic relations between Athenian aristocrats, and the massive presence of Socrates. Deleuze, to take a contemporary example, creates his concepts and embarks on his lines of flight between thinkers such as Nietzsche and Spinoza, artists and writers including Bacon, Lawrence, and Melville, and contemporary phenomena such as psychoanalysis and consumer capitalism. If we can speak of "Foucault's philosophy," it is in this sense of attempting to sketch out the philosophical universe in which Foucault's work and thought unfolds. What are the philosophical reference points that structure his thought? What are the questions and problems to which he tries to respond? How does he link up his thought with the actual concerns and struggles of both himself and others?

The essays in this volume offer a series of answers to these questions, while this introduction attempts to give a preliminary overview of the terrain to be covered.

Philosophical Curiosity

Philosophers are, understandably, reluctant to give an account of the nature of philosophy itself, or to pin down either its sources or its goals in relation to long-standing human concerns. However, sooner or later, many do; none more famously, perhaps, than Aristotle who identified the experience of "wonder" or "amazement" (*to thaumazdein*) as the origin of the philosophical drive (Aristotle 1998: 9). Foucault is a thinker whose early career, at least, would not lead one to expect any such pronouncements on his part;

however, he too came in his last years to embrace a particular view of the sources of philosophical motivation, and it was a view that is, surprisingly, rather close to that of Aristotle. Close, but also, of course, significantly different. In the Preface to the second volume of his *History of Sexuality* (1984a), Foucault explains the series of revisions and reconceptualizations that had led to the eight-year gap between the first and second volumes of that history. Why would he have subjected himself to such labor, he asks? The reason, quite simply, was "curiosity" (ibid.: 8). Curiosity is a quality that has at times been seen as a vice, but it is one that Foucault admires, not so much because it attests to a simple desire to know, but because it shows a desire "to get free of oneself" (ibid.). Curiosity, in this sense, displays a certain attitude of care, both toward the world and toward oneself (1997: 325). In fact, the word itself is derived from the Latin *cura*, as in *cura sui, le souci de soi*, the care of self.[1]

Foucault's understanding of curiosity distinguishes itself from Aristotle's understanding of wonder, however, in the particularly modern, or modernist, inflection that he gives it. For Foucault, curiosity may indeed begin with a sense of the marvelous and the extraordinary, or rather with the marvelousness of the ordinary, but it is by no means confined to a subsequent disinterested pursuit of knowledge about the world. It is also motivated both by a desire to change that world and to bring into question the relation between knowledge, the world, and the knowing subject. Curiosity, on this account, evokes a "sharpened sense of reality" and a willingness to "look otherwise at the same things"; it conveys "a passion for seizing what is happening now and what is disappearing" (2000: 325, modified). And it is also associated for Foucault with the modern attitude toward the present that he first finds in Baudelaire: a valorization of the present which is "indissociable from a desperate eagerness to imagine it, to imagine it otherwise than it is, and to transform it not by destroying it but by grasping it in what it is" (1997: 311).

For Foucault, the other side of this curiosity, as we saw, is the way in which it also draws the knowing subject into question. There would be no point in pursuing knowledge, Foucault tells us, if it only resulted in a certain knowledgeableness, and not "in one way or another and to the extent possible, in the knower's straying afield of himself" (1984a: 8). And, in a curious echo of Aristotle's statement that wonder gave rise to philosophy "both now and at first," Foucault asserts that if philosophy is "still now what it was in times past," then its "living body" consists in the essay (1984a: 9, modified). An essay is not to be thought of as a form in which, for example, students reformulate knowledge that they have been given by their teachers; rather, it is to be seen as a "test that transforms oneself in the game of truth"; it is an "ascesis," which is to say, "an exercise of self, in thought" (1984a: 9, modified).

Philosophy, then, would be the practice of thought that tries to grasp the present in all its complexity and fragility, the practice that brings into question the subject's own entanglement in games of truth, and, finally, the practice through which one seeks to modify one's own relation both to truth and to a present that is, in complex ways, a product of those forms of truth. This conception of philosophy, however, is not something that was present in Foucault's thought from the very beginning. In fact, as we will see, for much of his life Foucault rejected the title "philosopher" and claimed that his work had little, or nothing, to do with philosophy.

A Philosophical Trajectory

In the course of his career, Foucault demonstrated a fondness for remaining elusive and unclassifiable. As he famously wrote in the *Archaeology of Knowledge*, "do not ask who I am and do not ask me to remain the same: leave it to our bureaucrats and our police to see that our papers are in order. At least spare us their morality when we write" (2002: 19). And in a late interview, he expressed satisfaction that he had been located in so many squares of the political checkerboard: "anarchist, leftist … nihilist … new liberal, and so on" (1997: 113). But, more importantly, Foucault was always eager to avoid being captured by his own theoretical identity – witness the changes in direction as he distances himself from his archaeology (especially from its structuralist tendencies) in favor of a genealogical approach, and then abandons the initial plan for the genealogy of modern sexuality in order to undertake his genealogy of ethics. His justification for this constant turning and changing is his belief that the point of writing a book is precisely no longer to think the same thing as before. What would be the point in writing a book, he asks, if it didn't allow the person who wrote it to establish "a strange and new relation with himself" (ibid.: 205).

This elusiveness applies especially to the status of Foucault's work vis-à-vis philosophy. In fact, there is enough prima facie evidence to raise the question of whether he can usefully be seen in these terms. After all, his education and early career were in psychology as much as in philosophy. One of his undergraduate degrees, for example, was in psychology; one of his first positions was as a tutor in psychology at the École Normale in Paris (1951); and his first full-time academic job was as Assistant Professor of Psychology at the University of Clermont-Ferrand (1960).[2] Furthermore, his earliest publications (from the mid-1950s to the mid-1960s) were on existential psychology, the history of madness and medicine, and the works of various avant-garde novelists and theorists. And, subsequently, most of the books he published in his lifetime were histories of one kind or another.

Throughout his early and middle periods, until at least the late 1970s, his attitude toward the discourse of philosophy, especially in its professional guise, was generally either hostile and dismissive or self-deprecating. Before he was appointed to the chair of philosophy at the Collège de France in 1970, for example, he had the title of the chair changed to "History of Systems of Thought." Looking back from a later period (1978), he reflects that despite his early training in the "great philosophical machines" of Hegelianism and phenomenology, he doesn't consider himself to be a philosopher, nor does he think his work either recommends a way of doing, or of not doing, philosophy (2000: 240–1). In that same year, in a talk given to the French Society of Philosophy, he self-deprecatingly refuses to enter into a detailed discussion of Kant's critical project before such an audience, "not being a philosopher myself, hardly being a critic" (1996: 387). And, despite a growing number of philosophical speaking engagements in the US (for example, the Howison Lectures in Philosophy at Berkeley in 1980), he was also just as likely to turn up in a department of French literature (Berkeley, 1975) or a department of religion (Vermont, 1982). At one of these lectures he takes the opportunity to deny that he ever was a structuralist and, perhaps in response to the audience present, adds "and I confess, with the appropriate chagrin, that I am not an analytic philosopher. Nobody is perfect" (1997: 176).

However, none of this should be taken at face value. In fact, Foucault's entire work can usefully be read as philosophical in a number of ways. First of all, throughout his career, he undertook the traditional philosophical task of questioning the taken-for-granted in our thought and action, though in a new way, through the use of history. In this way he was able to engage with key philosophical themes: the nature of knowledge, the multiple relations between truth, power, and the subject, and questions about finding new ways to live in the contemporary world. Foucault pursued these aims, not by trying to grasp the timeless essences of things behind the shifting forms of appearance, or the necessary truths in apparently contingent features, but by trying to grasp notions and practices in their historical development. Fundamentally, he was interested in the specifically modern philosophical question: what is there that is contingent and local in the apparently necessary and universal?

More specifically, Foucault's unwillingness to discuss Kant's critical project, that we saw above, should be seen in light of the fact that he had in fact published a translation of a text by Kant and had written an extensive commentary on it as part of his doctoral studies (2008b). Admittedly, Foucault's public discussions of Kant were all of relatively minor texts, yet there is no doubt something disingenuous in his claim to be unqualified for any such discussion. Two other philosophers whose work was crucial for the development of Foucault's own thought were Nietzsche and Heidegger, although once again his public discussions of them are either limited or non-existent. In the case of Nietzsche, as we will see below, Foucault was always willing to acknowledge a debt and an affinity. Not only did he publish two papers on Nietzsche, but he appropriates the term "genealogy" and alludes to Nietzsche also in the French subtitle to the first volume of the *History of Sexuality* – "The Will to Know." In the case of Heidegger, as we will also see, the situation is rather less clear; but he did make important statements in some late interviews to the effect that Heidegger's influence had been formative for his own intellectual development. At least in the period up to the early 1980s, the only other major philosopher whom Foucault acknowledged to be important to him, was Deleuze.

What we see, then, at least up to the late 1970s, is a thinker who has a basic disciplinary training in philosophy, but also in psychology; who is attracted at first to questions about the history of the human sciences; who later plunges into the concrete political arrangements and micro-physical power relations that shape and are shaped by these forms of knowledge; and who pursues these interests primarily through archival research, with an increasing attempt to explain the methodological under-pinnings of his approach to knowledge, power, and history. At this time, Foucault's intellectual work is carried out as much in archives and in organizations such as the Group for Information on Prisons, as it is in philosophy seminar rooms. His major concern seems to be to forge the tools that will be used by others in their various struggles against contemporary forms of power (1980: 145). To the extent that the label "philosopher" might apply to Foucault at this stage, then, we can say that he is a philosopher who is always seeking for ways of making philosophy "permeable" (1988a: 311), as a discipline, as a form of thought, and as an order of discourse. It is almost as if he is a philosopher *malgré lui*, despite himself. This attitude of reluctance seems to change, however, when Foucault's work entered what was to be its final phase – the genealogy of ethics, or the exploration of the relations between subjectivity and truth.

There are two clear signs of this shift: first, Foucault's engagement with the idea of "critique" and its Kantian heritage; and, second, his close re-reading of ancient Greek and Hellenistic philosophers from Plato to the Cynics and Stoics. This first of these signs shows itself in a series of texts from the late 1970s and early 1980s, while the second appears in the second and third volumes of *The History of Sexuality* and in the newly published lectures from the Collège de France.[3] When Foucault returns to Kant in his late work he does so once again through a relatively minor text: in this case, Kant's essay "What Is Enlightenment?" What Foucault identifies as being important in this text is the idea that philosophy in the modern era is called upon to question its own time, both with respect to how it is different from what came before and also with respect to the future effects of this difference. In fact, Foucault suggests that modern philosophy as a whole can be characterized as both the questioning of, and the deepening of, the critical thought that emerges with "Enlightenment." Seen in this context, Kant's three *Critiques* can be taken to be laying the groundwork, or writing the rulebook, for the enlightened use of reason. While Foucault later assented that his own work fits within this project of a Kantian "critical history of thought" (1998: 459), there is no doubt that he also goes beyond Kant; in particular, beyond Kant's idea that the task of philosophy is to set the legit-imate *limits* of reason. For Foucault, rather, the task of philosophy would be to explore, both theoretically and practically, the possibility of going beyond the limits that may seem to be unbreachable.

This extra-Kantian aspect of Foucault's reflection comprises two strands in these writings. First, in the essay we have been discussing, Foucault appeals to Baudelaire's sense of modernity in order to complete the picture he is drawing. For Baudelaire, according to Foucault, the attitude of moder-nity is one of paying a heightened attention to the present, but in such a way that one imagines it otherwise than it is; one wishes to transform it by, pre-cisely, grasping it in its specificity. In Foucault's hands, this becomes the idea of a "critical ontology of ourselves," or of the present, coupled with a practical testing of the possibility of surpassing those limits that our present imposes (1997: 319). This historicizing inversion of the Kantian reflection on the limits of thought and action cements a shift in his engagement with Kant, which had been largely hostile in *The Order of Things*, but becomes increasingly productive later on, especially with respect to this exploration of the nature of critique.

The second strand that helps Foucault to push Kant in this direction is the way he traces the descent of the modern critical attitude from a range of early modern movements that opposed particular forms of government. The modern critical attitude, he argues, emerged as a direct counter-move to the growth of "governmentalization" in early modern society. Hence, he draws a line connecting the thinkers of the Reformation and of the Enlightenment and gives them a motto that differs from Kant's *sapere aude*. For these early practitioners of critique, the demand is that they should not be governed: "not like that, not for that, not by them" (1996: 384). Their concern is to cultivate "the art of voluntary inservitude" and "reflective indocility" (ibid.: 386). When these strands are combined, Foucault has a way of situating his own multidisciplinary research within a philosophical tradition that stretches from Kant, through Hegel and Marx, to Nietzsche and the Frankfurt School. This is a tradition, embodying the critical attitude, for which the diagnosis of our present condition is inseparable from the search for the means to alter that condition.

The second element in Foucault's apparent return to philosophy is one that allows him to extend this line of descent right back to the Socratic practice of philosophy that inspired and partly formed the thought of the Stoics and the Cynics. In ancient and Hellenistic Greece, Foucault finds a form of philosophy that practices something like the critical attitude, except in relation to the self and the mode of life that the thinker pursues. Through the cultivation of a whole range of techniques of the self, these seekers after wisdom tried to bring their lives into some kind of relation with the truth, whether this was the Stoic idea of living in accord with nature, or the Cynic idea of living a true life devoid of sophistication and deception. In the later volumes of *The History of Sexuality*, Foucault investigates this form of thought in its classical (Platonist) and Hellenistic (Stoic) forms. While he is careful not to propose these forms of ethics as solutions for us today, he clearly does think that their particular mode of problematization can be an aid toward our own efforts to think otherwise.

In several lectures from the early 1980s and also in his courses at the Collège de France from that time, we see another element of this engagement. In these lectures, Foucault investigates the concept and the practice of *parrhesia* (truth-telling) as it develops from classical Greek thought up to the practices of the Cynics in the early Christian era and even on to the figure of the artist, the poet, the revolutionary, and the philosopher in the modern era.[4] Once again, one has to be careful in interpreting this work. Is Foucault offering us an exemplary model for the relation between, let us say, the practice of the intellectual, speech, and truth? To what extent does he admire the single-minded pursuit of the "true life" that the Cynics embodied, their cultivation of a "philosophical militancy" (2009: 261–3)? Is he recommending a contemporary cultivation of *parrhesia* (but, in what sense?) in order to forge a more effective critical practice? No doubt these questions will attract sustained consideration now that his late courses are being published, but for the moment we can at least note Foucault's "excitement" (ibid.: 163) while lecturing on the Cynics and we can speculate that they, along with the Socratic tradition that the Stoics also continued, offered Foucault a way of linking his own central concerns with those of an admittedly marginal but important stream of philosophy. It is hard to imagine, in fact, that in 1984 Foucault could have repeated his claim that his work was neither a way of doing philosophy nor a way of telling others not to do it. What we see here, instead, is a process in which Foucault gives himself a philosophical lineage and invites others to take part in the same collective practice. This is a practice that he once summarized, in terms which Diogenes may have admired, as one of "refusal, curiosity, innovation" (1988b).

Reading Foucault's Philosophy

The essays in this collection explore Foucault's work as a philosopher, from his earliest publications to the recently edited courses at the Collège de France, both in relation to his engagement with philosophers who were important to him, and in relation to a range of important themes and problems in philosophy that his work can be taken to have a bearing on. While the essays typically deal with both aspects, they may be roughly divided up in terms of whether the first or the second aspect is predominant.

In the first group, Gary Gutting, in "Foucault, Hegel and Philosophy," directly addresses the question of whether Foucault should be regarded as a philosopher through a consideration of his relation to Hegel (as interpreted by the great French Hegelian Jean Hyppolite, one of Foucault's teachers in the early 1950s). Foucault himself raised the question of whether one could escape from Hegel and still be a philosopher. Gutting situates Foucault as standing opposed to Hegel the philosopher of absolute knowledge, but as nonetheless seeking to invent a non-Hegelian approach to the historical understanding of our situation; hence the archaeological and then genealogical approaches that he develops. Ultimately, Gutting argues,

Foucault does not contribute to philosophy in the sense that has defined the discipline since Kant and Hegel: a body of theoretical knowledge about fundamental human questions. There is only an ethical and political commitment to a life of continual self-transformation, unhindered by unnecessary conceptual and social constraints; and Foucault's intellectual enterprise is a critique of disciplines and practices that restrict the freedom to transform ourselves. Nonetheless, Gutting concludes, he can be seen as a philosopher "in the ancient sense of someone who sought, if not to know, then to live the truth."

Foucault sought to break away not only from Hegelianism but also from the existentialism and phenomenology that dominated French intellectual life in the 1950s, inasmuch as both preserved an emphasis on the philosophy of the subject. And Nietzsche was an important influence on Foucault's thinking here, particularly through his genealogical concern to understand the processes beyond ourselves through which we become subjects, which inspired Foucault's own genealogical histories of the present. But this is not to say that Foucault simply follows Nietzsche. In "I am Simply a Nietzschean," Hans Sluga offers an account of Foucault's relationship with Nietzsche by examining their respective understandings of the genealogical project, especially in connection with the 1971 essay "Nietzsche, Genealogy, History." On Sluga's analysis, Foucault, in contrast to Nietzsche, seeks a situated and partial, rather than complete, history of morality, and he seeks to dispel the inevitability that attaches to our values, rather than wanting to destroy morality to clear the way for a new valuation. Moreover, Foucault pays little attention to Nietzsche's ultimately political motivation in writing a genealogy of morals, being primarily concerned at this stage to contrast genealogy with traditional history, and with his own earlier archaeological form of history. Eventually, Foucault does adopt Nietzsche's conception of genealogy as a political undertaking, as is evident in *Discipline and Punish* and beyond. But particularly as Foucault's attention shifts from power to ethics, from social relations to the individual subject, it becomes clear that his genealogy is being undertaken with a different politics in mind, one that aims to open up the possibility not of new forms of domination, but of freedom.

Unlike Nietzsche, about whom Foucault has a good deal to say, Heidegger is a figure about whom Foucault says very little, but nonetheless indicates in a late interview to have been an important influence. In "Foucault, Heidegger, and the History of Truth," Timothy Rayner addresses the question of what Foucault owes to Heidegger's philosophy and points to a fundamental connection between them. Both sought to understand how, in the modern age, subjectivity became the epistemological and metaphysical locus of truth, and both used historical argument to challenge the notion of constitutive subjectivity. Rayner argues that Heidegger's history of being can be seen as a story of how the subject emerged through the process of the forgetting of the truth of being. And while power is usually seen as the primary theme of works of the 1970s like *Discipline and Punish* and the first volume of *The History of Sexuality*, it is also possible to see Foucault here as seeking to develop an approach to the history of truth. If so, Foucault's later turn to a genealogy of ethics can be seen not as a break from that work, but as a return to the problematic of the history of truth. In his account of the later work, Rayner brings out some interesting convergences between Foucault's and Heidegger's histories of truth, while also showing that there is a key difference between them. Foucault's history of subjectivity and truth represents a decisive critique of one of the fundamental presuppositions of Heidegger's thought: the idea of the preontological understanding of being.

Foucault's engagement with his contemporary, Habermas, is characterized by some convergence and considerable difference. Both rejected the Kantian paradigm of critique grounded in the notion of a transcendental subject; but, for Habermas, Foucault reduces the subject to an effect of power in a way that undermines the very possibility of critique. In "The Entanglement of Power and Validity: Foucault and Critical Theory," Amy Allen goes beyond the usual defenses of Foucault against Habermasian criticisms – that these are based on a partial reading of Foucault – to articulate a Foucauldian critique of Habermas, especially the latter's central notion of autonomy. In the process, she identifies what is central to the disagreement between them – their divergent accounts of the subject and its relation to power. In Foucault's genealogy of the autonomous subject as emerging through subjection to disciplinary power, power and freedom exist in a permanent "agonism." Habermas is too confident in the power of autonomy, understood as rational critique, to break free of the power relations that have made us who we are. Finally, Allen draws out the importance of Foucauldian insights for critical theory. Habermas's recourse to a position beyond power from which to critically assess the validity of norms opens him to the charge of theoretical authoritarianism. Foucault, for whom validity is always entangled with power, offers a more historically self-conscious stance toward our normative standards, including ways in which our conception of autonomy may be connected to disciplinary subjection.

Critique is not abandoned but becomes a self-consciously contextualized project, where there is always more for critique to do.

Finally, despite Foucault's confession, with "appropriate chagrin," that he was not an analytic philosopher, this by no means precludes connections between his work and that of Anglo-American philosophy. In "Foucault, Davidson, and Interpretation," C. G. Prado reveals an unexpected convergence between Foucault and the "model analytic philosopher" Donald Davidson. Prado argues that Foucault's understanding of the formation of subjectivity complements Davidson's account of linguistic interpretation. He rejects the idea that Foucault, at least post-archaeology, is a linguistic idealist, arguing that his understanding of truth as a practice-bestowed rather than world-bestowed property has no anti-realist ontological implications which would put him at odds with the realist Davidson. He then argues that Foucault's account of subject formation provides in effect an account of the acquisition of what Davidson calls the "prior and passing theories," the expectations that language users have regarding what to make of other speakers' statements and what listeners should make of their own statements. On this Foucauldian reading, how language users interpret what is said to them, and how they intend what they say should be interpreted, are functions of their being the subjects they are made to be.

If Foucault can be seen to engage, explicitly, silently, or potentially, with various philosophers, his work also addresses a range of philosophical themes and problems in philosophy. For the remaining essays in this volume, it is this aspect of Foucualt's philosophical engagement that comes to the fore. In "The 'Death of Man': Foucault and Anti-Humanism," Béatrice Han-Pile returns to the debate between humanism and anti-humanism in which the Foucault of the 1960s, of *The Order of Things*, played a major role. Her aim is to provide an analysis of the theoretical underpinnings of this debate. She argues that neither Foucault's opponents (e.g. Sartre, Garaudy) nor Foucault himself had any decisive arguments to offer for or against humanism. His opponents misunderstood the nature of archaeology as a method, and the associated characterization of "man" as the "empirico-transcendental double" in *The Order of Things*; while Foucault's attacks on humanism also failed because he did not provide any explicit account of how the various humanist conceptions of man are related to "man" the empirico-transcendental double. At the same time, it is shown how the later Foucault moves toward a rapprochement with humanism to the extent that, rather than simply rejecting the notion of the subject, he reformulates it in a non-metaphysical, non-essentialist way;

and, rather than simply rejecting such humanist values as freedom or self-creation, he upholds them as ideals but seeks to construe them in non-metaphysical ways.

Along with the issue of the subject, the question of knowledge and its critique also remains high on the agenda for modern philosophy; and Foucault engages with the question of knowledge not only in his archaeological phase but throughout his career. In "Foucault's Theory of Knowledge," Barry Allen offers an analysis of Foucault's views on knowledge as they emerge in both the archaeological and the genealogical phases of his work. In the former, knowledge is identified with discursive practice governed by analyzable rules; and the primary notion of knowledge as *connaissance*, the grid of rules, is distinguished from *savoir*, the actual statements put into circulation. In the shift to genealogy, knowledge comes to be connected with practices of disciplinary power, such that what is acknowledged as true, or discredited as false, "lines up with the major lines of social power." Overall, Allen draws attention to Foucault's indifference to a "normative concept of knowledge," to distinguishing knowledge from "what is claimed, believed, or said to be known (what passes for knowledge)." He also draws attention to parallels between Foucault's views on knowledge and those of American Pragmatism. He argues that the earlier Pragmatists, James and Dewey, can agree with Foucault that knowledge and truth are instrumentalities of social power, while avoiding his refusal to acknowledge differences of value, since they take pains to reconstruct the normative understanding of knowledge and truth. In contrast, Rorty rejects a normative understanding of knowledge and provides a form of "postmodern Pragmatism" that is much closer to Foucault's position.

In Timothy O'Leary's "Rethinking Experience with Foucault," the focus turns to Foucault's contribution to a philosophy of experience, as well as a consideration of the changes that the notion undergoes in Foucault's own thinking. Foucault's archaeological and genealogical approaches can be seen as ways of distancing himself from phenomenology's prioritization of the subject as a giver of meaning and foundation of experience. And with this, the notion of experience, present in an under-theorized form in Foucault's early *History of Madness*, all but disappears from his work, from *The Order of Things* to the first volume of *The History of Sexuality*. However O'Leary argues that in this phase Foucault lays the groundwork for a more sophisticated account of "lived experience" than is available through phenomenology, an account that comes to the fore in the late 1970s and is evident in the later volumes of *The History of Sexuality*.

In this account, the conscious subject loses primacy in the constitution of experience, which is understood to be made possible by larger epistemic, social, political, and ethical structures. At the same time, Foucault is also shown to be concerned with the historical transformations that our experiences undergo, through deliberate intervention in the form of experimental, critical practices. Overall, it is argued that Foucault's work, almost in its entirety, can be read as a contribution to a fully historicized philosophy of experience, in which experience is seen to have a history subject both to long-term modifications and to individual changes that arise through deliberate interventions.

In "Foucault, Queer Theory, and the Discourse of Desire," Jana Sawicki considers Foucault's contribution to a politics of transformation. She examines the later Foucault's genealogy of ourselves as desiring subjects, particularly in connection with the homosexual perspective, and argues that one of Foucault's aims is to transform the experience of being homosexual. In particular, Foucault turns to pleasure as a potential source of creative and open-ended processes of self-transformation. In so doing, he looks beyond identity politics and the demand for recognition, toward the project of creating new forms of sexual subjectivity, and thereby anticipates queer theory and its anti-identity politics. At the same time Sawicki questions efforts by queer theorists (e.g. Butler, Bersani) to explain Foucault's account of resistant pleasures within a psychoanalytic framework. These accounts rely on a model of desire that Foucault wanted to problematize because of its entanglement with the modern regime of sexual normalization through which individuals are integrated into society. Sawicki argues that, rather than appealing to psychoanalytic theory to explain the dynamics of power and pleasure, Foucault appropriated key concepts within psychoanalytic theory, especially the notion of pleasure, in order to "bend them to a new interpretive will." The particular target of his critique of the modern regime of sexuality was the idea that pleasures are to be tied to a deep causal principle discoverable within us called "sex," which underpins notions of normal and abnormal sexuality. The later volumes of *The History of Sexuality* were partly inspired by the prospect of unearthing alternate practices and discourses of bodily pleasure that might serve as a resource for those struggling against the modern regime of sexuality. They point toward the possibility of a different sexual ethics, concerned not with the scientific or moral truth about sexual desire, but with the cultivation of new forms of pleasurable experience that might be less bound up with processes of normalization.

Political philosophy is the focus of Paul Patton's "Foucault and Normative Political Philosophy," which explores the relationship of Foucault's genealogical approach to normative political philosophy through a consideration of his recently published lecture series *The Birth of Biopolitics*. Patton makes use of Rawls's political liberalism, with its strong normative focus on an ideal of public reason, as a framework to locate Foucault's analysis of neoliberal governmentality. Against the view that Foucault's descriptive analyses have no connection with normative issues, Patton argues that Foucault's studies of forms of governmental reason supplement Rawls's by providing an account of the nature, purposes, and methods of government, which Rawls neglects, and thus contributes to an historical understanding of contemporary political normativity. His analyses of liberal and neo-liberal governmentality enlarge our understanding of the discursive and normative frameworks within which much contemporary sovereign power is exercised. Moreover, he points to the manner in which resistance to particular ways of being governed is justified by recourse to elements of existing forms of governmental reason. Finally, because discourses about the nature, functions, and limits of government on occasion raise questions about the justification of political power and the acceptable limits to its exercise, normative questions about the legitimacy and limits of sovereign power arise in the course of Foucault's lectures.

Finally, Christopher Falzon considers another potential engagement on the part of Foucault. Although he hardly ever uses the term, Falzon considers how Foucault might be read as contributing to a "philosophy of dialogue," to a dialogical conception of social relations, both as a way of situating his notions of freedom and critique, and as a means of differentiating his position from the radical, individualistic subjectivism of Sartre, and from Habermas's collective rational discourse. Against the view that Foucault's rejection of a foundational subject capable of normatively grounding forms of thinking and practice leads only to a quasi-Sartrean notion of freedom as unconstrained, arbitrary autonomy, Falzon argues that Foucault can be read as turning to a fundamentally dialogical conception of the subject as both historically shaped, conditioned by circumstance, and influencing its circumstances in turn. It is in terms of this dialogue that the emergence and transformation of particular social forms, and their accompanying norms, can be understood. And against the view that Foucault's dialogue lacks the substance of Habermas's ideal vision of collective determination through unconstrained rational discourse, it is argued that Foucault offers a more concrete conception of dialogue as the encounters and struggles of finite human beings, constitutive of the social field. In this context, freedom is the resistance that drives dialogue, and the critique that gives impetus to the work of freedom is a means of facilitating that dialogue.

Overall, the Foucault who was motivated by a philosophical curiosity that drove him to get free of himself, who continually sought to avoid being captured by his own theoretical identity, and who for a long time refused the label of philosopher itself, can be seen to have been playing the philosophical game throughout his career. He is constantly engaged in a dialogue with the philosophers who were important to him, over a range of significant philosophical themes, from questions of ethics, epistemology, political normativity, and social critique, to the politics of sex and desire, and the transformative capacity of philosophy itself. In reflecting on these engagements, the essays in this volume show the relevance of Foucault's work to central concerns of philosophy – in both the "continental" and the "analytic" traditions.

Notes

1   See Foucault 1984b. The English title of this volume, *The Care of the Self* [*Le souci de soi*] is misleading; a more accurate rendition would be, "The Care of Self."
2   We are drawing on the extremely detailed "Chronologie" (Foucault 1994: 13–64) written by Daniel Defert. It is, unfortunately, untranslated.
3   For the discussions of "critique," see, for example, Foucault 1996, 2008a (lecture of Jan. 5). For the discussions of ancient philosophy, see 1984a, 1984b, 2008a, 2009.
4   See, especially, Foucault 2001, 2008a, 2009.

References

Aristotle (1998) *The Metaphysics*, trans. H. Lawson-Tancred. London: Penguin Books.

Foucault, M. (1980) *Power/Knowledge: Selected Interviews and Other Writings 1972–1977*, ed. C. Gordon. New York: Pantheon Books.

Foucault, M. (1984a) *The History of Sexuality*, vol. 2: *The Use of Pleasure*, trans. R. Hurley. Harmondsworth: Penguin Books, 1990.

Foucault, M. (1984b) *The History of Sexuality*, vol. 3: *The Care of the Self*, trans. R. Hurley. Harmondsworth: Penguin Books, 1990. [*Histoire de la sexualité: 3, Le souci de soi*. Paris: Éditions Gallimard, 1984.]

Foucault, M. (1988a) "The Functions of Literature." In L. Kritzman (ed.), *Politics, Philosophy, Culture*. London: Routledge.

Foucault, M. (1988b) "An Interview With Michel Foucault" (conducted by Michael Bess, San Francisco, November 3, 1980). *History of the Present* 4 (spring): 1–2, 11–13.

Foucault, M. (1994) *Dits et écrits 1954–1988*, vol. 1: *1954–1969*, ed. D. Defert and F. Ewald. Paris: Éditions Gallimard.

Foucault, M. (1996) "What is critique?" In J. Schmidt, (ed.), *What Is Enlightenment? Eighteenth-Century Answers and Twentieth-Century Questions*, trans. K. Geiman. Berkeley: University of California Press (pp. 382–98).

Foucault, M. (1997) *Essential Works of Foucault, 1945–1984*, vol. 1: *Ethics: Subjectivity and Truth*, ed. P. Rabinow. New York: The New Press.

Foucault, M. (1998) *Essential Works of Foucault, 1945–1984*, vol. 2: *Aesthetics, Method, and Epistemology*, ed. J. Faubion. New York: The New Press.

Foucault, M. (2000) *Essential Works of Foucault, 1945–1984*, vol. 3: *Power*, ed. C. Gordon. New York: The New Press.

Foucault, M. (2001) *Fearless Speech*, ed. J. Pearson. New York: Semiotext(e).

Foucault, M. (2002) *The Archaeology of Knowledge*, trans. A. Sheridan. London: Routledge.

Foucault, M. (2008a) *Le Gouvernement de soi et des autres; Cours au Collège de France, 1982–1983*, ed. F. Gros. Paris: Gallimard/Seuil.

Foucault, M. (2008b) *Introduction to Kant's Anthropology*, trans. R. Nigro and K. Briggs. New York: Semiotext(e).

Foucault, M. (2009) *Le Courage de la vérité; Cours au Collège de France, 1983–1984*, ed. F. Gros. Paris: Gallimard/Seuil.

1

Foucault, Hegel, and Philosophy

Gary Gutting

Was Foucault a philosopher? Bureaucratically, most certainly: he had advanced degrees in the subject up to the highest level, the *doctorat d'état*, and was a professor in several philosophy departments. But we know how little Foucault cared for what bureaucrats think, and he himself was ambivalent about his philosophical identity. In 1978, he said, "I don't regard myself as a philosopher. What I do is neither a way of doing philosophy nor a way of discouraging others from doing philosophy" (2000: 240–1). But in 1984 he said that his writings "are the record of a long and tentative … philosophical exercise" (1985: 9). An interesting answer to questions about whether X is a philosopher requires a relevant specific context, something most readily found through a paradigm example of a philosopher. For our modern age, Kant is an obvious choice, and Foucault's much discussed essay on Kant's "What Is Enlightenment?" provides a good opening for discussions of what might be his philosophical project (Gutting 2005b). Nonetheless, as I hope to show, Foucault's encounter with Hegel is even more significant for understanding his relation to philosophy. I shall begin with some background on Hegel's place in twentieth-century French philosophy.

The French warmed to Hegel very slowly, despite a number of attempts from the early nineteenth century on to import his thought. In particular, the neo-Kantianism that dominated the French university from the Franco-Prussian War until just before World War II had a strong antipathy to absolute idealism. The founder of the neo-Kantian school, Jules Lachelier, is said to have told his students: "There'll be no Hegel here as long as I'm around" (Sartre 1978: 25). This began to change with the publication of *Le Malheur de conscience dans la philosophie de Hegel* (Wahl 1929). Jean Wahl taught history of philosophy at the Sorbonne from 1927 to 1967. His books on Hegel and Kierkegaard were an important influence on the development of existentialism (Sartre also particularly mentions *Vers le concret* (Wahl 1932), which, however, oddly centered on William James, Alfred North Whitehead, and Gabriel Marcel – although there were frequent references in the footnotes to Heidegger). Later, Wahl worked closely with Foucault, Derrida, and Deleuze and was a good friend of Levinas. Jean Hyppolite's role came later, but was even more important. He became professor in the history of philosophy at the Sorbonne in 1949 and was also, from 1954, director of the École normale supérieure. Hyppolite held both positions until 1963 (when he was elected to the Collège de France), teaching influential courses on the history of philosophy (especially Hegel) and directing many theses, including those of Althusser, Foucault, Derrida, and Deleuze.

Wahl approached Hegel through the famous chapter in the *Phenomenology of Spirit* on the "unhappy consciousness." In Hegel's presentation, this chapter corresponds to just one stage in the dialectical development of spirit, the stage that Hegel calls "the Alienated Soul which is the consciousness of self as a divided nature, a doubled and merely contradictory being" (#207). The division is that between the contingent, multiple and changeable, self of my experience and the essential, simple and unchanging, self that I know I must be. On the one hand, this unhappy consciousness is the higher truth implicit in the preceding stage of skepticism, in which the doubting self unreflectively accepts the contradiction between its explicit effort to question everything and its implicit acceptance of truths essential for its life in the world. The "doubling" of the unhappy consciousness is its reflective awareness of both the explicit, contingent doubting self and the implicit, essential self that escaped genuine doubt. On the other hand, at the stage of unhappy consciousness, spirit continues to see the essential self as outside of its own contingent being in the world, thinking of it as an unattainable (though deeply desired) end (e.g., the transcendent God of Christianity). At the next stage, that of Reason, spirit realizes that the unhappy separation of its contingency from essential reality is an illusion: spirit itself *is* the essential nature from which it seemed to be separated. This, for Hegel, is the first stage of idealism, where the spirit begins to realize its identity with the essential, absolute truth.

Wahl, however, suggests that the unhappy consciousness, which Hegel presents as just one stage of spirit's development, can in fact be taken as the condition of consciousness at every stage of the dialectic short of the final synthesis in the Absolute's self-knowledge. At each point, there is a lived division between what spirit experiences itself as being and an apparently unattainable other that it aspires to be. From this standpoint, unhappy consciousness becomes a basis for interpreting the whole of the *Phenomenology*. Given such an interpretation, Wahl is led to what came to be called an "anthropological reading" of Hegel. Hegel's description of the unhappy consciousness is taken as corresponding to the quintessential human experience, as, for example, embodied in the great Greek and Shakespearean tragedies that we see as the fullest expression of our lived reality. Human experience, then, becomes the privileged model for the life of Hegel's spirit. The result, as Wahl puts it, is a "pantragicist" interpretation of Hegel, which extends the tragic vision of human life to Being itself.

Apart from its (debatable) merits as Hegel interpretation, the beauty of Wahl's book was that it showed how even philosophers who had no sympathy with Hegel's general approach or final conclusions could extract an attractive core from his system. Whether or not you accepted the dialectical method or the absolute idealism to which Hegel thought it led, you could appreciate the power of applying the method to the special case of human consciousness. Even if relentless dialectical self-negation is vapid as an account of nature or implausible as an account of history, it rings true of the endlessly self-reflective and self-questing of our lived experience. Whatever else Hegel achieved, he honed a language well suited – precisely because of its continual self-conflict – to describe the complex torsions of consciousness.

Wahl's approach also had the advantage of allowing French philosophers to assimilate Hegel's phenomenology – construed as the careful description of concrete experience – to that practiced by Husserl and also by Heidegger in *Being and Time*. (The last two were closely connected, because the Husserl imported into France – e.g., by Koyré and Levinas – was read through Heideggerian lenses.) Add the vocabulary of Hegelian unhappy consciousness to a Heideggerized Husserlian phenomenology and you have the means to carry out Sartre's ontology of freedom. For example, the key formulation that *human consciousness is not what it is and is what it is not* came to Sartre from Hegel through Wahl.

Although Wahl's strategy for appropriating Hegel fit perfectly with the project of existential phenomenology, it lost its charm when, in the wake of structuralism, the French turned away from subjectivity and lived experience as royal road to philosophy. But the new "death-of-man" orientation was well served by the reading of Hegel put forward by Hyppolite.

In the very beginning of the chapter on "The Unhappy Consciousness" in his magnum opus, *The Genesis and Structure of Hegel's Phenomenology of Spirit*, Hyppolite (1974: 190) acknowledges the validity of Wahl's interpretation, saying that "unhappy consciousness is the fundamental theme of the

Phenomenology. Consciousness, as such, is in principle always unhappy consciousness." But he goes on to point out that "nonetheless unhappy consciousness, in the strict sense of the term, is the result of the development of self-consciousness" (ibid.), thus implicitly distinguishing Wahl's broad sense of "unhappy consciousness" from the narrow sense Hegel has in mind in his chapter explicitly on the topic, which treats unhappy consciousness as due simply to reflection on the specific form of self-consciousness that makes explicit the contradiction of skepticism. Wahl, he implies, is right because "this reflection implies a split with life, a separation so radical that consciousness of it is consciousness of the unhappiness of all reflection" (ibid.). But Hyppolite restricts his own detailed discussion to Hegel's narrow sense.

Later in his chapter, Hyppolite alludes to the use made of Wahl's interpretation by the existentialists. He points out that in Hegel's idealism there is eventually a synthesis whereby the division of the unhappy consciousness is overcome and spirit achieves an "objectivity that is no longer the pure and simple in-itself; it has become the in-itself for-itself or the for-itself in-itself." The result is "a substance that is at the same time subject, a substance that poses itself as what it is" (ibid.: 204). Hyppolite then notes that "most contemporary thinkers deny the possibility of such a synthesis of the in-itself and the for-itself, and it is precisely on this ground that they criticize Hegel's system as a system" (ibid.). Instead:

> [T]hey generally prefer what Hegel calls "unhappy consciousness" to what he calls "spirit." They take up Hegel's description of self-certainty which fails to be in-itself; but they abandon Hegel when, according to him, specific self-consciousness – subjectivity – becomes the universal self-consciousness – thingness – a movement through which being is posed as subject and subject is posed as being.

In other words, "they accept Hegel's phenomenology but reject his ontology" (ibid.: 204–5). Hyppolite diplomatically says that his brief here is not to debate this issue, but simply "to elucidate as clearly as possible the endeavor of the *Phenomenology*." In this regard, he concludes, "there can be no doubt about the meaning of the dialectic of unhappy consciousness. As Hegel put it explicitly: 'Self-consciousness that reaches its fulfillment in the figure of unhappy consciousness is only the torment of spirit struggling to rise again to an objective, but failing to reach it'" (ibid.: 205). Hyppolite at least makes it entirely clear that the existentialist reading is not Hegel's own.

Hyppolite's later book on Hegel, *Logic and Existence* (1952), moves more decisively away from the existentialists' anthropological reading and gives central place to language rather than to human consciousness. He begins with the idea that there are aspects of being that are ineffable and so not accessible to knowledge but only to some sort of non-cognitive apprehension. The ineffable might take the form of an immediate sensation "beneath" knowledge, which Hegel discusses at the beginning of the *Phenomenology*, or, at the other extreme, a faith in an absolute that transcends knowledge, which Hegel discusses in his early critique of Jacobi (in *Faith and Knowledge*). As Hyppolite emphasizes, the existence of an ineffable contradicts Hegel's fundamental assertion that knowledge is absolute; that is, complete and all-encompassing.

To appreciate this point, Hyppolite briefly recalls some basic features of Hegel's project in the *Phenomenology*. In that book, Hegel tries to demonstrate through a detailed analysis of various sorts (stages) of experience that all being is pervaded by conceptual structures that make it exhaustively knowable. Of course, the subject that has this knowledge is not the finite human consciousness as we experience it in everyday life but rather the spirit that the *Phenomenology* ultimately reveals as identical with being itself, which thus turns out to be its own self-knowledge. But the project of the *Phenomenology* is to examine successive forms of finite human experience, starting with the immediate certainty of our sensations and moving through perception of physical objects, the understanding achieved by experimental and theoretical science, etc., to the highest cultural forms of experience (art, religion). For each stage of experience, Hegel develops arguments purporting to show that the stage contains contradictions, resulting from the fact that the knowledge it achieves leaves out something that appears to be essentially unknowable. The process of working through these contradictions is what Hegel calls "dialectic."

For example, the certainty of sensation derives from what seems to be the sheer immediacy of the sensory experience; that is, the experience is apparently not "mediated" by interpretive concepts, which would open up the possibility of our misunderstanding the experience's content. We are, we think, certain because we are in direct contact with a unique object (a "this") in its full concrete singularity. But, Hegel argues, the exclusion (in the name of certainty) of conceptual content is inconsistent with the singularity of the "this" we are experiencing. For if there is no conceptual content in our experience, there is nothing to distinguish the "this" from any other concrete "this" of which we might have a sensation. As a result, the "this," which seemed to apply to a unique singularity, applies universally to all possible sensations. But this result contradicts the claim that we are in direct contact with a unique object and thereby undermines the certainty of the experience. Later stages of consciousness can be analyzed in a parallel way. One that Hyppolite (1997: 16) discusses (##360–3) is illustrated by an episode from Goethe's *Faust*, in which "consciousness, weary of the universality of knowledge and of the burden of mediation, … claims to back completely to ineffable pleasure." Another is that corresponding to the development of philosophical empiricism (#558).

After working through many successive stages of experience in this way, Hegel eventually reaches the stage of "absolute knowledge"; that is, an experience that encompasses unlimited knowledge of all being. Each successive stage resolves the contradictions of the preceding stage by reconciling ("sublating") them under a higher, synthesizing concept. For example, the stage of unhappy consciousness, discussed above, resolves the contradiction between the doubt and the certainty of skeptical consciousness by ascribing the doubts to a finite self and the certainty to an infinite self from which the finite self is separated. The final stage, the experience of absolute knowledge, effects a total synthesis, a total reconciliation, of the contradictions of all the preceding stages. The subject of this experience is, as we noted above, not our ordinary human consciousness but "absolute spirit," the totality of all being existing as the historical process of its knowledge of itself. Since absolute spirit contains literally everything in its total self-knowledge, there is no ineffable that would escape its final conceptual synthesis.

So far, we have spoken of knowledge as knowledge of being. Such knowledge is universal, which means that, in particular, "it sublates and absorbs all the consciousnesses of singular selves" (Hyppolite 1997: 10). On Hyppolite's reading of Hegel, this implies "the possibility of a universal recognition, of an intelligible discourse which is simultaneously this 'I' and all 'I's.'" In other words, "language … is the universal instrument of mutual recognition" (ibid.). It follows that "knowledge … is not only knowledge of being, it is also what makes the instituted community of consciousnesses possible," which means that knowledge is essentially linguistic, since language is the instrument of communication. Nor is language present only in the final synthesis that is absolute spirit. Each stage of Hegel's dialectic can be understood as a process of dialogue ("originally, what does the word dialectic mean, if not the art of discussion and dialogue?"). "Human life is always language, sense, without which human life loses its character and returns to animal life." At any stage, "dialectical discourse could be interrupted, and skepticism [about the conceptual synthesis that moves the dialectic forward] is in effect always possible." This happens when consciousness "rejects language and discourse and claims to reach an ineffable absolute." But such a claim either "says the opposite of what it intends [by trying to say anything at all], and [then] it is language which is right"; or else, if a consciousness "stubbornly renounces language, this consciousness can only get lost, dissolved." What is supposed to be the ineffable is merely "the abstraction of nothingness" (ibid.: 11).

Granted that Hegel has established that language is the engine of his dialectic, the "*Dasein* [*l'être-là*] of spirit" (ibid.: 19), the next question is just how to understand language in this sense. Hyppolite rejects the "humanistic" interpretation (which is just a variation on the anthropological interpretation in terms of lived experience). Even "in the *Phenomenology*, Hegel does not say man, but self-consciousness. The modern interpreters who have immediately translated this term by man have somewhat falsified Hegel's thought." Hyppolite agrees that, for Hegel, "the Logos appears in the human knowledge that interprets and says itself." But he emphasizes that, nonetheless, "man is only the intersection of this knowledge and this sense. Man is consciousness and self-consciousness, but consciousness and self-consciousness are not man." We need to understand "that Hegel's philosophy results at least as much in a speculative logic as in a philosophy of history" (ibid.: 20).[1] Correspondingly, the language that drives the dialectic is not that of ordinary "natural" human speech; it is, rather, "the authentic language of being" (ibid.: 26). Nonetheless, natural human language is not separate from the "language of being," any more than finite human consciousness is separate from absolute spirit. According to Hegel, spirit is not a transcendent reality, existing outside human history; on the contrary, it is ultimately identical with that history. Accordingly, as Hyppolite puts it, the language of being exists "within natural language," even though it is not the same as the merely human language spoken in any particular stage, short of absolute knowledge, of Hegel's phenomenology of consciousness. What we need to understand, however, is "how is this language, which is no longer that of anyone, which is being's universal self-consciousness, to be distinguished from human, all-too-human language? In other words how does the passage from Phenomenology to absolute Knowledge work?" (ibid.: 26–7). This, Hyppolite tells us, "is the Hegelian question par excellence" (ibid.: 27).

Even at the end of Hyppolite's detailed reflection on this question, the answer is not entirely clear. What is clear is that "Hegel believed himself able to comprehend human reflection in the light of absolute knowledge," and Hyppolite allows that "the principle of this comprehension is contained in the meaning of Hegelian ontology." In other words, given Hegelian dialectic, we are able to understand how finite human existence is included (sublated) into the final synthesis of spirit's absolute knowledge. But Hegel also believed that he could "exhibit human consciousness's becoming-absolute-knowledge, as if this becoming were a history"; that is, an occurrence within the temporal framework of human history. If this were not the case, how could we, who exist in human history, move to the level of absolute knowledge? Hyppolite (ibid.: 189) agrees that human history "is the place of this passage" of human consciousness to absolute knowledge, but he notes that "this passage is not itself a *historical fact.*" This is because, for Hegel, although absolute knowledge does not exist outside of the historical world (the historical world is the only world), there is still a priority of the absolute over history: "The Logos [absolute knowledge] is absolute genesis, and time is the image of this mediation, not the reverse" (ibid.: 188). But the passage of human consciousness to absolute knowledge is precisely the genesis of absolute knowledge, so if this passage were an event of human history, time would be the ultimate source of absolute knowledge. Hegel seems to have no answer to this final question about how we reach absolute knowledge.

The young French philosophers, including Foucault, who studied Hegel with Hyppolite were not concerned with saving the self-consistency of the Hegelian system. Like their existentialist predecessors, they found no plausibility or even charm in the idea of absolute knowledge and, indeed, insisted on giving priority to the finite world of human existence. But, again like the existentialists, they found Hegel's vocabulary of dialectical negation a perspicuous medium for philosophical reflection, particularly in fact for exploring the differences ("contradictions") that remain irreducible given the failure of absolute knowledge. On the other hand, they rejected the existentialists' prioritization of human consciousness and accordingly found attractive Hegel's emphasis (at least in Hyppolite's interpretation) on language, which they could use to de-center lived experience. Indeed, they thought they could use dialectical arguments à la Hegel to refute existentialist claims about the absolute position of human consciousness. Such arguments could, moreover, show that consciousness existed only in an ontological field of linguistic structures, which themselves had to be understood in terms of broadly Hegelian differences. The result was a domain of investigation that occupied, to adapt a phrase of Leonard Lawler's (2003), the Hyppolitean middle: a turbulent space delimited by the two unacceptable resting points of existential phenomenology and Hegelian absolute knowledge. It is this domain that, for the young Foucault, would have defined his possibilities as a philosopher.

This focus on the Hyppolitean middle reflects a long-standing concern of French philosophy with the tension between the concrete experience of the lifeworld and the universal concepts of rational thought. Alain Badiou (2005), for example, has recently emphasized the role of this tension in French thought at least from the days of Bergson and Brunschvicg (with roots as far back as Descartes) and, in particular, proposed reading the story of French philosophy since 1940 as an effort to combine a philosophy of concrete life with a philosophy of the abstract concept.[2] After about 1960, younger philosophers who had found existentialist reductions of Hegel to the endless dialectic of unhappy consciousness philosophically inadequate (and likewise, as the French always had, rejected a culmination of dialectic in absolute knowledge) were naturally drawn to a rethinking of the role of the concept (rational structure) in Hegelian terms.

In 1969, in his eulogy for Hyppolite at the École normale, Foucault formulates the problem in terms of the fundamental question Hyppolite posed for Hegel: how to unite the standpoint of the *Phenomenology* and that of the *Logic*. "M. Hyppolite has always, from the beginning," focused his work on "the point where the tragedy of life finds its meaning in a Logic, where the genesis of a thought becomes the structure of a system, where existence itself is articulated in a Logic" (Foucault 1969: 134; my translation). This, indeed, was the theme of Hyppolite's *Logic and Existence*, which Foucault calls "one of the great books of our time" (ibid.: 136; my translation).

About two years later, in his inaugural lecture at the Collège de France, where he succeeded Hyppolite, Foucault (1972), in a warm and informative concluding tribute to his former teacher, put the matter in more personal terms. Hyppolite, he said, was crucial for his own effort to "truly escape from Hegel," an enterprise requiring "an exact appreciation of the price we must pay to detach ourselves from him" and of "the extent to which our anti-Hegelianism is possibly one of his tricks directed against us, at the end of which he stands, motionless, waiting for us" (ibid.: 236). The price of escaping Hegel (and the risk of failure), Foucault suggests, arises from what he sees as the central concern of Hyppolite's study of Hegel: "Can one still philosophize where Hegel is no longer possible? Can any philosophy continue to exist that is no longer Hegelian? Are the non-Hegelian elements in our thought necessarily non-philosophical? Is that which is antiphilosophical necessarily non-Hegelian?" (ibid.: 236–7). In short, is being a Hegelian a necessary and sufficient condition of being a philosopher?

We may well wonder why Foucault thinks there's a serious question of whether there can be a non-Hegelian philosophy. For Foucault, at least, a clue to the answer immediately follows in his text where he makes reference to modernity. Hyppolite, he says, "wanted to turn Hegel into a schema for the experience of modernity (is it possible to think of the sciences, politics and daily suffering as a Hegelian?) and he wanted, conversely, to make modernity the test of Hegelianism and, beyond that, of philosophy" (ibid.: 236). Foucault accepted the (Hegelian) idea that philosophy, at any given time, must "comprehend its age in thought," which for us means the age we call "modern" – in the Kantian sense of an age of free individuals who strive to define their own identity rather than accept the definitions of external authorities. But, although Foucault's broad characterization of modernity is Kantian, he rejects Kant's view that the role of philosophy is to discover universal transcendental principles for understanding and grounding our freedom. In the essay, "What Is Enlightenment?" Foucault embraces the modernity of Baudelaire rather than of Kant: "Modern man, for Baudelaire, is not the man who goes off to discover himself, his secrets and his hidden truth, he is the man who tries to invent himself" (2000: 311) For this project of invention, we need to invert the Kantian method of finding the necessary conditions for the possibility of our knowledge and ask, instead, "In what is given to us as universal, necessary, obligatory" what is in fact merely "singular, contingent, and the product of arbitrary constraints?" (ibid.: 315). In short, we need a philosophical approach tuned to the full historicity of our current situation. Who but Hegel offers such an approach?

But, at the same time, Foucault's modernism leaves no room for Hegelian absolute knowledge, which, from the viewpoint of the historical individual, is the ultimate threat to free self-invention. The question, then, becomes, as Hyppolite saw, whether the Hegelian dialectic can be adapted to provide a philosophical understanding of our modernity, or will our effort to deploy it either lead us back to the illusion of absolute knowledge ("motionless, waiting for us") or be inadequate to the realities of our situation? Further, given that Hegelian dialectic is, de facto, the only current philosophical approach geared to a genuinely historical understanding, will its failure mean the failure of philosophy as such? Or will we be able to invent a new, non-Hegelian approach? On Foucault's reading of Hyppolite, these are genuine questions, which will determine the fate of philosophy in the modern period: Hyppolite "never saw the

Hegelian system as a reassuring universe; he saw in it the field in which philosophy took the ultimate risk" (Foucault 1972: 236).

In formulating these questions, Hyppolite, Foucault tells us, effected five fundamental alterations "not within Hegelian philosophy, but upon it." First, he gave up Hegel's claim that philosophy could culminate in a "totality" that synthesized and reconciled all oppositions, and instead presented philosophy, as Husserl did, as "an endless task, against the background of an infinite horizon." Second, and following from the first, he replaced the finality of absolute knowledge with the idea of "continuous recommencement," thereby transferring "the Hegelian theme of the end of self-consciousness into one of repeated interrogation" (recalling Kierkegaard's category of repetition). Third, rather than absorbing all non-philosophical experience and knowledge into spirit's final philosophical synthesis, Hyppolite, in the manner of Bergson, "reestablish[ed] the contact with the non-philosophical" in a non-reductive manner. Fourth, the irreducibilty of the non-philosophical led him to look back, like Fichte rather than Hegel, to the question of how philosophy might find its beginning in the non-philosophical. Specifically (and this is the last alteration), Hyppolite invoked the challenge of Marx, and asked: "[I]f philosophy must begin as absolute discourse, then what of history and what is this beginning which starts out with a singular individual, within a society and a social class, and in the midst of struggle?" (ibid.). This invocation of the "singular individual" refers to the fixed point of French philosophy throughout the twentieth century, the irreducibility of the free individual, which had always stood as the fundamental obstacle to a French appropriation of Hegel's thought. Although, for Foucault (as for Deleuze and Derrida), this obstacle was, in moral and political terms, as strong or stronger than ever, Hyppolite had led them to an appreciation of Hegel's power as a thinker of historical realities that required their coming to terms with his dialectic. Hyppolite's five "alterations" provided the matrix from which Foucault hoped to effect this "coming to terms" with Hegel.

The first two alterations suggested a philosophical project that gave up the goal of final truth and became an "infinite task" continually starting over (what we might call Sisyphean philosophy). The second two alterations proposed giving up the goal of autonomy and admitting that philosophy itself originates from and is in constant interaction with irreducibly non-philosophical domains of experience and understanding. The last alteration in effect sums up all the others by recognizing that a philosophy that is neither final nor autonomous provides no escape from the vicissitudes of human history.

It is clear that Foucault himself accepted all of these alterations. But concretely, what were the alternatives to Hegelianism in its absolute form? In a 1978 interview with Duccio Trombadori, Foucault describes the "intellectual panorama" presented to him in his student days (the early fifties) as he tried to choose his own approach. The two extremes of the panorama were "Hegel's theory of systems" and "the philosophy of the subject … in the form of phenomenology and existentialism." Outside the university, "it was Sartre," with his particular version of the philosophy of the subject, "who was in fashion." Within the university, Hegelianism was dominant, although "it was a Hegelianism permeated with phenomenology and existentialism, centered on the theme of the unhappy consciousness." A third alternative, "establishing a meeting point between the academic philosophical tradition and phenomenology, was the work of Merleau-Ponty (friend of Sartre but also a Sorbonne professor), "who extended existential discourse into specific domains" (Foucault 2000: 247).

In assessing these alternatives, the young Foucault, already reflecting the viewpoint of his late essay on Enlightenment, sought an approach that offered "the broadest possible mode of understanding the contemporary world " (ibid.: 246). Nor was this just a vague matter of wanting a philosophy that was "up-to-date." Foucault saw an urgent need to escape from the mistakes that had led to the horrors of World War II. "The experience of the war had shown us the urgent need of a society radically different from the one in which we were living, this society that had permitted Nazism, that had lain down in front of it, and that had gone over en masse to de Gaulle." Foucault shared the "total disgust toward all that" with "a large sector of French youth" (ibid.: 247). As a result, "we wanted a world and a society that were not only different but that would be an alternative version of ourselves: we wanted to be completely other in a completely different world" (ibid.: 247–8).

This desire for a complete break with the past excluded "the Hegelianism offered to us at the university," since Hegel's dialectic, "with its model of history's unbroken intelligibility," required the continual inclusion of the past in the future (ibid.: 248). But, at the same time, Foucault was firmly opposed to existential phenomenology, whether formulated by Sartre or by Merleau-Ponty, because he questioned "the category of the subject, its supremacy, its foundational function" (ibid.: 247). *The Order of Things* deploys philosophical critiques of the subject, but apart from such critiques, Foucault found a philosophy of the subject incapable of taking him beyond the self that the society he rejected wanted to mold for him:

> The phenomenologist's experience is basically a way of bringing a reflective gaze to bear on some object of "lived experience," on the everyday in its transitory form, in order to grasp its meanings. … Moreover, phenomenology attempts to recapture the meaning of everyday experience in order to rediscover the sense in which the subject that I am is indeed responsible, in its transcendental functions, for founding that experience together with its meanings. (Foucault 2000: 241)

Foucault did not deny that there is a subject in this phenomenological sense. No doubt, "the subject dispenses significations"; "that point was not called back in question." Rather, he says, "the question was: Can it be said that the subject is the only possible form of experience? Can't there be experiences in the course of which the subject is no longer posited, in its constitutive relations, as what makes it identical with itself?" (ibid.: 248).

Foucault saw postwar society as turning its youth into subjects who would continue the sordid history that had produced the war. Mere descriptions of the essential characteristics of all subjects, à la phenomenology, would do nothing to stop this process. What was needed, rather, were "experiences in which the subject might be able to dissociate from itself, sever the relation with itself, lose its identity" (ibid.). It was the need for such radically transformative experience that turned Foucault away from the Hegelian and existentialist ways of understanding his world.

What he turned to were two avant-garde literary figures, Georges Bataille and Maurice Blanchot, who then referred him to Nietzsche, who, because of the way the Nazis had used him, "was completely excluded from the academic syllabus" (ibid.). "What struck me and fascinated me about those authors," Foucault tells us, "and what gave them their capital importance for me, was that their problem was not the construction of a system but the construction of a personal experience." Whereas "phenomenological work consists in unfolding the field of possibilities, related to everyday experience," the personal experiences constructed by Bataille, Blanchot, and Nietzsche are "limit-experiences" that "have the function of wrenching the subject from itself, of seeing to it that the subject is no longer itself, that it is brought to its annihilation or its dissolution." This is what Foucault calls "the project of desubjectivation" (ibid.: 241) and makes the purpose of all his books: "however boring, however erudite my books may be, I've always conceived of them as direct experiences aimed at pulling myself free of myself, at preventing me from being the same" (ibid.: 241–2).

His emphasis on such extreme experiences might suggest that Foucault's books are anti-Hegelian in the very strong sense of evoking ineffable states that cannot be expressed through the shared categories of language and so escape the rational structures of philosophical explanation. Nonetheless, limit-experiences themselves play little role in his books. The *topics* of these books are things associated with extreme experiences: madness, sickness and death, crime and punishment, sexuality. Even the apparently more sober topic of knowledge in *The Order of Things* deals with radical differences in fundamental frameworks of thought – as in Borges's fictional "Chinese encyclopedia," of which "we apprehend in one great leap … the stark impossibility of thinking *that*" (Foucault 1970: xv). But, despite a certain amount of evocative prose (e.g., in the original Preface, later dropped, of *History of Madness*), the bulk of Foucault's discussion is about how (quite ordinary) people in various ages viewed madness, death, sex, etc., not the actual limit-experiences of the mad, the dying, the sexually ecstatic, etc. Since, according to Foucault, outside perceptions of madness and the like were, no longer ago than the eighteenth and nineteenth centuries, radically different from our own, his explications of these perceptions can help shake us out of the dogmatic doze that hides alternatives to our conventional ways of thinking. But such increased alertness to possibilities is far from the explosion of identity Foucault says he was seeking. Even if the process of writing his books had such an effect for him, this was not expressed in their contents.

Rather than evocations of limit-experiences, we typically find analyses of the deep rational structures that Foucault eventually calls epistemes: conceptual systems underlying the thought and language of a given historical period. In his earlier works – up through *The Order of Things* – Foucault avoids Hegelianism by ignoring questions about the transition from one system to another, restricting his discussion to the excavation of the implicit cognitive rules (hence his label, "the archaeology of knowledge"). But although this synchronic focus blocks the dialectic, it is tempting to regard Foucault's project as a historicized version of transcendental philosophy, a temptation reinforced by his frequent claim that his archaeology is concerned with the "historical a priori."

Béatrice Han (2002), in particular, has made an elaborate and instructive case for a transcendental Foucault. In my view, however, she does so by taking with a high philosophical seriousness what are in fact just Foucault's heuristic (and sometimes ironic) use of a variety of vocabularies, especially Kantian and Heideggerian, to characterize what are his essentially historical projects. (We will return to Han's interpretation below.) I say that Foucault's projects are essentially historical because their success or failure depends ultimately on their fidelity to the total body of contingent historical details. It is true, as I have argued elsewhere, that, as histories, Foucault's accounts are not simple empirical generalizations open to instant refutation by a few pointed counter-examples (Gutting 2005a: 65–9). Rather, they provide broad interpretive frameworks – characteristic of what we might call idealist rather than empiricist history – that must be judged by their ability to understand an overall body of data, not to accurately reflect each single data-point. So, for example, when Foucault, in *History of Madness*, says that confinement of the mad in asylums was a distinctive feature of the classical age's treatment of the mad, he is not asserting (as certain critics have assumed) that there were no asylums prior to the seventeenth century. His point is that, in the classical age, confinement was, for the first time, regarded as the canonical way of treating the mad. Such a claim is not inconsistent with earlier examples of confinement and with the existence of other classical ways of treating the mad. Nonetheless, it remains empirically refutable by, for example, evidence that confinement was merely an occasional ancillary to medical treatment. Even the most comprehensive views about how people thought in the past are not distinctively philosophical – and certainly not transcendental – if their justification requires the support of specific bodies of empirical data. Since Foucault's general claims about thinking in the classical and modern ages do require such support, those claims are essentially historical, not transcendental.

After *The Order of Things*, beginning with *Discipline and Punish*, Foucault finally turned to questions about the diachronic, causal development of thought, questions he had earlier avoided because he found the standard ways of treating them – by evoking a broadly Hegelian "spirit of the times" or Marxist references to technological and social changes or academic historians' appeals to intellectual influences – were "more magical than effective" (Foucault 1970: xiii). His rejection of the first two approaches also no doubt reflects his fear of slipping into the totalizing syntheses of the Hegelian system or similar "grand narratives." Eventually, however, Foucault developed what, with an overt nod to Nietzsche, he called his genealogical method for explaining changes in ways of thinking.

This method decisively escaped anything resembling Hegelianism by insisting on explanations that were multiple, contingent, and corporeal. Epistemes shifted, he claimed, not because of pervasive monolithic forces such as spirit's elimination of contradiction or Marxist materialist equivalents, but because of the chance convergence of specific practical techniques for, e.g., teaching children how to write, training soldiers in the use of their rifles, making factory workers more efficient producers. Genealogy, accordingly, provides historical explanations without any reference to anything approaching the general, a priori principles of Hegelian thought.

Some (both critics and supporters) have found a grand narrative – philosophical or at least high-level social scientific theorizing – in Foucault's views on the relation of power and knowledge. In particular, it is claimed that Foucault presents knowledge as so dependent on the power structures of the society in which it is produced that it has no independent cognitive authority. Consequently, he is either hailed or denounced as a proponent of epistemological relativism or skepticism. But Foucault has no interest in skepticism as a general philosophical thesis or attitude. His skepticism is directed toward quite specific and local claims to cognitive authority on the part of psychiatrists, criminologists, sexologists, etc. He has no brief against the authority of, say, mathematicians, physicists, chemists, or evolutionary biologists; or, for that matter, most historians and economists. Further, the general remarks he does make (e.g., in the first volume of *History of Sexuality*) about the nature of power are designed to emphasize the diverse forms and locations of power in a society (his "micro-physics" of power) and thereby oppose any monolithic account of its operation and effects – hardly the basis for a general skepticism based on the distorting effects of power. Even so, some may maintain that the mere fact that Foucault presents all knowledge as intimately tied to power structures implies a global skepticism. This is not prima facie obvious; it is hard to think that, for example, its support and direction by government agencies undermines the cognitive authority of nuclear science. More generally, there may well be a viable epistemic compatibilism that reconciles knowledge and social causation. In any case, apart from any suggestive speculations he may offer on how to think about power/knowledge in general, Foucault's specific histories do not require a global skepticism.

It is also possible to read Foucault's last two books (on ancient Greek and Roman sexuality) as implying a return, in an ethical context, to a philosophy of the subject. Here Foucault's histories work along not just the previous two axes of knowledge (archaeology) and power (genealogy) but add an axis of the individual subject, which "constitutes" itself in the context of the first two axes. But, of course, merely bringing into the discussion the individuals who are the subjects of knowledge and power hardly requires accepting a transcendental standpoint, which requires a very particular conception of the subject (that which Foucault denotes in *The Order of Things* as "man"). Han (2002: 187), however, maintains that Foucault's subject is a transcendental ego: "Foucault reactivates the perspective of a constitutive subjectivity and understands the constitution of the self by means of the atemporal structure of recognition," a position which would put him firmly back into the philosophy of the subject.

Han takes Foucault to be making this surprising move because he presents the subject as forming itself by a process of reflection and action, as, for example, when he says that thought (that whereby the subject gives itself a specific meaning) is "freedom in relation to what one does, the motion by which one detaches oneself from it, establishes it as an object, and reflects on it as a problem." On Han's reading, such passages imply that Foucault's subject is "autonomous" (ibid.: 172), even, she suggests, in the radical sense of Sartrean existentialist humanism (ibid.: 169). She goes so far as to claim that:

> [Foucault's] insistence on the importance of problematization and recognition as *voluntary* and *reflective* activities leads Foucault to envisage the relationship to the body in a purely unilateral manner, as an action of the self on the self, where the body only appears as material for transformation while consciousness seems to be paradoxically reinstalled in the sovereign position that genealogy had criticized. (Ibid.: 165)

As I see it, Han's reading of Foucault ignores the fact that freedom and reflection need not be read as the technical terms of idealist philosophy but may refer to everyday features of human life (the metaphysical equivalent to Freud's famous reminder that sometimes a cigar is just a cigar). In their everyday sense, freedom and reflection do not imply Kantian (or Sartrean) autonomy. They may, for example, represent the small spark of subjectivity in a context heavily constrained by the social system of power-knowledge. In his books on ancient sexuality, Foucault of course often uses Platonic vocabulary, which smacks of strong autonomy. Moreover, since the power-knowledge constraints of ancient Greece and Rome are no longer relevant to us, he has little to say about them. He is simply looking for modes of thinking about the self (e.g., in terms of an aesthetics of existence) that might suggest strategies in our struggle with modern disciplinary society. None of this provides grounds for concluding that Foucault has lapsed into transcendentalism.

Foucault's work is not a contribution to philosophy in the sense that has defined the discipline since at least Kant and Hegel: a body of theoretical knowledge about fundamental human questions. He had no such theoretical conclusions to offer us, just ethical and political commitments to the kind of life he wanted to live. This was a life of continual free self-transformation, unhindered by unnecessary conceptual and social constraints. His intellectual enterprise was the critique of disciplines and practices that restrict the freedom to transform ourselves. He did not object to those who continued to build new theoretical structures, and, in some cases, such as Deleuze, he seemed to endorse their results. But he was not really a philosopher in the modern sense. Of course, Foucault's books, like other classics of intellectual history, exhibit enormous philosophical talent and are often of great interest to philosophers. Moreover, as his final work makes clear, he was a philosopher in the ancient sense of someone who sought, if not to know, then to live the truth.

Notes

1   By "speculative" here, Hegel does not mean "improbable" or "unwarranted" but, rather, "operating at a level of reason, above ordinary human consciousness."
2   This recalls Foucault's similar distinction between the philosophy of experience and the philosophy of the concept, although, speaking of his student days, he presented this as a choice between existential phenomenology and philosophy of science (as developed by Bachelard and Canguilhem), not a project of reconciliation. From a broader perspective, however, the choice between, say, Merleau-Ponty and Canguilhem was between two ways of resolving Badiou's tension, the first giving priority to experience and the second to concepts.

References

Badiou, A. (2005) "The Adventure of French Philosophy." *New Left Review* 35: 67–77.
Foucault, M. (1969) "Jean Hyppolite (1907–1968)." *Revue de Métaphysique et de Morale* 14 (2): 131–6.
Foucault, M. (1970) *The Order of Things*, trans. A. Sheridan. New York: Random House.
Foucault, M. (1972) "The Discourse on Language." Included as an appendix to *The Archaeology of Knowledge*, trans. A. Sheridan. New York: Pantheon.
Foucault, M. (1985) *The History of Sexuality*, vol. 2: *The Use of Pleasure*, trans. R. Hurley. New York: Pantheon.

Foucault, M. (2000) *Essential Works of Foucault, 1945–1984*, vol. 3: *Power*, ed. C. Gordon. New York: The New Press.

Gutting, G. (2005a) "Foucault and the History of Madness." In G. Gutting, ed., *The Cambridge Companion to Foucault*, 2nd edn. Cambridge: Cambridge University Press.

Gutting, G. (2005b) *Foucault: A Very Short Introduction*. New York: Oxford University Press.

Han, B. (2002) *Foucault's Critical Project*, trans. E. Pile. Stanford, CA: Stanford University Press.

Hyppolite, J. (1974) *Genesis and Structure of Hegel's Phenomenology of Spirit*, trans. S. Cherniak and J. Heckman. Evanston, IL: Northwestern University Press.

Hyppolite, J. (1997) *Logic and Existence*, trans. L. Lawler and A. Sen. Albany: State University of New York Press.

Lawler, L. (2003) *Thinking Through French Philosophy: The Being of the Question.* Bloomington, IN: Indiana University Press.

Sartre, J.-P. (1978) *Sartre by Himself*, trans. R. Seaver. New York: Urizen Books.

Wahl, J. (1929) *Le Malheur de conscience dans la philosophie de Hegel*, 2nd edn. Paris: Presses Universitaires de France.

Wahl, J. (1932) *Vers le concret*. Paris: Vrin.

2

"I am Simply a Nietzschean"

Hans Sluga

Anyone who sets out to determine Foucault's debt to Nietzsche will have to take his last interview ("The Return of Morality") into account in which he characterized himself as "simply a Nietzschean" (1989: 327). The claim deserves notice because Foucault never expressed himself in an equally forceful manner about anyone else. But it provokes also an immediate question. How could he have been "*simply* a Nietzschean" given the remarkable fluidity of Nietzsche's thought and his own unwillingness to be pinned down once and for all? ("Leave it to our bureaucrats and our police to see that our papers are in order," he had written, after all, in *The Archaeology of Knowledge* (1972: 17).) Foucault understood, of course, that "there is not just *one* Nietzscheanism" and he was sure therefore that "one cannot say that there is a true Nietzscheanism and that this one is truer than the other" (1989: 247). In his final interview he had emphasized, moreover, that he had never sought to reproduce Nietzsche's thinking. Instead, he said, he had tried "as far as possible, on a certain number of issues, to see with the help of Nietzsche's texts – but also with anti-Nietzschean theses (which are nevertheless Nietzschean!) – what can be done in this or that domain" (ibid.: 327). These carefully formulated qualifications raise some additional questions. What in Nietzsche's texts had he made his own? What specifically anti-Nietzschean theses had he entertained? And how had these been nevertheless still Nietzschean? Those questions may lead us, in turn, to consider how Foucault had come to his interest in Nietzsche in the first place, how his take on Nietzsche had changed along the wide arc of his intellectual journey, and how, finally, his professed Nietzscheanism relates to the affinity with Heidegger also invoked in the last interview. I have tried to answer some of those questions in an earlier essay (Sluga 2005) but I am no longer certain that my discussion went far enough in probing the complexity of Foucault's relationship to Nietzsche. What is needed, I now think, is more attention to their respective understanding of the genealogical project. I will try to fill this lacuna without repeating what I have earlier said on the matter. This will still leave many other aspects of the relation of these two thinkers to be explored.

Asked by Alessandro Fontana in 1984 whether he would describe his work as "a new genealogy of morals," Foucault replied famously: "If not for the solemnity of the title and the imposing mark that Nietzsche left on it, I would say yes" (1989: 310–11). But we must note that he could hardly have said this before 1970. Until then he had dubbed himself, instead, an archaeologist of the structures of discourse. But soon after the publication of *The Archaeology of Knowledge* in 1969 he began to characterize his approach as genealogical in Nietzsche's sense – a shift marked by the publication in 1971 of the essay "Nietzsche, Genealogy, History." In that piece of writing Foucault voiced what I take to be a threefold agreement with Nietzsche: (1) with regard to the genealogical method, (2) with regard to the goals of the genealogical enterprise, and (3) with regard to its broad implications.

Every serious student of Foucault will know, however, that the use he makes of the distinction between archaeology and genealogy is not at all easy to describe. There is disagreement between the interpreters, for instance, over the question whether the genealogical method is meant to supersede the archaeological one or is supplementary to it. It is not that genealogy is historically oriented while archaeology is concerned with rigid structures; it is also not that genealogy takes a dynamic view of human knowledge whereas archaeology considers discursive structures to be static. It is also not that genealogy examines transitions between discourses, whereas archaeology studies only their internal characteristics. In *The Archaeology of Knowledge*, Foucault writes, indeed, that events which involve "the substitution of one discursive formation for another … are, for archaeology, the most important: only archaeology, in any case, can reveal them" (1972: 171). Archaeology is, thus, very much concerned with historical change, as should, indeed, be obvious to any reader of *The Order of Things* and of Foucault's other early books. But Foucault also writes in *The Archaeology of Knowledge* that the archaeological enterprise is not intended "to isolate mechanisms of causality," that it does not ask "before a set of enunciative facts … what could have motivated them (the search of contexts of formulation); nor does it seek to rediscover what is expressed in them (the task of hermeneutics); … it seeks to define specific forms of articulation" (ibid.: 162). The archaeological enterprise describes, in other words, historical changes, but offers no account of what brings them about. Genealogy, on the other hand, concerns itself precisely with the mechanisms of historical change. In "Nietzsche, Genealogy, History," Foucault declares accordingly that genealogy establishes "the hazardous play of dominations," that it "must delineate the struggle these forces wage against each other," and that it examines "the perpetual instigation of dominations and the staging of meticulously repeated scenes of violence" (1977: 148, 149, 151). Genealogy, in contrast to archaeology, thus makes use of notions of domination, force, and violence. Foucault conceives in this way of his own genealogy as akin to the Nietzschean project of a genealogy of morals understood as a study of the operations of the will to power. Nietzsche writes in his *Genealogy*:

> I lay stress on this major point of historical method, especially as it runs counter to just that prevailing instinct and fashion which would much rather come to terms with absolute randomness, and even the mechanistic senselessness of all events, than the theory that a power-will playing is acted out in all that happens. (1994: 2:13)

This will to power manifests itself, so Nietzsche also writes, in "spontaneous, aggressive, expansive, re-interpreting, re-directing and formative powers" (ibid.). It takes on everywhere the terrible hues of violence.

Such words may suggest that Nietzsche and Foucault are of one mind in their conception of the genealogical project. One is, nevertheless, forced, on a closer reading of the essay "Nietzsche, Genealogy, History," to the conclusion that Foucault departs from Nietzsche (deliberately or unwittingly) in three significant respects. He definitely downplays Nietzsche's interest in the question of the *origin* of morality; he appears to think of genealogy primarily in relation to history rather than to politics; and he seems determined to minimize Nietzsche's interpretational conception of the genealogical method. I want to argue here that we can reach a more adequate, more fully articulated understanding of Foucault's relation to Nietzsche by considering to what extent those charges are just.

Origin vs. Descent

Foucault declares in his essay that Nietzsche uses the term "origin" (*Ursprung*) often in an "unstressed" fashion as a straight alternative to the terms "formation," "descent," "parentage," "birth" – *Entstehung, Herkunft, Abkunft,*

Geburt (1977: 140). He goes on to claim without further qualification that "in the main body of *The Genealogy*, *Ursprung* and *Herkunft* are used interchangeably in numerous instances" (ibid.: 142, fn.19). This is surely an unlikely assertion since the two terms cannot easily be substituted for each other in Nietzsche's formulations. Nietzsche begins *Genealogy* II.2, for instance, with the words: "*Eben das ist die lange Geschichte der Herkunft der Verantwortlichkeit*" and he is surely speaking there of the long history of the emergence or formation of responsibility, not of a long history of the origin of this phenomenon since an origin cannot literally have a long history.[1] In II.8 of the same text, he writes, on the other hand: "*Das Gefühl der Schuld … hat, wie wir sahen, seinen Ursprung in dem ältesten und ursprünglichsten Personen-Verhältnis.*" This should be translated to say that "the feeling of guilt has its origin, as we saw, in the oldest and most original [or, primordial] personal relationship."[2] The word "descent" cannot without distortion be substituted for that of "origin" in this context. Such linguistic observations are, perhaps, not by themselves conclusive, but they point to deeper disagreements between Foucault and Nietzsche.

In order to see how far Foucault departs from Nietzsche in his refusal to accept a real difference between *Ursprung* and *Herkunft*, we must look more closely at Nietzsche's programmatic preface to *The Genealogy of Morals*. Nietzsche writes there that his ultimate goal is to construct a "real history of morals," and he warns us accordingly against an "English hypothesis-mongering into the blue." Against such speculative hypothesizing, he wants us to consider "that which can be documented, which can actually be confirmed and has actually existed" (1994: 7). There is no doubt about Foucault's attraction to this kind of labor. Identifying himself, so it seems, with the Nietzschean project, Foucault speaks of genealogy approvingly as "gray, meticulous, and patiently documentary." Such genealogy, he continues, "operates on a field of entangled and confused parchments, on documents that have been scratched over and recopied many times. … Genealogy, consequently, requires patience and a knowledge of details and it depends on a vast accumulation of source materials. … In short, genealogy demands relentless erudition" (1977: 139–40). Even before becoming a genealogist, Foucault had practiced this kind of sustained scholarship, and he was subsequently to speak fondly (and somewhat self-ironically) of his membership in "one of the more ancient or more typical secret societies of the West … the great warm and tender Freemasonry of useless erudition" (1980a: 79).

Despite this broad agreement with Nietzsche, Foucault did not, however, make Nietzsche's envisaged goal for such scholarship his own. He never attempted the reconstruction of "the whole, long, hard-to-decipher hieroglyphic script of man's moral past" that Nietzsche (1994: 7) had in mind. The latter did not, of course, believe it easy to deliver such a complete history and he certainly did not imagine that he had delivered it in his *Genealogy of Morals*. The "*On*" in the full title of the work suggests, rather, that he intended it as a first exploration of the scope, nature, and possibility of such a comprehensive inquiry. The book was, in other words, not to be understood as providing a completely worked-out genealogical deduction. The three essays that make it up are, indeed, only episodic in character. While the first concentrates largely on the shift from pagan to Christian culture, the second jumps to a much earlier moment in time when our forebears first became human, and the discussion of asceticism in the third essay focuses on no particular era. Nietzsche was, in any case, certain that no single person could realize the entire genealogical project. In an appendix to the first essay he expressed, rather, the hope that his book "might serve to give a powerful impetus in such a direction" and he called for the combined effort of many scholars to advance the genealogical study of morality (ibid.: 1).

But such programmatic remarks make evident that Nietzsche was quite seriously aiming for a complete rather than a partial history of morals. We may, of course, suspect that such an undertaking is impossible and conclude that Nietzsche was caught up here in a characteristically nineteenth-century, encyclopedic mode of thinking, one that no longer appeals to us. The thoroughly twentieth-century Foucault certainly never embarked on such a treacherous project. This may, indeed, be one of the strengths of his work, but it may also, on further consideration, prove to be one of its limitations. Foucault's genealogy is, in any case, always temporally, culturally, and subject-matter specific (it is, e.g., in the first volume of *The History of Sexuality* that we find a study of the emergence of sexuality in seventeenth- to nineteenth-century Europe). Nietzsche, by contrast, never intended to be a "specific" intellectual of the sort that Foucault sought to be. He was, instead, after the largest possible perspective on morality (alternating that with the most close-up, frog-like, intimate view of it). It is useful to remember here the first sentence of Nietzsche's essay "On Truth and Lies in a Nonmoral Sense," which reads: "Once upon a time, in some out of the way corner of that universe which is dispersed into numberless twinkling solar systems, there was a star upon which clever beasts invented knowing" (1979: 79). Such a sentence would be impossible out of Foucault's mouth. Nietzsche, we can see from this and similar formulations, was, in contrast to Foucault, after a global perspective on the human condition and, *a fortiori*, a complete history of morals. As part of this project, he genuinely wanted to determine the origin, the start, the beginning, the birth (he uses all those terms) of morals. It remains to be seen what sense he sought to give this notion of origin.

Foucault is, of course, right in distinguishing different understandings of this origin – loaded and less loaded ones. The believer who holds God to be the origin of the ten commandments intends thereby to validate those moral principles. The origin claims to vindicate the moral principle. Nietzsche's account of the origins of modern slave-morality, on the other hand, is meant to invalidate that morality. His genealogy is, thus, first of all destructive in character, but it is meant to clear the ground at the same time for a new kind of valuation. "[A]ll sciences," he writes in his note to the first essay of the *Genealogy*, "are henceforth to do preparatory work for the philosopher's task of the future. For reasons to be explained, I will call this task political" (1994). Nietzsche's genealogy is thus meant to be both destructive and political. This has led to the charge that he is guilty of a "genetic fallacy." It is said that he assumes that we can invalidate a system of values simply by establishing that it has arisen from dubious origins. But this charge must be confronted with the fact that Nietzsche himself has repeatedly acknowledged that the mere tracing of an origin does not as such determine the value or disvalue of a moral principle. He allows, in fact, that a morality may have grown out of an error, but that "the realization of this fact would not as much as touch upon its value" (1974: 345). Clearly, more is required for a destructive genealogy to work than a proof that a particular kind of value has come from a disreputable source. What is needed, for instance, is showing that our whole system of values rests on such errors and that there is nothing else to support the entire structure of values. Nietzsche evidently thought that the critique of our particular values requires a comprehensive genealogy. Thus, showing that our modern system of values originates from a moment of social resentment is not sufficient to dismantle those values. It might still be held that those values are true. What is needed then in order to complete the genealogical destruction of modern morality is a comprehensive genealogy which includes a genealogy of our concept of truth. But this can be achieved only by taking a complete view of human understanding. It appears that only a comprehensive genealogy, one that uncovers the origins of our entire system of valuation, can succeed in the destructive task that Nietzsche has set himself (ibid.: 110–15). Nietzsche's genealogy must, in other words, be understood, precisely, as an attempt at a historical uncovering of the origin of our moral system.

Since Foucault refuses to consider the possibility of such a comprehensive undertaking – perhaps for good reasons – we can't take his genealogies to be either destructive or vindicatory in character. Neither a destruction nor a vindication of our values is, in fact, Foucault's goal. His specific genealogies are designed, rather, to remove the impression of inevitability that generally attaches to our values. He wants to open spaces where new possibilities, potentialities for new valuations, become apparent. He insists for this reason that "the work of the intellect is to show that what is, does not have to be, what it is" (1989: 252). And he admonishes us for that same reason "to dig deep to show how things have been historically contingent, for such and such reasons intelligible but not necessary" (ibid.: 209). In "Nietzsche, Genealogy, History," Foucault writes in the same spirit that the genealogist must seek to find behind things "not a timeless and essential secret, but the secret that they have no essence or that their essence was fabricated in a piecemeal fashion from alien forms" (1977: 142). Genealogy, understood in Foucault's sense as a history of descent, does therefore not involve the "erecting of foundations; on the contrary, it disturbs what was thought unified; it shows the heterogeneity of what was imagined consistent with itself" (ibid.: 147). Specific genealogies are certainly not excluded by Nietzsche, but his type of genealogy goes further in wanting to destroy the entire system of hitherto existing values in order to erect on its ruins the edifice of a new kind of valuation.

Politics vs. History

In the second half of "Nietzsche, Genealogy, History," Foucault sets out to examine the relation of genealogy to "history in the traditional sense." This is (to my mind) the least compelling part of his essay. For one thing, it is largely written in an unsatisfactorily hyperbolic style – as if Foucault were trying to channel Nietzsche's voice. The result is, however, quite unlike the ironic, incisive tone of Nietzsche's writing (and is also not indicative of the much more sober style of Foucault's own later genealogical work).

According to Foucault, genealogy in contrast to traditional history is "*wirkliche Historie*" – a term he renders repeatedly and dubiously as "effective history" ("*l'histoire 'effective'*" – 1994a: 147).[3] How are we to understand this supposed contrast? Foucault's characterization is far from compelling if it is meant to give expression to Nietzsche's conception of genealogy and it does not even conform to his own later genealogical practice. Traditional history, Foucault writes, "transposes the relationship ordinarily established between the eruption of an event and necessary continuity"; genealogy, on the other hand, "deals with events in terms of their unique characteristics, their most acute manifestations" (ibid.: 154). One might object that Nietzsche's sought-after comprehensive genealogy and his attempted integration of genealogy into the larger narrative of the world as will to power are precise opposites of an isolation of "a profusion of entangled events." The notion of the event, of "countless lost events, without a landmark or a point of reference" (ibid.: 155) plays, in any case, no role in Nietzsche's thought. Foucault's counterclaim can only be understood in terms of his refusal to accept the comprehensive nature of Nietzsche's genealogical project. His emphasis on the isolated event takes us back, in any case, to *The Archaeology of Knowledge*, where archaeology is described as "the project of a pure description of discursive events" (1972: 27) an investigation that "in the name of methodological rigor" concerns, in the first instance, "a population of dispersed events" (ibid.: 22). This kind of archaeology requires that the "pre-existing forms of continuity" and all the usual "syntheses that are accepted without question, must remain in suspense." Insofar as continuities are accepted, "we must show that they do not come about of themselves, but are always the result of a construction the rules of which must be known" (ibid.: 25). We can't object to this in Nietzsche's name, if Foucault means only to say that the continuities that traditional history recognizes may need to be replaced by others. That is, indeed, part of Nietzsche's undertaking. But Nietzsche does not subscribe to the event-atomism that for Foucault is basic to *The Archaeology of Knowledge*. We can conclude, however, that in "Nietzsche, Genealogy, History," Foucault's characterization of the genealogical project is still colored by his own earlier archaeological mode of thought and as such does justice to neither Nietzsche's nor his own subsequent understanding of the genealogical enterprise.

Foucault's assertion that Nietzsche wants to contrast genealogy as *"wirkliche Historie"* to traditional historical scholarship is, moreover, based on a misreading. The preface to Nietzsche's *Genealogy* which serves here as reference point differentiates genealogy as real history not from traditional scholarship but from the imaginative inventions perpetrated by Paul Rée and the English moralists. The late Nietzsche says, in fact, little about the relation of genealogy to historical scholarship of the traditional sort. He makes no attempt, in particular, to connect what he says about genealogy to his own earlier considerations in the second of his *Untimely Meditations*, the essay "On the Use and Abuse of History" and its dissection of the various forms of historical consciousness. That comparison is, on the other hand, one of Foucault's major concerns in "Nietzsche, Genealogy, History." While focusing on these two moments in Nietzsche's thought, Foucault pays little attention to Nietzsche's ultimate motivation in writing *The Genealogy of Morals* which is, as I have already remarked, political rather than historical in character. It is helpful to note at this point that the closest antecedent to Nietzsche's *Genealogy* is not the essay "The Use and Abuse of History," but his book *The Birth of Tragedy*. That work operates, of course, with a different timeframe from the *Genealogy;* it is not at all concerned with the rise of Judeo-Christian morality (out of "malice," Nietzsche claims in the preface to the second edition of that work); but, like *The Genealogy of Morals, The Birth of Tragedy* tells a story of the formation of our modern system of values. In the earlier work, that value-system is called scientific rationalism and Socratic optimism, in the later it is called slave-morality – terms which are not altogether unrelated in Nietzsche's mind. Both works can be considered genealogical in character since both mean to undermine the values whose genesis they describe; and both advance in place of the discredited system of values a new "life-affirming," tragic world-view that they see prefigured in early Greek civilization. I emphasize these deep similarities, because that allows us to get clearer also on Nietzsche's motivation for writing *The Genealogy of Morals*. The crucial point here is that *The Birth of Tragedy* is clearly a political treatise. Nietzsche wrote it in the aftermath of the Franco-Prussian war and under the stimulus of Richard Wagner's revolutionary sentiments in order to advance a radically new politics. The *Genealogy* is motivated by those same concerns. When Nietzsche writes in it that "the earth has been a madhouse for too long" (1994: II.22) and that in a stronger age than our decaying present a redeeming man will appear (ibid.: II.24), we must not forget that he refers us to Napoleon as well as to Zarathustra as such redeeming figures (ibid.: I.16). The political context of the *Genealogy* becomes even clearer when we read the book together with the aphorisms that Nietzsche composed at more or less the same time. Genealogy, it then becomes evident, is to be a tool in the emergence of a "great new European politics." This new kind of politics involves "more comprehensive forms of dominion, whose like has never existed." We see the appearance of "a master race, the 'future masters of the earth,'" who take hold of "the destinies of the earth, so as to work as artists upon 'man' himself" (Nietzsche 1968: 960). These "legislators of the future will say: 'Thus it shall be!' And they alone determine the 'whither' and the 'wherefore,' what is useful and what constitutes utility for men" (ibid.: 972). The formulations are well known and notorious and they must surely be read together with other Nietzschean thoughts that point in altogether different directions. They make clear, however, that, at the time of writing his *Genealogy of Morals*, Nietzsche was preoccupied with a large-scale (even megalomaniac) political agenda and that the question of how genealogy relates to his earlier tripartite division of history is of little concern to him at this point. None of that is, however, visible from Foucault's essay.

We should not be surprised then that there is no single reference to either *The Birth of Tragedy* or *The Will to Power* in Foucault's essay, even though the piece contains more than 60 references to Nietzsche's writings and quotes him copiously from a variety of sources. Foucault's own genealogical investigations will, of course, turn political in due course, though never on the scale that Nietzsche envisages. Where Nietzsche thinks (in a characteristically nineteenth-century fashion) in terms of great radical ruptures, Foucault prefers to consider "mobile and transitory points of resistance, producing cleavages in a society that shift about, fracturing unities and effecting regroupings" (1980b: 96). But this later concern with politics is still to come. In "Nietzsche, Genealogy, History," the view of genealogy as a political undertaking has still to take shape. We must wait for the pointedly political tone of *Discipline and Punish*, the first volume of *The History of Sexuality*, and the lecture course *Society Must be Defended* for this to occur.

I am emphasizing this divergence of Nietzsche's actual goals from those that Foucault ascribes to him in "Nietzsche, Genealogy, History" not in order to attack his scholarly acumen, but in order to raise the question how the second part of that essay is to be understood. To put it differently: why is Foucault so concerned with asking what kind of historical inquiry genealogy is meant to be? My answer is that his reading of Nietzsche stands at this point still in the shadow of his own earlier archaeological work. We can read the second part of Foucault's essay, indeed, as a piece of self-criticism directed at his own earlier practice of writing history. What he says about Nietzsche serves him, in other words, to advance a new and more radical view of writing history. Foucault's work in the early, archaeological period had, of course, also been historically oriented (as I have already emphasized) just as the work of the genealogical period would prove to be. But in the archaeological period Foucault had had nothing to say about the role of the archaeologist himself – this in addition to his silence about the forces that move the historical process. In his preface to the English edition of *The Order of Things* Foucault had written, for instance: "In this work, then, I left the problem of causes to one side. I chose instead to confine myself to describing the transformations themselves, thinking that this would be an indispensable step if, one day, a theory of scientific change and epistemological causality was to be constructed" (1994b: xiii). But *The Order of Things* is characterized also by its description of the development of modern thought from a majestically objectifying point of view. Foucault writes thus: "I tried to explore the scientific discourse not from the point of view of the individuals who are speaking, nor from the view of the formal structures of what they are saying, but from the point of view of the rules that come into play in the very existence of such discourse." It is understandable enough that he wants to avoid the "phenomenological approach" which gives "priority to the observing subject," and even more that he shuns an approach that might lead to postulating a transcendental consciousness (ibid.: xiv). But setting all this aside, we are still left with the question: what is the position, the qualification, the place of knowledge from which the archaeologist is so majestically describing the changing scenery of the Western episteme? From what epistemic position is Foucault himself speaking? If every episteme structures, determines, and delimits a field of discourse, what is the status of the discourse in which we survey and commensurate different and incommensurable epistemes? These are questions to which the archaeological Foucault provides no answer, and it is difficult to imagine how he could provide them.

It appears to have taken Nietzsche's genealogy to alert Foucault to this blind spot in his archaeological undertaking. In "Nietzsche, Genealogy, History," he reveals, in any case, a new awareness of the need to determine the place of the historian himself. He can write now almost as if he were commenting on his own earlier self: "Historians take unusual pain to erase the elements in their work which reveal their grounding in a particular time and place, their preferences in a controversy – the unavoidable obstacles of their passion" (1977: 156–7). Foucault's initial conclusions from this insight are radical, indeed more radical than they need to be. In contrast to the traditional historian – but in contrast also to the Foucauldian archaeologist – the genealogist, so he insists now, has a historical sense that "is parodic, directed against reality, and opposes the theme of history as reminiscence and recognition" (ibid.: 160). The genealogist turns this sense of parody, moreover, immediately on himself. He "will push the masquerade to its limit and prepare the great carnival of time where masks are constantly reappearing. No longer the identification of our faint individuality with the solid identities of the past, but our 'unrealization' through the excessive choice of identities" (ibid.: 160–1). Foucault seeks to make out that this is also Nietzsche's view. This impression is reinforced in the English translation when it makes Nietzsche proclaim: "Perhaps, we can discover a realm where originality is again possible as parodists of history and buffoons of God" (ibid.: 161), as if Nietzsche was identifying with this particular form of "historical spirit." We must observe, however, first of all, that Nietzsche's German says simply "perhaps, we discover" which Foucault renders as "perhaps, we will discover" ("*Peut-être découvrirons-nous*") and which our translator, in turn, makes into "perhaps, we *can* discover," thus making Nietzsche express the hope that such a state might come about. But the original German sentence says no such thing; it is uttered, rather, on behalf of "the hybrid European – a rather ugly plebeian, all in all" who "definitely requires a costume" (Nietzsche 1973: 223). The "parodic" conception of genealogical history does not, fortunately, survive into Foucault's subsequent genealogical work. Though his comments about the status of his genealogical investigations are sometimes self-deprecatory, there is no reason to think that these investigations are meant to be mere parodies, directed against reality.

There is, of course, a great deal of continuity in Foucault's thinking about the subject that also surfaces in these words. Even in his archaeological period, he had spoken of the need to deconstruct the subject. But in "Nietzsche, Genealogy, History" he was doing something more. He was turning, in effect, to the deconstruction of the subject that writes history and thus to the destruction of his own earlier work as an archaeologist. Genealogical inquiry is, he was saying now, meant to deprive the self of the reassuring stability of life and nature. Two points stand out from Foucault's dense formulations. The first is that the genealogical inquiry cannot lay claim to a detached, objective, and timeless truth, but must understand itself as a practical tool. "Knowledge," Foucault writes accordingly, "is not made for understanding; it is made for cutting" (1977: 154). The second is that such an undertaking destroys altogether the idea of a fixed human identity. The genealogical enterprise, far from being a search for such an identity, is, in fact, committed to its dissipation. Instead of postulating solid identities we are told in the last sentence of the essay that we must turn to "the destruction of the man who maintains knowledge by the injustice proper to the will to knowledge" (ibid.: 164). The violence of these formulations reflects, perhaps, here most directly the violence of Foucault's turn against his own earlier work and scholarly self. But the real insight that he derived from this transitional moment still needed to be refined until finally he could write in the second volume of his *History of Sexuality*:

> There is irony in those efforts one makes to alter one's way of looking at things, to change the boundaries of what one knows and to venture out from there. Did mine actually result in a different way of thinking? Perhaps at most they made it possible to go back through what I was already thinking, to think it differently, and to see what I had done from a new vantage point and in a clearer light. Sure of having traveled far, one finds that one is looking down on oneself from above. The journey rejuvenates things, and ages the relationship with oneself. (1985: 11)

The calmly reflective tone of these words takes one far beyond anything Nietzsche (or, for that matter, a "simple" Nietzschean) could have said; they reveal, instead, Foucault's deepening attachment to the ancient world, to stoic values and attitudes, to the classical care of the self. With their help, so it seems, he has come to a post-Nietzschean moment. But that he should have reached this point was, of course, due once more to Nietzsche and his intensive concern with antiquity. I am inclined to read Foucault's last interview as an expression of the same post-Nietzschean spirit. His generous recognition of the thought of Heidegger and Nietzsche, never before put into words, his broad vision of his own work, the equanimity of his voice – they all speak of an advance beyond Nietzsche. In his modest characterization of himself as "simply a Nietzschean," he is at once acknowledging the significance of Nietzsche for the trajectory of his thinking and gesturing beyond the Nietzschean origins.

Interpretation

There is yet another point at which we can discern Foucault's peculiarly post-Nietzschean stance. For that we must turn to his characterization of Nietzsche's interpretational method in "Nietzsche, Genealogy, History." Nietzsche considers it a crucial insight that genealogy must employ a method of interpretation. Foucault's essay, on the other hand, speaks of this matter in only one short paragraph when he writes that "the development of humanity is a history of interpretations" and that genealogy is concerned with "the emergence of different interpretations" of such things as "morals, ideals, and metaphysical concepts" and specifically also "of the concept of liberty or of the ascetic life" (1977: 152). But he dismisses as purely metaphysical the thought that such interpretations might bring about "the slow exposure of the meaning hidden in an origin." Instead, he characterizes interpretation as "the violent surreptitious appropriation of a system of rules, which in itself has no essential meaning, in order to impose a direction, to bend it to a new will, to force its participation in a different game" (ibid.: 151–2). We may take this to be a plausible summary of Nietzsche's views, but, whereas the idea of interpretation is absolutely central to Nietzsche, Foucault's rudimentary treatment of it reveals a degree of skepticism toward the whole hermeneutic enterprise. This skepticism is well known to us from his earlier work. Thus, Foucault had written in *The Archaeology of Knowledge* that archaeological investigation is certainly not meant to uncover an interpretation: "It is to establish what I am quite willing to call a *positivity*. To analyze a discursive formation therefore is to deal with a group of verbal performances at the level of the statements and of the form of positivity that characterizes them" (1972: 125).

Interpretation plays, of course, a very different role in Nietzsche's thought. This is most evident from the provocative formula that "there are no moral phenomena at all, only a moral interpretation of phenomena" (Nietzsche 1973: 108). The aphorism is crucial to understanding Nietzsche's genealogical enterprise, but one must admit that it is not without difficulties. These arise from its distinction between phenomena and their moral interpretation, a distinction Nietzsche appears to question elsewhere when he objects bluntly to a positivism that takes phenomena to be basic facts with the words: "No, facts, is precisely what there is not, only interpretations" (1968: 481). And in another passage he writes: "There are no facts, everything is in flux, incomprehensible, elusive; what is relatively most enduring is – our opinions," and, thus, presumably our interpretations (ibid.: 604). One might argue, of course, that in denying moral phenomena and allowing only moral interpretations of phenomena, Nietzsche does not mean to separate phenomena from their moral interpretation, that he is saying only that the sphere of the moral is a sphere of interpretation. But this is not quite correct. In *The Genealogy of Morals* his account of punishment, for instance, clearly distinguishes between the practices that enter into our system of punishment and our varying moral interpretation of them. The correct reading is, rather, that Nietzsche knew of different kinds of interpretation. This allows him to distinguish between (historical, social) phenomena, on the one hand, and their moral interpretation, on the other. The phenomena of which his aphorism speaks are thus not identifiable as uninterpreted, bare facts of the kind the positivist postulates; they present themselves to us, rather, as interpreted, but not yet as interpreted in moral terms. There are for Nietzsche, in other words, different strata of interpretation, and distinguishing them is crucial in genealogical inquiry.

The formula that there are no moral phenomena at all, only a moral interpretation of phenomena, is important for a number of reasons. It tells us, first of all, that the history of morals is a history of interpretation and that this history originates, in consequence, where interpretation originates, i.e., in the human sphere. If Nietzsche did not make this assumption, his attempt to trace "the whole, long, hard-to-decipher hieroglyphic script of man's moral past" would, indeed, be outlandish. According to Paul Rée and the English theorists, a comprehensive history of morals would have to include an account of the entire process of biological evolution; it would have to study the slow emergence of altruistic and egoistic drives in social animal species; and it would also have to search for the origins of sentience in animals, and for the growth of their capacity to experience pleasure and pain. But these natural, biological phenomena have no moral significance as such for Nietzsche. Nietzsche subscribes accordingly to neither an ethological nor a utilitarian ethics. He is no moral naturalist. He holds, rather, that morality appears only when the natural phenomena are subjected to moral interpretation. He writes in this spirit in *The Gay Science*:

> The distinctive invention of the founders of religion is, first: to posit a particular kind of life and everyday customs … – and then: to bestow on this life style an *interpretation* that makes it appear to be illuminated by the highest values so that this life style becomes something for which one fights and under certain circumstances sacrifices one's life. (1974: 354)

Jesus (or, more likely, Paul) discovered the life of small people living in the Roman provinces and "he offered an exegesis, he read the highest meaning and value into it – and with this also the courage to despise every other way of life." The origin of a religion is, in other words, always to be found in "a long festival of recognition" (ibid.). The assumption that the moral resides at the level of our interpretation of the phenomena explains, furthermore, why Nietzsche's *Genealogy* is so much concerned with the terms of our moral language and why he proposes an academic essay contest in furtherance of the genealogical project on the question: "What signposts do linguistics, especially the study of etymology, give to the history of the evolution of moral concepts?" (1994: 1). It is true that he calls also for the participation of physiologists and physicians, for ethnological, psychological, and medical studies in addition to philosophical and historical ones, but even then the decisive question is for him that of a "physiological illumination and interpretation" of all tables of values. The entire *Genealogy* must, in fact, be read as a hermeneutics of the history of moral interpretations. The passage from master- to story of the slave-morality reveals, for instance, how the same social reality (that of relations of domination) can receive two different, and indeed opposed, interpretations. The history of punishment is a long history of our interpretation of human suffering and cruelty. The analysis of asceticism has to be conducted in terms of the question what ascetic ideals might mean. They have, in fact, many historical meanings and interpretations. Nietzsche's fundamental insight is that human beings "would rather will nothingness than not will" for the will to nothingness still provides an interpretation of the human condition, whereas not to will is to give up on the whole enterprise of giving meaning to the phenomena.

This kind of consideration plays, however, a negligible role in Foucault's "Nietzsche, Genealogy, History." It was nonetheless to bear fruit later on in Foucault's own genealogical work; but it did so in a radically transformed fashion that makes it difficult for us to identify the Nietzschean roots. One of the insights of Nietzsche's hermeneutics is that we put interpretations on interpretations, and that moral interpretation, in particular, always presupposes other interpretations from which we can and must separate it in order to gain a proper view of the moral. An analogous thought can be found in Foucault's characterization of political power in the late 1970s and his overall characterization of power in the 1980s. Political power, he said in this first period, is power acting on power relations, and in the second he described power in general as action acting on actions. While Nietzsche understood moral interpretation as supervening on others, Foucault treated political power, or even power itself, as supervenient on other relations. The parallels are significant, since interpretation and the will to power are for Nietzsche related phenomena. Interpretation is, according to him, "introduction of meaning – not 'explanation'"; it is in most cases not the recovery of a meaning that is already there but the adding of a new interpretation "over an old interpretation that has become incomprehensible, that is now itself only a sign" (1968: 605). He concludes: "Our values are interpreted *into things*. Is there then any *meaning* in the thing in itself? Is meaning not necessarily relative meaning and perspective? All meaning is will to power (all relative meaning resolves itself into it)" (ibid.: 590).

Foucault came to the idea that power relations are layered on top of each other and that political power is always supervenient on other power relations in the late 1970s. Shortly after the publication of the first volume of *The History of Sexuality*, Lucette Finas interviewed him in the hope of getting him to expand on the theme of sexuality. But Foucault declared quickly that the whole point of the book had for him in reality been "a re-elaboration of the theory of power," adding sarcastically: "I'm not sure that the mere pleasure of writing about sexuality would have provided me with sufficient motivation" (Foucault 1980a: 187). The impetus for thinking about the problem of power, he added, had come to him "during the course of a concrete experience that I had with prisons, starting in 1971–72" (ibid.: 184). This had left him realizing that one needed to substitute a "technical and strategic" understanding of power for the traditional, "judicial and negative" one. The experience had taught him to reject thinking of power in terms of "exclusion, rejection, denial, obstruction, occultation, etc." (ibid.: 183), and to focus, instead, on its capacity to "make positive mechanisms appear" (ibid.: 186). Such a perspective could, in fact, help to analyze institutions "from the standpoint of power relations, rather than vice versa," as he was to put it elsewhere (2000: 243). And this would make evident in particular that the institution of the state could not account "for all the apparatuses in which power is organized" (Foucault 1980b: 188). There existed, in fact, relations of power "between all points of the social body," as, for instance, "between a man and a woman, between the members of a family, between a master and his pupil, between everyone who knows and everyone who does not" (1980a: 187). One needed, in other words, to assume the existence of a myriad particular mechanisms of power.

But if power relations are ubiquitous and politics is to be conceived in terms of them, does it not follow that everything is political? By 1977, some of Foucault's more adventurous readers were, indeed, drawing that sweeping conclusion. The same thought was clearly also on the mind of Foucault's interviewer when she asked: "Can one adopt a political standpoint regarding power? You speak of sexuality as a political apparatus. Could you define the sense you give the word 'political'?" (Foucault 1980a: 189). But Foucault was not to be trapped into endorsing the simplistic formula that was being ascribed to him. He responded cautiously instead: "To say that 'everything is political' is to affirm this ubiquity of relations of force and their immanence in the political field but this is to give oneself the task, which as yet has scarcely been outlined, of disentangling this indefinite knot" (ibid.). One had to remember, he added, that "political analysis and criticism have in a large measure still to be invented" (ibid.: 190). This was not meant to express ignorance of the long history of political thought, but to affirm the belief that political analysis had to be radically recast, that it could not rely on the old understanding of politics in terms of the institutional order of a polis or state and their rule or government, and that we needed to reconceptualize the domain of politics instead in terms of the concept of power. Such a rethinking of the basic concepts of politics had, in fact, been on Foucault's mind at least since the beginning of the 1970s when he had told Gilles Deleuze that the concepts of domination, rule, and government "are far too fluid and require analysis" (1977: 213).

Foucault obviously understood that there was something seductive in the formula that everything is political, just as there is in saying "everything is sexual," or "everything is in the mind," or "all action is selfish," or even "everything is beautiful in its own way." Each of these utterances seems at first sight illuminating in its stark generality (the "Wow!" effect), but each of them proves on closer examination to be empty of meaning. Each robs, indeed, its crucial term (be it political, sexual, mental, selfish, or beautiful) of its discriminatory power. This is not where Foucault was going. He was ready to grant that all social relations belonged to "a political field," he said to Lucette Finas, but he meant instead to speak of politics itself very precisely as a "more-or-less global strategy for coordinating and directing those relations" (ibid.: 189).

The simplest picture of politics that one might derive from this formulation would involve a division between a domain of inherently non-political relations (the "political field") and a second level of "strategic" political relations of power that coordinate and direct relations within this domain. But this two-tiered picture is for two reasons insufficient. First, the relations within the domain of power relations, the political field, are for Foucault by no means to be considered "elementary and by nature 'neutral'" (ibid.). They are, rather, typically the outcome of other and earlier strategic interventions. Second, the strategic relations that constitute politics are once more relations of power and so themselves are once again potentially subject to strategies of coordination and direction. Relations within a family, for instance, constitute a political field in Foucault's sense and we are, in principle, able to distinguish within this field among relations that are subject to strategic, supervenient interventions and those relations that constitute such interventions even though the distinction may, in practice, be often invisible in this relatively informal environment. The difference between political strategies of coordination and direction and the domain to which they are said to apply becomes, however, evident when we consider more organized institutions. Take, for instance, the case of law-making. Legislating is a political activity which issues in laws that concern prescribed, permitted, or forbidden activities. Thus traffic rules regulate the relations between people engaged in driving behavior; economic legislation organizes and legitimates business relations. Here the distinction between the supervenient, strategic, political intervention (the legislating) and the power relations that are being coordinated and regulated (the subject of the legislation) is straightforward. Power relations within a particular social sphere may at times seem immune to political intervention. Family life may at some point have been considered immune in this fashion, but the relations between parents and children and between marriage partners have today become highly politicized. Foucault tells Lucette Finas that for this reason it is necessary now to oppose a process of politicization to the use of existing techniques and mechanisms of power. The basic political challenge of our time is not for him the choice between political positions in "a pre-existing set of possibilities." It is, rather, "to imagine and to bring into being new schemas of politicization." He illustrates this by adding: "To the vast new techniques of power correlated with multinational economies and bureaucratic states, one must oppose a politicization which will take new forms" (1977: 190). Corporate and bureaucratic power have been for too long outside the purview of politics and must now be subjected to political intervention. Ever new areas of social relations may in this way become politicized over time, while others may cease to be so. Foucault had made a similar point already some years earlier when he had said in an another interview that "the frontier of the political has shifted, and so now subjects such as psychiatry, internment, or the medicalization of a given population have become political problems" and politics has in this way "colonized areas that had been almost political yet not recognized as such" (Eribon 2004: 293).

The idea that power relations are layered on top of each other to form a complex web of interconnections and that power – in particular, political power – must always be understood as supervenient on other power relations was to take a new turn when Foucault came to think more about action at the end of the 1970s. Eventually he even declared that it had never been his goal "to analyze the phenomena of power, nor to elaborate the foundations of such an analysis" (2000: 326). Instead, he claimed now to be interested in "the problematizations through which being offers itself to be, necessarily, thought" and such problematizations concerned, in turn, "those intentional and voluntary actions by which men not only set themselves rules of conduct, but also seek to transform themselves" (1985: 243). This momentous change in language indicates a shift of Foucault's attention from politics to ethics, that is, from social relations to the individual subject. Hence, he could also write that "it is not power, but the subject, that is the general theme of my research" (2000: 327). The shift did not mean, however, that he had completely given up on the concept of power or lost politics altogether from view. As late as 1983, he maintained "that all human relationships are to a certain degree relationships of power" (ibid.), but where he had previously tried to conceive action in terms of power relations, he now went about it in the opposite direction. Power was now to be understood in terms of action, politics in terms of ethics, and social relations in terms of an aesthetics of existence (the care of others in terms of the care of the self).

The move became first apparent in the late 1970s when Foucault began to speak of political power "as a mode of action upon the actions of others" (2000: 341 and *passim*). This formulation retained the earlier insight that politics involves supervenient relations; it added, in fact, nothing new to *that* idea; but the relations in question were now to be understood as relations in action rather than as effects of power. This marked a profound change in the way in which Foucault now understood politics and a dramatic advance in his analysis of the concept of the political. This is explicit in the essay "The Subject and Power" of 1982 which we can summarize in the following terms: (1) "What defines a relationship of power," Foucault writes succinctly, "is that it is a mode of action" (2000: 340). (2) And the exercise of power is to be understood specifically "as a mode of action upon action" (ibid.: 341). (3) Power "exists only as exercised by some on others." The term designates, in fact, "relationships between 'partners'" (ibid.: 340). (4) "Power relations are rooted in the whole network of the social" (ibid.: 345). To live in a society means to live in such a way that some individuals act on the actions of others. "A society without power relations can only be an abstraction" (ibid.: 343). (5) The exercise of power is concerned with "government" in a broad sense of the word. It is characteristic of our own period – not of all "government" – that power has become "progressively governmentalized, that is to say, elaborated, rationalized, and centralized in the form of, or under the auspices of, state institutions" (ibid.: 345).

With this new conception of power in hand, Foucault could now also articulate the difference between power and force – terms he had used almost indiscriminately earlier on – and explicate the relation between power and freedom, which had previously been mysterious. "A man who is chained up and beaten is subject to force being exerted over him, not power," he could now argue. But if the man can be induced to talk, rather than submit to death, "then he has been caused to behave in a certain way. ... He has submitted to government" and thus has submitted to power. As such the individual remains free – however marginal his freedom may be – and it is this freedom which guarantees that "there is no power without potential refusal or revolt" (ibid.: 324). The proposition "where there is power, there is resistance," which he had so dogmatically asserted in the first volume of *The History of Sexuality*, was thus finally receiving its justification. At the same time Foucault was also now able to identify the role of freedom in politics and the puzzling relation between power and freedom. He could write now that "power is exercised only over free subjects and only insofar as they are 'free'" (ibid.: 342). At the same time, he thought it characteristic of power, as "a certain type of relation between individuals ... that some men can more or less entirely determine other men's conduct" (ibid.: 324).

In conceiving of power relations that supervene on other relations of power and subsequently of actions that supervene on other actions, Foucault was, in effect, elaborating what Nietzsche had said about the stratification of supervenient interpretations. But he was, in this way, also making progress beyond Nietzsche. Nietzsche's language of interpretation suggests the image of genealogy as part of a scholarly hermeneutics; in speaking of the supervenience of power and action, the later Foucault said more clearly than Nietzsche that genealogy is above all a political undertaking. At the same time he was moving beyond a Nietzschean viewpoint. In focusing increasingly on action rather than power, he set aside Nietzsche's global perspective of the world itself as will to power in favor of a more limited, more distinctly human view of our form of life.

Conclusion

Now at the end of this painstaking investigation, I ask myself how important it is to determine the exact relations between Nietzsche and Foucault. What is to be gained from identifying the similarities and differences in their respective conception of genealogy? Are these questions of interest only for the historian of ideas?

Their real significance lies elsewhere: in the fact that genealogy is still an incomplete project. While we possess today all kinds of genealogical studies, it is still not clear what genealogy as such can deliver. Does it necessarily lead to the critical destruction of the values it examines? Is it meant to establish, perhaps, only the contingency of individual systems of values? Can it sometimes also vindicate values?[4] More broadly, we can ask: what is the range of genealogical research? Should there not be a genealogy of politics as well as of morality, of aesthetics as well as of religion? Do the concepts of will, of will to power, of power not also all call for genealogical investigation? Does the genealogical enterprise not also itself require genealogical dissection? What is meant to be the ultimate outcome of our efforts in the genealogical field? Nietzsche writes:

> To introduce a meaning – this task still remains to be done, assuming there is no meaning yet. Thus it is with sounds, but also with the fate of peoples: they are capable of the most different interpretations and direction toward different goals. On a yet higher level is *to posit a goal* and mold facts according to it; that is, active interpretation and not merely conceptual translation. (Nietzsche 1968, 605)

Genealogy here turns out to be critical history in the face of a politics of the future. Foucault came to see the matter eventually in similar terms. There was, for him, first of all the critical part of genealogy. "In its critical aspect ... philosophy is that which calls into question domination at every level and in every form in which it exists, whether political, economic, sexual, institutional, or what have you," he said in January of 1984 (1998: 300–1). But he realized also that "since the nineteenth century, great political institutions and great political parties have confiscated the process of political creation." And he thought that this should be combated. Needed instead was "political innovation, political creation, and political experimentation outside the great political parties, and outside the normal or ordinary program" (ibid.: 172). This process had to include the production of "instruments for polymorphic, varied, and individually modulated relationships." Foucault concluded:

> We have to dig deeply to show how things have been historically contingent, for such and such reasons intelligible but not necessary. We must make the intelligible appear against a background of emptiness and deny its necessity. We must think that what exists is far from filling all possible spaces. To make a truly unavoidable challenge to the question: What can be played? (ibid.: 139–40)

He adopted thus, eventually, Nietzsche's conception of genealogy as a political undertaking. But the kind of politics he envisaged differed radically from the one Nietzsche had in mind. Where, for Nietzsche, genealogy was meant to open up the possibility of new forms of domination, Foucault meant it to open up new spaces of freedom. Coming close to Nietzsche in one respect, he remained at the same time far from being "simply a Nietzschean." The qualifications that he added to that claim in his last interview prove to be much to the point.

Notes

1   Curiously enough, Maudemarie Clark and Alan J. Swensen translate the sentence as: "Precisely this is the long history of the origins of responsibility." (*On the Genealogy of Morality*, Indianapolis: Hackett Publishing, 1998, p. 36.) But this is surely just a sloppy bit of translation as the unaccounted-for plural ("origins") indicates.
2   Clark and Swensen are again careless when they render Nietzsche's "ursprünglichsten Personen-Verhältnis" as "most primitive relationship" (ibid.: 45).
3   I note in passing that the concept of the "effective" statement (not "effective history") belongs to the vocabulary of *The Archaeology of Knowledge*.
4   An intriguing attempt at a vindicatory form of genealogy is made by Bernard Williams (2002).

References

Eribon, D. (2004) *Insult and the Making of the Gay Self,* trans. M. Lucey. Durham, NC, and London: Duke University Press.

Foucault, M. (1972) *The Archaeology of Knowledge,* trans. A. M. Sheridan. New York: Pantheon Books.

Foucault, M. (1977) *Language, Counter-Memory, Practice: Selected Essays and Interviews,* ed. D. F. Bouchard, trans. D. F. Bouchard and S. Simon. Ithaca, NY: Cornell University Press.

Foucault, M. (1980a) *Power/Knowledge. Selected Interviews and Other Writings 1972–1977,* ed. C. Gordon. New York: Pantheon Books.

Foucault, M. (1980b) *The History of Sexuality,* vol. 1: *Introduction,* trans. R. Hurley. New York: Vintage.

Foucault, M. (1985) *The History of Sexuality,* vol. 2: *The Use of Pleasure,* trans. R. Hurley. New York: Pantheon.

Foucault, M. (1989) *Foucault Live (Interviews, 1966–84),* ed. S. Lotringer, trans. John Johnston. New York: Semiotext(e). Foreign Agents series.

Foucault, M. (1994a) *Dits et Ecrits, 1954–1988,* vol. 2. Paris: Gallimard.

Foucault, M. (1994b) *The Order of Things.* New York: Vintage Books.

Foucault, M. (1998) *Aesthetics, Method, and Epistemology. Essential Works of Foucault, 1945-1984,* vol. 2, ed. J. D. Faubion. New York: The New Press.

Foucault, M. (2000) *Power. Essential Works of Foucault, 1945–1984,* vol. 3, ed. Colin Gordon. New York: The New Press.

Nietzsche, F. (1968) *The Will to Power,* trans. W. Kauffman and R. J. Hollingdale. New York: Vintage Books.

Nietzsche, F. (1973) *Beyond Good and Evil,* trans. R. J. Hollingdale. London: Penguin Books.

Nietzsche, F. (1974) *The Gay Science,* trans. W. Kaufmann. New York: Vintage Books.

Nietzsche, F. (1979) "On Truth and Lies in a Nonmoral Sense." In D. Breazeale, ed. and trans., *Philosophy and Truth. Selections from Nietzsche's Notebooks of the Early 1870s.* Atlantic Highlands, NJ: Humanities Press.

Nietzsche, F. (1994) *On the Genealogy of Morality,* ed. K. Ansell-Pearson, trans. C. Diethe. Cambridge: Cambridge University Press.

Sluga, H. (2005) "Foucault's Encounter with Heidegger and Nietzsche." In G. Gutting, ed., *The Cambridge Companion to Foucault,* 2nd edn. Cambridge: Cambridge University Press.

Williams, B. (2002) *Truth and Truthfulness.* Princeton, NJ: Princeton University Press.

3

Foucault, Heidegger, and the History of Truth

Timothy Rayner

What does Foucault owe the philosophy of Martin Heidegger? Despite considerable interest in this question in recent years, the answer remains unclear. One problem is that commentators don't know where to look to find the answer. Without any prima facie evidence of the nature of Foucault's investment in Heideggerian thought, it is unclear at what points of his career Foucault was engaging with Heidegger, if at all. It is well known that Foucault was interested in Heidegger's work in the early 1950s, a period in which he flirted with a career in psychiatry. Foucault also cites Heidegger as an "essential philosopher" in his final interview, a few weeks before his death (Foucault 1988: 250). But Foucault's early work on existential psychology is widely perceived as a false start, and the final interview is contentious enough to have been excluded from the English version of his *Essential Works*. In light of this, it is easy to accord Heidegger a marginal status in Foucault's work. Foucault's engagement with Heidegger appears to stand in relation to his work in the same manner as bookends stand to a shelf of books – located adjacent to and outside the bounds of his *oeuvre* proper.

Such an interpretation does not stand up to scrutiny. It is impossible to exclude Heidegger from Foucault's *oeuvre*, since he leaks in from both sides. Approaching Foucault's *oeuvre* from the point of view of his early works, we find traces of Heidegger's conception of the human being in relation to language filtering into Foucault's publications of the 1960s. Hubert Dreyfus has argued that *Mental Illness and Psychology* (1962) (a revised version of Foucault's existential psychology-inflected *Mental Illness and Personality* (1954)) combines "early Heideggerian hermeneutics" with "a variation on Heidegger's later account of the stages by which the Western understanding of being covered up the truth of being" (Dreyfus 1987: ix). The same variation on Heideggerian history runs through the *History of Madness* (1961). Just as Heidegger argues that modernity has forgotten the truth of being, which lies obscured today behind technical discourse and metaphysical concepts of human experience, Foucault in this book presents madness, understood as the "absence of work" (*l'absence d'oeuvre*), as an original experience, covered over by the scientific language of mental illness and awaiting its Dionysian revival. The concept of madness as *l'absence d'oeuvre* remains a guiding theme for Foucault's inquiries into the ontology of literature in the 1960s. If we grant that Heidegger had a role in Foucault's formulation of this concept, it follows that a certain Heideggerian influence persists in his work at least until 1966, when Foucault published "The Thought of the Outside."[1]

Approaching matters from the other end of Foucault's *oeuvre*, we find that Heidegger becomes significant for Foucault at least four years prior to his final interview. Foucault commented on his relationship to Heidegger in 1980 and 1982. Independently, these comments may sound like off-the-cuff remarks. Together, they form the coordinates of a unique perspective on Heidegger's work with decisive implications for our interpretation of Foucault's career and the nature of his philosophical project.

Foucault delivers the first comment in a seminar at Berkeley in 1980. The point of the comment seems to be to shed light, by contrast with Heidegger, on his own approach to the history of modern subjectivity. Foucault states:

> For Heidegger, it was through an increasing obsession with *techné* as the only way to arrive at an understanding of objects that the West lost touch with being. Let's turn the question around and ask which techniques and practices form the Western concept of the subject, giving it its characteristic split of truth and error, freedom and constraint. I think that it is here that we will find the real possibility of constructing a history of what we have done and, at the same time, a diagnosis of what we are. (1997c: 178–9)

Given that he had not previously suggested that he was engaging Heidegger's work to understand the history of subjectivity (or anything else), we might be forgiven for thinking that Foucault refers to Heidegger at this point simply for the benefit of Heideggerians in the audience, such as Dreyfus. This perspective is harder to sustain with respect to the second comment Foucault makes on Heidegger, in a 1982 lecture at the Collège de France. Once again, Foucault makes the comment in the context of reflecting on his approach to the history of subjectivity. He prefaces the comment with a question: "What is the subject of truth, what is the subject who speaks the truth?" Foucault declares: "I have tried to reflect on all this from the side of Heidegger and starting from Heidegger" (2005: 189).

Foucault was notorious for extravagant extemporization, some of which must be taken with a grain of salt. Yet these comments on Heidegger are worth taking seriously. When we consider the nature of Foucault's research at the time of making the comments, keeping in mind, on the one hand, his claim in his final interview concerning the impact of Heidegger on his work, and, on the other, his indebtedness to a Heideggerian-inflected approach to history in his early publications, a clear perspective on his relationship to Heidegger comes into view. This concerns Foucault and Heidegger's shared interest to write a history of subjectivity and truth. Both these philosophers sought to understand how, in the modern age, subjectivity became the epistemological and metaphysical locus of truth. Both used historical argument to challenge our conception of the subject, with the aim of undermining the concept of constitutive subjectivity that has to a large extent defined modern thought and culture. In light of this, it is hardly surprising to find that Foucault approached the question of the history of the subject "starting from Heidegger." Heidegger, more than any other twentieth-century philosopher, took a historical and ontological perspective on the being of modern subjectivity.

My argument in this essay is that Foucault developed his own perspective on the history of the subject through a critical confrontation with Heidegger's history of being. This is not to suggest that Foucault came to accept the substance of Heidegger's philosophical ontology (cf. Han 2002: 13). As we shall see, in writing the history of truth, Foucault sought not only to distance himself from Heidegger's ontological project, but to counter and undermine it. Yet the fact that he was critical of Heidegger does not preclude the possibility that, in developing his historical narrative, he used Heidegger as a philosophical foil. Such is the position I take in this essay. By counterposing his account relative to the major steps in Heidegger's history of being, Foucault was able to define his reading of the history of subjectivity and truth, while undercutting Heidegger's philosophical conclusions. The outcome is a practice-based history of the modern subject *in its being*, which, while fragmentary, can be seen to stand alongside Heidegger's history of being as genuine philosophical contribution to understanding the present.

Heidegger and the History of Truth

Construed from the perspective of modernity, Heidegger's history of being is a story of how the subject emerged through the process of the forgetting of the truth of being. To appreciate Heidegger's historical argument, it is best that we begin with his account of truth as disclosure in *Being and Time* (1927).

Heidegger opens his account of truth as disclosure with a phenomenological critique of the traditional concept of truth as *adaequato intellectus et rei* – the agreement, or correspondence, between intellect and thing. Heidegger notes that for such a correspondence to occur, it is necessary that the judgment or assertion pertain to the thing as the thing it is – that is, in its being. More importantly, the judgment or assertion must somehow manifest, or "uncover" (*Entdecken*), the thing in its being. Heidegger insists on this point: "To say that an assertion '*is true*' signifies that it uncovers the entity as it is in itself" (1962: 261).

Heidegger's objective in this argument is to refocus reflection on truth away from judgments and assertions toward the being for whom truth exists: *Dasein*, the human being. *Dasein* ("there-being") is Heidegger's term for the being that finds itself in a world, presented with a manifest realm of things. Crucially, *Dasein* is not just *in* the world – it *is* its world or "clearing" (*Lichtung*) (Heidegger 1962: 401–2). This "world" is not a geographical space of objects, but an existential-temporal realm created through the implicit projection of a set of values, ends, and ideals inherited from the past into the future. Most of the time, Heidegger claims, *Dasein* is oblivious of the world it creates. The world fades into the background of human experience, manifested only as a vague and oppressive nothingness. But *Dasein* retains a "pre-ontological" understanding of the world. It is on this basis that *Dasein* understands beings in their meaningfulness and truth. For the purposes of appreciating Foucault's critique of Heidegger, we should underscore that *Dasein*'s pre-ontological understanding of being is essentially an understanding of *itself* as a world-disclosing entity. As Heidegger claims, *Dasein* – the being that discloses truth in judgments or assertions – "*is* its disclosedness" (ibid.: 263).

Following *Being and Time*, Heidegger amended his account of *Dasein*'s role in the disclosure of truth. By the 1930s, he had come to the position that the world or clearing is not the creation of *Dasein* at all, but the product of the "destining" (*Geschick*) of being as such. The projective-disclosive horizon that grants meaning and significance to things in the world is thereafter construed as a function of the truth of being – an epochal process of "unconcealment" that "shows and makes visible without showing or becoming visible itself" (Heidegger 1972: 30). *Dasein* is relegated to a supporting role in the revealing-concealing economy of the truth of being.

By taking a questioning stance toward the concealment of being, *Dasein* holds open the clearing and establishes its place of existence. Heidegger claims that *Dasein* is summoned to this task by the force of the withdrawal of the truth of being into concealment. But since the truth of being is inherently self-concealing, *Dasein* inevitably forgets its role in the economy of being and thus, even while participating in the event, forgets its essential nature. *Dasein*'s "forgetfulness," in Heidegger's view, has world-historical implications. From ancient times to the present day, he argues, human beings have become *increasingly* forgetful of the truth of being, to the point that they have forgotten being as such. This is how Heidegger thinks the modern subject came into existence. The modern subject is the product of a history of forgetting – the forgetting of the truth of being.

We are now in a position to understand the history of being. Heidegger's narrative begins in pre-Socratic Greece. He claims that the pre-Socratics enjoyed an originary proximity to the truth of being on account of their word for truth, *alētheia*. As the privative of *lēthe* (forgetting or concealment), *alētheia* connotes the unconcealment of beings in a manner which places appropriate emphasis on the primacy of concealment in the truth of being. Heidegger insists that subjectivism is "impossible" in the pre-Socratic locale (1977a: 147). Greek existence centered on an ecstatic experience. To be is to stand in the midst of the irruptive unconcealment of being.

Plato is responsible for the initial mistake that set the West on a course to subjectivism. Plato transformed the language of truth, substituting the term *eidos* (form or image) for *alētheia*. *Eidos*, Heidegger argues, lacks the lexical advantages of *alētheia* for conceiving the truth of being, since it merely connotes "the outward aspect that a visible thing offers to the physical eye" (1977b: 20). Thanks to Plato, Heidegger argues, "[t]ruth becomes … the correctness of apprehending and seeing … a characteristic of human comportment toward beings" (1998: 177).

The rise of Platonic philosophy established a new metaphysical approach to ontological inquiry focused on beings as opposed to being as such. Locating the essence of truth in the relationship between the human being and beings, the metaphysical tradition consigned the truth of being to obscurity. Aristotle's reinterpretation of the Platonic *eidos* put the tradition on an empirical path, locating the *eidos* in individual, material things. By the time the Romans translated Aristotle's term *energeia* as *actualitas*, the concept of truth as *alētheia* had faded into a mythical past. Truth had become actual truth and the inquiry into truth a debate over what counted as actuality.

Medieval Christian philosophers took a clear position in this debate. The medievals defined God as *actus purus*, "pure actuality" (Heidegger 2003: 23). This further transformed the nature and experience of truth. With the rise of the Church, Heidegger claims, the "locus of truth" is transferred to "faith – to the infallibility of … the doctrine of the Church" (1977a: 122). Heidegger argues that an experience emerged at this point with decisive implications for modern science and culture. Faith in the actuality of God enabled humans to become *certain* of the possibility of salvation and the means to its achievement (2003: 21–2). This experience was fundamental for medieval Christian culture (ibid.: 22). The ultimate implications of this experience, however, only begin to unfold in the seventeenth century. Modernity takes over the idea of Christian certainty, now construed as a property of subjective judgments. Heidegger claims: "Modern culture is Christian even when it loses its faith" (ibid.: 24).

Descartes' *Meditations* mark the beginning of the modern epoch in the history of being. Building on Platonic metaphysics and Christian certainty, Descartes identifies subjective self-representation as the most certain of experiences, that which cannot be doubted. Subjectivity, as a result, becomes the basis for understanding substance and being in general. The human being becomes "the relational center of that which is at such" (Heidegger 1977a: 128). Heidegger argues that "[t]he whole of modern metaphysics taken together, Nietzsche included, maintains itself within the interpretation of what it is to be and of truth that was prepared by Descartes" (ibid.: 127). Yet the Cartesian moment remained incomplete until Kant drew out its implicit representational content. Kant argues in the first *Critique* that "being" is not a predicate, "merely the positing of a thing, or of certain determinations, as existing in and of themselves" (1965: 504). The upshot is that being exists only in acts of subjective representation. For Heidegger, Kant's thesis about being marks the culminating moment in the history of the forgetting of being. It is the moment when "being" becomes pure subjectivity, and the truth of being becomes nothing at all.

Foucault and the History of Truth: First Pass

Foucault first signaled his intention to write a history of truth in 1970, in his inaugural lecture at the Collège de France. He presents results of this research in 1973 in lectures at the University of Rio and some methodological observations in 1974 at the Collège de France. After this, Foucault appears to abandon the history of truth as a framing perspective for his research until 1980. At this point it becomes central again, cast as a history of subjectivity and truth. We will consider this later work in the following section with a view to determining how much the project owes to Heidegger. First, let us reflect on Foucault's initial forays in this area.

In 1970, Foucault is mainly concerned to indicate the direction of future research. His first objective is to understand the transformation in the nature of truth between Archaic and classical Greece. In the Archaic period, Foucault claims, truth was a "ritualized act" inseparable from the "exercise of power." Poets and oracles were sanctioned to speak truth "as of right," determining justice and attributing "to each his rightful share" (1972: 218). Through the fifth and fourth centuries BC, this paradigm of ritual discourse was confronted by a new distinction between true and false discourse. Foucault agrees with Heidegger that Socrates and Plato were instrumental to the success of this latter conception of truth: "[B]eginning with Socrates, or at least with Platonic philosophy … effective, ritual discourse, charged with power and peril, gradually arranged itself into a disjunction between true and false discourse" (ibid.: 232). This transformed the nature of true-speaking: "the highest truth no longer resided in what discourse *was*, nor in what it *did*: it lay in what was *said* … its meaning, its form, its object and its relation to what it referred to. … And so the Sophists were routed" (ibid.: 218).

It is clear from these comments that Foucault's perspective on the history of truth in 1970 is informed by the Nietzschean understanding of power–knowledge relations that defines his subsequent work. Foucault makes an explicit case for a Nietzschean approach to the history of truth when he returns to the topic in lectures at Rio in 1973 (2000b: 5–14). Remarkably, Foucault here describes the goal of his research in precisely the terms he will use to describe his 1980s work: to write a history of *subjectivity and truth*. Foucault rejects the idea of the "subject of representation as the point of origin from which knowledge is possible and truth appears" (ibid.: 3). He claims: "The subject of knowledge itself has a history; the relation of the subject to the object; or, more clearly, truth itself has a history" (ibid.: 2).

Of the five lectures Foucault delivers at Rio, the second is the most relevant for our purposes. Here, Foucault uses Sophocles' *Oedipus Rex* to frame the political stakes of the ancient rupture in the history of truth. In Foucault's reading, *Oedipus Rex* dramatizes the demise of the ancient Assyrian god-king, all powerful and all-knowing, about whose mythical presence the Archaic paradigm of truth revolved (ibid.: 31). The ancient rupture in the history of truth reflects a fundamentally political event – "the dismantling of that unity of a magico-religious power which existed in the great Assyrian empires; which the Greek tyrants … tried to restore for their own purposes" (ibid.). Foucault points out how, at the start of *Oedipus Rex*, Oedipus behaves as if he has special access to knowledge. Of the citizens of Thebes, he was the only man capable of deciphering the riddle of the Sphinx. By the end of the play, Oedipus has discovered that he is the most deceived of men and blinds himself accordingly. The moral, Foucault concludes, is that power is blind. Truth is no longer the ritualized expression of power. From this point on, "the man of power would be the man of ignorance" (ibid.: 32).

Sophocles and Plato, on this account, are plebeian heroes of the democratization of truth. Without downplaying the importance of their victory, Foucault suggests that the demise of the ancient paradigm produced a new form of blindness – a blindness concerning the historical relationship between power and knowledge. Plato gave rise to "a great Western myth: that there is an antinomy between knowledge and power" (ibid.). Yet the relationship between power and knowledge, Foucault claims, is precisely what we must appreciate in order to understand the history of truth.

Foucault devotes the final three lectures at Rio to discussing the role of power relations in the emergence of two key scientific practices: inquiry and examination. While he doesn't return to the topic of the history of truth in these lectures, the fact that he chose to frame the lectures in these terms is itself significant. In the last two lectures of the series, Foucault locates the origins of examination as a scientific technique in the context of the emergence of modern disciplinary society. This is essentially the same argument that he develops in detail in *Discipline and Punish* (1975). What is remarkable about Foucault's treatment of this material in 1973 is that he frames it in light of the more general inquiry into the history of truth. This suggests that he initially conceived *Discipline and Punish* as a chapter in a history of truth, and not simply as a contribution to a history of power and power–knowledge relations.

The third and final time that Foucault addresses the topic of the history of truth in his 1970s work is in a lecture at the Collège de France in 1974. This discussion is particularly salient for our purposes, since Heidegger appears here, more or less explicitly presented as a philosophical interlocutor and foil.

Foucault, in 1974, is concerned to define his approach to the history of truth. To this end, he distinguishes what he describes as two different "series" of truth. On the one hand, there is *demonstrative* truth – truth as something that can be shown, demonstrated, and established. On the other hand, there is *truth as event* – truth as something that is commanded, coaxed, or provoked into existence. Foucault's examples of truth-events span history: "the oracle who speaks the truth at Delphi," the "Greek, Latin and medieval medicine of crises," and "alchemical practice," where truth is linked "to the *kairos*, and must be seized" (Foucault 2006: 236–7). For our purposes, however, Foucault's most provocative example of a truth-event is the ancient concept of truth itself, *alētheia*.

Rather than propose a Heideggerian definition of *alētheia*, Foucault refers to the work of the French classicist, Marcel Detienne. *Alētheia*, for Detienne, is "non-forgetting." But this is not the originary forgetting of the truth of being. Detienne points out that in a non-literate society such as that of ancient Greece, forgetting implies non-existence. The role of the ancient masters of truth, Detienne argues, was to perpetuate the non-forgetting of cultural exemplars, cultivating the remembrance of cultural ideals through their religiously sanctioned speech (1996: 47–8). Notably, this interpretation grants no special ontological knowledge to the master of truth, such as an understanding of the truth of being. As Foucault claims: "The relationship between [the] truth-event and the person who is seized by it … [is] not a relationship of knowledge [*connaissance*], but one of power" (2006: 237).

Once again, we are presented with a Nietzschean perspective on ancient truth. Yet something of a Heideggerian aspect comes into view in Foucault's discussion of how truth-events figure in the history of the sciences. Foucault argues that truth-events lie at the genealogical origins of the sciences. Demonstrative truth, he asserts, "derives in reality from the truth-ritual, truth-event, truth-strategy." As such, demonstrative truth is shaped and defined by a species of truth-productions it can scarcely acknowledge; it is "an aspect or a modality of truth as event and of the technology of the truth-event" (ibid.: 238). The Heideggerian aspect to this discussion comes sharply into view in Foucault's account of the overlap between these series of truth. Far from having superseded the truth-event series, demonstrative truth, Foucault claims, has "colonized" the truth-event series, occupying its space while appropriating its function and effects (ibid.: 236). As a result, demonstrative truth is perceived today as the only form of truth, while truth-events are roundly dismissed. This echoes Heidegger's account of the history of being, where the truth of being winds up both presupposed and concealed by a subsequent paradigm of scientific-representational truth.

Foucault was obviously aware of the resonance between his account and the dynamics of Heidegger's history of being. Immediately having presented this account, he moves to distinguish it from Heidegger's approach to the history of being. Foucault claims:

> There are those who are in the habit of writing the history of truth in terms of the forgetting of Being, that is to say, … they assert forgetting as the basic category of the history of truth … [However] forgetting can only take place on the ground of the assumed knowledge relationship, laid down once and for all. Consequently, I think [these people] only pursue the history of one of the two series I have tried to point out, the series of apophantic truth, of discovered, established, demonstrated truth, and they place themselves within this series. (ibid.: 238)

This passage reflects a keen critical understanding of Heidegger's history of truth, understood as a history of the forgetting of being. What is decisive about the passage is that it indicates precisely what Foucault rejects in Heidegger's approach to the history of truth. Foucault rejects the idea of "an assumed knowledge relationship" running through the history of truth – the idea of a pre-ontological understanding of being. Such an approach, in Foucault's view, reflects an implicit reliance on the idea of truth as something that can be demonstrated – here, now, or anytime. Contrary to Heidegger, Foucault thinks that the forms of truth that are most important to our history are not truths that are available to all people at all times, but iterative practices that are singular and rare, linked to power formations as opposed to onto-logical structures, discrete personal transformations rather than world-historical shifts in the experience of being. These intuitions were central to Foucault's final researches into the history of truth. Here, the critical engage-ment with Heideggerian history becomes apparent.

Foucault and the History of Truth: Second Pass

Foucault's ethical turn in the 1980s is usually perceived as marking a break in the trajectory of his research. After almost a decade of focusing on mod-ern power structures, Foucault revived the project of a history of sexuality – which he had commenced and then set aside in 1976 – focusing on the theme of ethical self-cultivation in Greek and Roman antiquity. If one assumes that the analysis of modern power structures is the defining fea-ture of Foucault's research in the 1970s, then the ethical turn certainly appears to mark a break in that work. If, on the other hand, one emphasizes

Foucault's attempt to develop an approach to the history of truth in the early 1970s, reflecting in particular on his framing of the research for *Discipline and Punish* in this light in 1973, a different picture emerges. Foucault's ethical turn amounts to a *return* – a return to the problematic of the history of truth.

This, to be sure, is how Foucault came to see his work at the end of his life. In the introduction to *The Use of Pleasure* (1984), he describes his work as "fragments" toward a history of truth. The shifts and changes in his final years, Foucault suggests, enabled him to appreciate this project "from a new vantage point and in a clearer light" (1992: 11). Nowhere is the perspective sharper than in Foucault's 1982 lectures at the Collège de France, *The Hermeneutics of the Subject* (2005). Here, Foucault presents a broad overview of the history of truth from Plato to the present day – a history, moreover, that he claims to have developed "starting from Heidegger" (2005: 189). Foucault's history of truth in 1982 converges with Heidegger's history of being at crucial points. At the same time, Foucault's argument presents a devastating challenge to Heidegger's line of historical interpretation, calling into question a fundamental presupposition of Heidegger's history and, indeed, his philosophical project.

In the 1980 and '81 series at the Collège de France ("Subjectivity and Truth"), Foucault had analyzed the "truth-games" involved in the regimen of sexual life in Greek and Roman antiquity. Here, Foucault identified the ancient principle of *epimeleia heautou*, or "care for self." In the 1982 series, care for self becomes the guiding theme of Foucault's research. Foucault argues that in antiquity the principle of care for self was more important than the Delphic principle, "know yourself" (*gnōthi seauton*). Where these two principles coincide, Foucault claims, "know yourself" was subordinated to "care for self" (2005: 4–5). Foucault argues later in the series that, despite the pre-eminence of the principle of care for self in the ancient world, attempts to reflect on the history of Western thought tend to take self-knowledge as their guiding theme for research. In this way, Foucault suggests, scholars are able to trace a straight line of development from "Plato to Husserl, though Descartes" (ibid.: 461). This, of course, is precisely how Heidegger read the history of truth. Heidegger presents a distinguished example of how to misread the history of truth, presupposing the constancy of self-knowledge in the form of the pre-ontological understanding of being.

Foucault, for his part, takes a Nietzschean approach to the history of truth. Rather than presuppose the human capacity for self-knowledge as a given, he asks how we came to be creatures that are capable of self-knowledge. To answer this question, he seeks to map the history of the relationship between the subject and truth *starting* with the principle of care for self – where care for self is seen to involve "technologies of the self" through which the self is created, transformed, and presented to the world as an object of knowledge.

Foucault takes his lead in this history from the ethical practices of the ancient Greeks. Much as Heidegger sees pre-Socratic life as indicating a purer, more authentic, relation to being, Foucault treats pre-Socratic ethics as a kind of naive template that subsequent concepts and practices have served to obscure. For the Greeks, Foucault argues, caring for oneself entailed the adoption of a *techné tou biou*, or "art of life." The objective of this *techné* was self-mastery – to keep oneself from being carried away by passions and desires, thus "to achieve a mode of being that could be defined by the full enjoyment of oneself, or the perfect supremacy of oneself over oneself" (Foucault 1992: 31). Foucault emphasizes that this work upon the self was not undertaken simply for the sake of self-cultivation. It was a question, instead, of preparing young men for a role in public life, by equipping the individual with the self-mastery required to take care of others.

The first point of convergence between Foucault and Heidegger's histories is the Platonic moment in the history of truth. Heidegger argues that Plato transformed the meaning of truth. Foucault presents a more nuanced perspective, arguing that Plato transformed the relationship to truth. Foucault argues that all forms of care for self involve an indispensable relation to truth. For the pre-Socratics, care for self involved assimilating a set of rules that functioned as both truths and prescriptions (Foucault 1997a: 285). The Platonic innovation was to introduce a new relation to truth – a *conversion to self* with decisive implications for the subsequent history of subjectivity. For the Platonic school, Foucault argues, care for self entailed the "ontological recognition" of self (1992: 88–9). Importantly, this was not the recognition of the soul as *substance*, but the recognition of the soul as *subject*, i.e., "the subject of instrumental action, of relationships with other people, of behavior and attitudes in general" (2005: 57). Plato, in short, introduced the form of subjectivity into the practice of care for self – not as a concept, but as a mode of relation, or conversion, to the ontological reality of self.

A second convergence can be seen in Foucault and Heidegger's accounts of the shift in ancient culture from Greece to Rome. Foucault argues that there were a number of significant developments in the practice of care for self in this period. While the Hellenes and Romans continued to work upon themselves, the idea of a freely chosen *techné tou biou* faded from view. Increasingly, the care for self became a universal task and obligation, to the extent that imperial Rome was defined by "a veritable culture of the self" (ibid.: 205). At the same time, the obligation to care for others that provided the original reason for the care for self slowly disappeared. Care for self became an end in itself, with the self as such as its reward (ibid.: 177).

Foucault remains strictly focused on the relations between subjectivity and truth in the 1982 lectures, and tends not to comment on the "truth-effects" of the practices under discussion. Still, it is easy to appreciate how the accumulated effects of the Hellenistic and Roman care for (and conversion to) self brought the experience of being-a-subject into relief. Foucault's account of the "absolutization" of the self in this period echoes Heidegger's argument that the Romans knew an experience of actuality that simply did not exist for the Greeks (ibid.). Yet, Foucault disagrees with Heidegger that these developments involved the entrenchment of a technological perspective on life. Heidegger, as Foucault notes, thinks that we lost touch with being through our obsession with technical mastery. As a result we became subjects. Foucault argues for the contrary perspective to this. In Foucault's view, human beings became subjects when life ceased to demand the application of a *techné*, calling instead for an ongoing test and cultivation of self. Foucault makes this point in his conclusion to the 1982 series. Heidegger is not mentioned but his presence is palpable – the themes speak for themselves.

> [I]f we accept … that if we want to understand the form of objectivity peculiar to Western thought since the Greeks we should perhaps take into consideration that at a certain moment, in certain circumstance typical of classical Greek thought, the world became the correlate of a *techné* … [and we accept that] the form of objectivity of Western thought was … constituted when, at the dusk of thought, the world was considered and manipulated by a *techné*, then I think we can say this: that the form of subjectivity peculiar to Western thought, if we ask what this form is in its very foundation, was constituted by a movement that was the reversal of this. It was constituted when the *bios* ceased being what it had been for so long in Greek thought, namely the correlate of a *techné*; when the *bios* (life) ceased being the correlate of a *techné* to become instead the form of a test of the self. (Ibid.: 486)

The third point of convergence between Foucault and Heidegger's histories concerns the link between medieval Christianity and modernity.

Foucault and Heidegger agree that medievalism and modernity are linked through an intensification of the experience of knowledge. Heidegger argues that the medieval concept of God enabled a new certainty regarding salvation. This experience provided the genealogical firmament for the self-certainty that underpins modern representationalism. Foucault develops a coordinate point of view, focusing on the role of self-knowledge in medieval confessional practices. Medieval pastoral power, Foucault argues, could not be deployed "without knowing the insides of people's minds, without exploring their souls, without making them reveal their innermost secrets" (2000a: 333). The Christians drew on Roman techniques of self-interrogation to enable individuals to participate in the generation of this knowledge through a "hermeneutics of the self." Foucault describes this as "an absolutely crucial moment in the history of subjectivity in the West" (2005: 364). By dramatizing the stakes of the Platonic conversion to self in light of questions of eternal salvation and damnation, Christianity intensified subjective experience to an absolute degree. While the objective of confessional practice was to encourage the penitent to renounce the sinful self, it is plain how these practices served to deepen the experience of psychological interiority and thus contributed to the formation of a positive subjectivity.

The final point of convergence between Foucault and Heidegger's histories concerns their respective treatments of Descartes and Kant. Descartes, for Heidegger, reflects the ultimate forgetting of being. Gathering the threads of Platonic and Christian metaphysics, Descartes lays down the fundamental principle of de-worlded, alienated humanity – that the human being is constitutive subjectivity. Foucault also associates Descartes with a uniquely modern experience of constitutive subjectivity. And, in a sense, he sees Descartes as guilty of an ontological forgetting. What Descartes forgets, however, is not the truth of being, but the historical ontological conditions for the existence of constitutive subjectivity. Supremely confident in the ontological fact of the *cogito*, Descartes is able to reject the care for self as a precondition of access to truth. For Descartes, the subject can access the truth through representational knowledge alone. Foucault perceives this as a threshold moment in the history of subjectivity. He claims:

[W]e can say that we enter the modern age (I mean, the history of truth enters its modern period) when it is assumed that what gives access to truth ... is knowledge (*connaissance*) alone. ... [T]he "Cartesian moment" takes on its position and meaning at this point, without in any way my wanting to say that

> it is a question of Descartes, that he was the inventor or that he was the first to do this. I think the modern age of the history of truth begins when knowledge itself and knowledge alone gives access to truth. That is to say, it is when the philosopher (or the scientist, or simply someone who seeks the truth) can recognize the truth and have access to it in himself and solely through his activity of knowing, without anything else being demanded of him and without him having to change or alter his being as subject. (2005: 17)

There is an irony to Descartes' position. Descartes represents the moment in the history of truth at which the subject assumes the right to claim authorship of its being and experience. Descartes takes this position oblivious to the history of practices of the self that are responsible for the creation of this experience. As Foucault notes, however, "we must not forget that Descartes wrote 'meditations' – and meditations are a practice of the self" (1997b: 278). While rejecting practices of the self as precondition of access to truth, Descartes uses these practices as part of his work. Foucault had previously discussed the role of transformative practice in Descartes' *Meditations* in his reply to Derrida, in 1972. In this earlier essay, Foucault argued that the *Meditations* are premised on a transformative exercise, which functions to qualify the subject as an entity capable of independently knowing the truth (1998: 405–6). A decade later, there is little evidence that Foucault had changed his point of view.

Foucault, however, has changed his point of view on how to situate Descartes in the history of thought. By locating Descartes at the onset of philosophical modernity, he implicitly alters the periodization of modernity that he had presented a decade and a half earlier in *The Order of Things*, thereby bringing his account of the modern phase in the history of truth into line with Heidegger's history of being. In *The Order of Things*, Foucault had distinguished classicism and modernity, with Descartes as the figurehead of the former period and Kant as the paradigmatic philosopher of the latter. But in 1982, Foucault transforms this periodization, presenting Descartes and Kant as the "two major moments" in the history of philosophical modernity (2005: 190). Descartes is responsible for the inauguration of the universal knowing subject and the idea of truth as the representation of the real. Kant, Foucault claims, adds a "supplementary twist" to the Cartesian innovation, arguing that the limits of knowledge "exist entirely within the structure of the knowing subject" (ibid.: 190, 26). It is almost as if Foucault were correcting Heidegger's reading of Descartes and Kant's relationship in the history of truth – affirming the perspicuity of Heidegger's insight, while rejecting the framework in terms of which Heidegger thought the matter through.

The convergences between Foucault and Heidegger's historical narratives go a long way toward explaining how Foucault, in his later work, approached the history of subjectivity and truth starting with Heidegger. At the same time, Foucault's history of truth brings to light one major philosophical difference between these thinkers. This concerns the role of self-knowledge in their respective historical accounts. Heidegger presents a story about how human beings, through metaphysical error and the will to mastery, lost touch with their essential truth and nature. Qua subjects, modern humans have forgotten being and thereby forgotten themselves – they must rediscover their *Dasein* in a fundamental act of ontological self-recognition. Foucault's account of the history of subjectivity and truth decisively undermines this point of view. Foucault argues, first of all, that ontological self-recognition is not an originary capacity but a historically determined practice. This practice can be traced back to the Platonic conversion to self. Furthermore, in Foucault's view, it is precisely this practice that is responsible for creating the modern subject. The upshot is that Heidegger's insistence that *Dasein* must remember what it has forgotten and recognize itself in its ontological truth places him within the very tradition that he seeks to oppose. Heidegger's strategy for overcoming the Platonic tradition *in thought* recapitulates that tradition *in practice*, inadvertently working to sustain that tradition rather than undermine it.

Far from a simple variation on Heideggerian history, Foucault's history of subjectivity and truth represents a decisive critique of one of the fundamental presuppositions of Heideggerian thought – the idea of the preontological understanding of being. Working with and against Heidegger, Foucault shows how the self-reflexive knowledge that Heidegger takes as a given has been created through a history of practices of the self. The fact that Foucault had indicated his opposition to the idea of the preontological understanding of being in 1974 suggests that his critical engagement with Heideggerian thought predates the history of subjectivity and truth by at least a decade. Once we add to this Foucault's encounter with Heidegger's ontology of language in the 1960s, we can begin to appreciate why Foucault claimed in his final interview that Heidegger had "always" been important for his work (1988: 250). Far from occupying the margins of Foucault's *oeuvre*, Heidegger was a central philosophical figure. It is high time that Foucauldian scholarship acknowledged the profundity of this philosophical debt.

Note

1   I develop an interpretation of Heidegger's role in Foucault's early concept of
    madness in *Foucault's Heidegger* (Rayner 2007: 37–43). The central thesis of this
    book is that the style of thinking that characterizes *l'absence d'oeuvre* informs
    the objectives of Foucault's work to the end of his career.

References

Detienne, M. (1996) *The Masters of Truth in Archaic Greece,* trans. J. Lloyd.
New York: Zone Books.

Dreyfus, H. (1987) "Foreword to the California Edition." In M. Foucault, *Mental
Illness and Psychology,* trans. A. Sheridan. Berkeley and Los Angeles: California
University Press.

Foucault, M. (1972) "The Discourse on Language." In *The Archaeology of Knowledge
and The Discourse on Language,* trans. A. M. Sheridan. New York: Pantheon,
pp. 215–37.

Foucault, M. (1988) "The Return of Morality." In L. D. Kritzman, ed., *Michel
Foucault – Politics, Philosophy, Culture: Interviews and Other Writings 1977–
1984.* New York: Routledge, pp. 242–54.

Foucault, M. (1992) *The History of Sexuality,* vol. 2: *The Use of Pleasure,* trans.
R. Hurley. London: Penguin.

Foucault, M. (1997a) "The Ethics of the Concern for Self as a Practice of Freedom."
In P. Rabinow, ed., *Ethics: Essential Works of Michel Foucault 1954–1984,* vol. 1.
London: Penguin, pp. 281–301.

Foucault, M. (1997b) "On the Genealogy of Ethics." In P. Rabinow, ed., *Ethics:
Essential Works of Michel Foucault 1954–1984,* vol. 1. London: Penguin,
pp. 253–80.

Foucault, M. (1997c) "Subjectivity and Truth." In S. Lotringer and L. Hochroth,
eds., *The Politics of Truth.* New York: Semiotext(e), pp. 171–98.

Foucault, M (1998) "My Body, This Paper, This Fire." In J. D. Faubion, ed., *Aesthetics,
Method and Epistemology: Essential Works of Michel Foucault 1954–1984,* vol. 2.
London: Penguin, pp. 393–417.

Foucault, M. (2000a) "The Subject and Power." In C. Gordon, ed., *Power: Essential
Works of Michel Foucault 1954–1984,* vol. 3. New York: New Press, pp. 326–48.

Foucault, M. (2000b) "Truth and Juridical Forms." In C. Gordon, ed., *Power:
Essential Works of Michel Foucault 1954–1984,* vol. 3. New York: New Press,
pp. 1–89.

Foucault, M. (2005) *The Hermeneutics of the Subject: Lectures at the Collège de France
1981–1982,* trans. G. Burchell. New York: Palgrave Macmillan.

Foucault, M. (2006) *Psychiatric Power: Lectures at the Collège de France 1973–1974*, trans. G. Burchell. New York: Palgrave Macmillan.

Han, B. (2002) *Foucault's Critical Project: Between the Transcendental and the Historical*. Stanford, CA: Stanford University Press.

Heidegger, M. (1962) *Being and Time*, trans. J. Macquarrie and E. Robinson. Oxford: Blackwell.

Heidegger, M. (1972) "Summary of a Seminar on the Lecture 'Time and Being.'" In *On Time and Being*, trans. J. Stambaugh. New York: Harper and Row, pp. 25–54.

Heidegger, M. (1977a) "The Age of the World Picture." In W. Lovitt, ed., *The Question Concerning Technology and Other Essays*. New York: Harper and Row, pp. 115–54.

Heidegger, M. (1977b) "The Question Concerning Technology." In W. Lovitt, ed., *The Question Concerning Technology and Other Essays*. New York: Harper and Row, pp. 3–35.

Heidegger, M. (1998) "Plato's Doctrine of Truth." In W. McNeill, ed., *Pathmarks*. Cambridge: Cambridge University Press, pp. 155–82.

Heidegger, M. (2003) "Metaphysics as History of Being." In *The End of Philosophy*, trans. J. Stambaugh. Chicago: University of Chicago Press, pp. 1–54.

Kant, I. (1965) *The Critique of Pure Reason*, trans. N. K. Smith. New York: St Martin's Press.

Rayner, T. (2007) *Foucault's Heidegger: Philosophy and Transformative Experience*. London: Continuum.

4

The Entanglement of Power and Validity: Foucault and Critical Theory

Amy Allen

Thus far, the Foucault/Habermas debate has been a rather lop-sided affair, with the bulk of the contributions to this topic consisting of substantial – if often unpersuasive – Habermasian critiques of Foucault (see Fraser 1989; Habermas 1987b; Honneth 1991; McCarthy 1991). As much recent work on Foucault has shown (including some of the contributions to this volume), the standard picture that Habermasians paint of Foucault as the anti-humanist, anti-Enlightenment, anti-modern nihilist is based at best on a partial reading, at worst on a misreading, of his work. In the context of the Foucault/Habermas debate, much less attention has been devoted to developing detailed Foucauldian critiques of Habermas (with the notable exception of Ashenden and Owen 1999). As a result, this side of the "debate" is considerably less well developed; hence the "debate" is not really a debate at all.

In an attempt to level the playing field, this paper has two primary aims: first, to articulate and develop a Foucauldian critique of Habermas, in particular of his account of autonomy, which forms the normative core of his social and political theory; and, second, to defend Foucault against the genetic fallacy objection that Habermasians have raised in response to this line of argument. As I hope will become clear, framing the debate in this way will allow us to get to the heart of their disagreement, which concerns their divergent accounts of the subject and its relation to power. I start by presenting a Foucauldian critique of Habermas's conception of autonomy, a critique that draws on Foucault's genealogical account of subjection to disciplinary power. I then go on to defend Foucault against the charge that his critique of the link between disciplinary subjection and autonomy commits the genetic fallacy. My ultimate goal, however, is not to exacerbate the split between Foucauldians and Habermasians by giving the former additional reasons to reject Habermas's view. Rather, my goal is to show, contra Habermas's own positioning of Foucault as the French poststructuralist Other, the importance of Foucauldian insights for the project of critical theory. I shall conclude by sketching out (too briefly, to be sure) what I take to be the most important of those insights.

Subjection and Autonomy: Foucault contra Habermas

In a wonderfully rich and important essay on the Foucault/Habermas debate, James Tully (1999) argues that the principal objections that Habermas and Habermasians have raised against Foucault – the charges of presentism, unreasonableness, relativism, and cryptonormativism – can be successfully turned around against Habermas. Drawing on the resources found in Foucault's work from 1977 forward, Tully articulates each of these Foucauldian criticisms of Habermas, arguing that Habermas's approach is insufficiently critical of its own present, rests on unreasonable assumptions about the superiority of a decentered view of the world, takes as universal a form of subjectivity that is both historically contingent and potentially problematic, and is excessively utopian (ibid.: 109–39). Without engaging directly with the specifics of Tully's argument, I would like here to adopt a similar argumentative strategy. Unlike Tully, I shall limit my focus to one – admittedly very broad – Habermasian criticism of Foucault that I think can productively be turned around to raise important Foucault-inspired questions about Habermas's own view. The crux of the criticism is Habermas's claim that Foucault's conception of the social is unsociological. As I hope will become clear, framing the dispute around this issue will allow us to get to the heart of a central strand of the Foucault/Habermas debate: their divergent accounts of the subject and its relation to power.

Twice in *The Philosophical Discourse of Modernity*, Habermas accuses Foucault of being "unsociological," first with respect to his concept of the social, later with respect to his Nietzschean conception of power (1987b: 242, 249). By this he seems to mean at least two things. First and foremost is the charge that Foucault understands power as a set of strategic relations that are coextensive with the social body; hence, Foucault equates a strategic conception of power with the social itself. According to Habermas, this leaves Foucault unable to explain the possibility of social order, for such an explanation depends upon the realization that our sociocultural form of life is dependent upon the "*communicative use* of propositionally differentiated language," a use that is "constitutive for the level of a genuinely social reproduction of life" (ibid.: 312). Inasmuch as Foucault's "genealogical historiography deals with an object domain from which the theory of power has erased all traces of communicative action" (ibid.: 286), Foucault is incapable of explaining how social order is possible, even as he assumes that power is institutionalized in more or less stable social orders. The second and related point is that Foucault conceives of individuals as "mechanically punched out" by a discourse formation (ibid.: 293). After all, Habermas argues, if one equates the social with power relations and power relations with strategic interactions, then "the socialization of succeeding generations can also be presented only in the image of wily confrontation. Then, however, the socialization of subjects capable of speech and action cannot be simultaneously conceived as individuation, but only as the progressive subsumption of bodies and of all vital substrata under technologies of power" (1991: 254). Rather than offering a genuinely sociological account of individuation through socialization, as Habermas (1992) himself aspires to do, Foucault is charged with viewing the individual as nothing more than the effect of power.

Habermas is correct, I think, to say that Foucault understands power in strategic terms. Indeed, as Arnold Davidson (2003: xviii) has argued, the strategic model of power "is one of the major achievements of Foucault's thought during [the middle of the 1970s]." By defining power in terms of strategic relations, Foucault seems to be making two claims: first, that power relations involve a confrontation or struggle between opposing forces (Foucault 1978: 92–3); and, second, that there is an instrumental logic to these struggles, such that each party to the struggle aims to get the other to do what he or she wants. Despite the other shifts in emphasis and approach between the middle and the late Foucault, the strategic model of power remains constant. As Foucault succinctly put the point in an interview a few months before his death, "power is not evil. Power is games of strategy" (1997a: 298). What is less clear is whether Habermas is right to suggest that Foucault's adherence to the strategic model of power, combined with his claim that power is omnipresent, renders Foucault incapable of explaining the possibility of social order, a possibility that his own analyses necessarily presuppose. Foucault, for his part, did not see the omnipresence and inescapability of strategic power relations as incompatible with either the communication relations that Habermas thinks ground stable social orders or the freedom that such orders seek to preserve. "When I speak of relations of power," Foucault insists, "I mean that in human relationships, whether they involve verbal communication …, or amorous, institutional, or economic relationships, power is always present: I mean a relationship in which one person tries to control the conduct of the other" (ibid.: 291–2). Far from denying the possibility of freedom, power relations so conceived *presuppose* freedom: "if there are relations of power in every social field, this is because there is freedom everywhere" (ibid.: 292).

Regarding his second charge, even a cursory reading of Foucault's late work shows that Habermas's claim that Foucault views the individual as nothing more than a mechanically punched out copy is, to say the least, problematic. To be fair to Habermas, the lectures that make up Habermas's *Philosophical Discourse of Modernity* were composed in 1983 and 1984 (the volume appeared in German in 1985), so Habermas's reading of Foucault obviously could not encompass Foucault's late work on ethics. However, even as an interpretation of Foucault's middle period genealogies of power, *Discipline and Punish: The Birth of the Prison* (1977) and the first volume of *The History of Sexuality* (1978), Habermas's reading is certainly debatable. As I have argued in more detail elsewhere (Allen 2000), although Foucault does claim that the individual is an effect of power, he does not regard the individual as merely or nothing more than an effect of power. Far from deterministically undermining the subject, Foucault's middle period works should be understood as articulating a series of contingent and historically specific conditions of possibility for subjectivity (see Allen 2003; 2008). Thus, Habermas (1994) is wrong to suggest, as he does in his final reflection on the occasion of Foucault's death, that Foucault's late work on ethics and the Enlightenment stands in contradiction to his earlier work on discourse and power-knowledge regimes.

As I have already indicated, I think that Foucault can be successfully defended against this Habermasian line of criticism. However, I shall not pursue this defense any further here. Rather, I would like to consider how this line of criticism might be turned around and deployed against Habermas, by exploring the worry that Habermas has a strangely unpolitical or de-politicized conception of the lifeworld.[1] Now, it turns out that this claim has already been raised by prominent critics of Habermas, in particular Axel Honneth and Nancy Fraser, both of whom take issue with Habermas's problematic tendency in his two-volume magnum opus, *The Theory of Communicative Action* (1984; 1987a), to use the term "power" to refer only to the functionally integrated administrative political system. For example, Honneth (1991) criticizes Habermas's distinction between system and lifeworld on the grounds that it presents a problematically norm-free system domain and a problematically power-free lifeworld. Similarly, Fraser maintains that it is "a grave mistake to restrict the use of the term 'power' to bureaucratic contexts" (1989: 121), for this renders Habermas's theory of communicative action incapable of fully illuminating gender dominance and subordination, which is secured largely through the lifeworld domain of the traditional nuclear family. The upshot of this line of criticism is that Habermas pays insufficient attention to the way that power operates in the core domains of the lifeworld: cultural meanings, social practices and norms, and socialization of individual and group identities. With his conception of the lifeworld, one might say, Habermas presents an object domain from which all traces of power have been erased.

In response to this line of criticism, Habermas clarifies his position: "[T]he lifeworld," he insists, "by no means offers an innocent image of 'power-free spheres of communication'" (1991: 254). To the contrary, Habermas specifies two ways in which his theory of communicative action enables an analysis of the role of power in the lifeworld. The first is his colonization of the lifeworld thesis, explored in detail in the second volume of *The Theory of Communicative Action*. This thesis highlights the ways in which increasingly complex systems-theoretical forms of power intrude upon lifeworld contexts, producing pathological effects. However, this response fails to meet the full force of Honneth and Fraser's objection, since their objection concerned the lack of an account of power relations that are internal to the lifeworld itself, not whether or not Habermas was willing to admit that power relations grounded in political systems could impinge on the lifeworld from the outside.

Habermas's second response, which appeals to his notion of systematically distorted communication, is, for our purposes, both more promising and more interesting. As Habermas explains in the first volume of *The Theory of Communicative Action*, systematically distorted communication is a case of concealed strategic action, in which "at least one of the parties [to an interaction] is deceiving himself about the fact that he is acting with an attitude oriented to success and is only keeping up the appearance of communicative action" (1984: 332). Because they give the appearance of an orientation toward mutual understanding when in fact they surreptitiously undermine that orientation, instances of systematically distorted communication "disrupt the validity basis of speech" (Habermas 2001: 147). Hence, in instances of systematically distorted communication, power relations, in the form of a strategic orientation to success, penetrate the structures of communicative action themselves. As a result, this account of power in the lifeworld gets Habermas much closer to an answer to Honneth and Fraser's objection.

However, the ability to meet this objection is purchased at a high price for Habermas. Because systematically distorted communications are latently and unconsciously strategic, they are neither fully strategic nor fully communicative. Habermas remarks that they are "confounding" because in them "the same validity claims that are being violated … at the same time serve to keep up the appearance of consensual action" (ibid.). The difficulty is that Habermas needs to rely on the distinction between strategic and communicative interactions in order to diagnose and critique systemic distortions of communication as distortions. Habermas must appeal to the notion of communicative action – that is, to the validity basis of speech – in order to distinguish between interactions that are genuinely communicative and those that are merely apparently so. Although this circle is not necessarily a vicious one, it does raise the difficult question of how confident we can ever hope to be in our judgments that communications are or are not systematically distorted. In the background here is the Foucauldian worry that it is not possible to disentangle power from validity (which is not the same thing as reducing the latter to the former). I shall return to this issue below.

In addition to these two ways in which Habermas explicitly acknowledges a role for power in the lifeworld, there is a third, largely unnoticed, account of power in the lifeworld. This account is implicit in Habermas's view of individuation through socialization, and it concerns the role that power plays in socialization processes, in particular in the formation of moral autonomy. Following Freud and Mead, Habermas maintains that the internalization of structures of authority is necessary for formation of moral autonomy. As he puts it: "[T]he task of passing to the conventional stage of interaction consists in reworking the arbitrary will of a dominant figure of this kind [that is, a parent] into the authority of a suprapersonal will detached from this specific person" (1990: 153). Through a process of internalization, the social sanctions that accompany norm violations "are assimilated into the personality of the growing child and thus made independent of the sanctioning power of concrete reference persons" (ibid.: 154). Although ideally the child continues to develop beyond this conventional stage and attains post-conventional autonomy – and with it the ability to reflectively and critically assess the validity of norms whose validity is accepted without question at the conventional stage – the interesting point is that Habermas views the internalization of the superior power and authority of the parent to be a necessary step in the formation of the autonomous post-conventional self. Hence, power turns out to be a condition of the possibility of autonomy. The autonomous subject emerges only through a process of subjection to the superior power of the parent (though it does not, in Habermas's view, emerge through that process *alone*).

To be sure, Habermas's use of the term "authority" is crucial here, since it signals that he sees the superior power of the parent as legitimate (or at least not obviously illegitimate). But his use of this term also raises the difficult issue of whether the child is able genuinely to assess the legitimacy of those power relations, given that she must first internalize them in order to become autonomous, and thus to be capable of assessing their legitimacy. Habermas is aware of this problem; as he notes: "[F]or the growing child this question [of whether a norm is valid] has already been given an affirmative answer before it can pose itself to him as a question" (1987a: 39). Still, he has faith that that the attainment of post-conventional autonomy allows him to avoid the pessimistic consequences that might seem to follow from this. Although the generality of the generalized other is rooted in the "the de facto power of a generalized imperative" insofar as "the concept is constructed by way of internalizing a concrete group's power to sanction," the very same "moment of generality *also* already contains the claim – aiming at insight – that a norm deserves to be valid only insofar as … it takes into account the interests of everyone involved" (ibid.). But the question remains: just how does the internalization of structures of power make them legitimate, especially given that the child must first internalize them in order to become capable of assessing them critically?

One possible answer to this is suggested, somewhat obliquely, by Habermas in *The Future of Human Nature* (2003). There, he acknowledges the fundamental asymmetry between parents whose communicatively structured interactions are "connected with internal reasons" and the child to whom the "'space of reasons' is not yet widely open" (ibid.: 62). Even though autonomy is only attained through a process of asymmetrical dependency, what we get out of that process is precisely autonomy, which includes the capacity to reflect on and break free of the power relations that have made us who we are. As Habermas puts it: "[Adolescents] can retrospectively compensate for the asymmetry of filial dependency by liberating themselves through a critical reappraisal of the genesis of such restrictive socialization processes" (ibid.). One might object at this point not only that this is an altogether too rosy picture of adolescence, but also that Habermas places too much faith in the power of autonomy understood as rational critique. As Judith Butler (1997) has argued, extending Foucault's analysis of subjection by integrating it with a Freudian account of the psyche, a stubborn attachment to and desire for our own subordination can perfectly well persist alongside a rational critique of the power relations that have formed us (see also Allen 2006; 2008). The worry is that Habermas's robust account of autonomy is plausible only insofar as we are overly sanguine about the depth and complexity of the relationship between power and the autonomous subject, a phenomenon that Foucault and Butler analyzed under the heading of subjection. If the subject only becomes a subject in and through a subjection to power relations – as Habermas's own account of individuation through socialization implicitly acknowledges – then we must confront the possibility that what looks like autonomy may in fact be something else entirely.

What Is Fallacious About the Genetic Fallacy?

But why, one might wonder, should it matter how the autonomous subject comes to be autonomous? If the result of the process that Habermas describes is autonomy, then what does it matter how that capacity was achieved? If we define autonomy as the ability or capacity for critical reflexivity, then doesn't the attainment of this capacity by definition give us the ability to reflect critically on our own subjection? And isn't any assumption to the contrary the result of a mistake in reasoning known as the genetic fallacy?

In one of her incisive and influential contributions to the Foucault/ Habermas debate, Fraser forcefully presents this objection against Foucault. She summarizes his position on the relationship between autonomy and disciplinary subjection as follows:

> Imagine a perfected disciplinary society in which normalizing power has become so omnipresent, so finely attuned, and so penetrating, interiorized, and subjectified, and therefore so invisible, that there is no longer any need for confessors, psychoanalysts, wardens, and the like. In this fully "panopticized" society, … the disciplinary norms would have become so thoroughly internalized that they would not be experienced as coming from without. The members of this society would, therefore, be autonomous. … But, it is claimed, this would not be freedom. (1989: 49)

Fraser argues that Foucault's critique presents no problem whatsoever for Habermas's (or, for that matter, any other) defense of autonomy. According to Fraser, a fully disciplinary society "seems objectionable only because

Foucault has described it in a way that invites the genetic fallacy, that is, because he has made it the outcome of a historical process of hierarchical, asymmetrical coercion wherein people have been, in Nietzschean parlance, 'bred' to autonomy" (ibid.: 50). Thus, even if Foucault is correct in claiming that autonomy is the result of a process of subjection to disciplinary power, the proper response for Habermas, according to Fraser, is simply to bite the bullet and say: "If that's discipline, I'm for it" (ibid.: 49).

It is worth noting first of all that Fraser's criticism implicitly suggests that Foucault is somehow *against* discipline, and that he is attempting to persuade his readers that they should be as well.[2] As I shall try to show, Foucault's position is much more complicated than this. But for the moment, let's stick with the debate as Fraser has framed it. Her charge is that Foucault's genealogical critique of the link between subjection and autonomy, a critique that also formed the basis of our Foucault-inspired critique of Habermas's account of individuation through socialization in the previous section of this paper, commits the genetic fallacy. (How) can Fraser's charge be answered?

The genetic fallacy is said to be committed when the source or origin of a belief, proposition, theory, or value is taken to be relevant to its evaluation (Cohen and Nagel 1934). Underlying the labeling of this fallacy as a fallacy is the assumption that how a belief, proposition, theory, or value originated is logically irrelevant to our appraisal of it. Fraser interprets Foucault as arguing that, in the fully panopticized society, the internalization of disciplinary power relations is necessary for the achievement of autonomy. Her claim that he commits the genetic fallacy stems, then, from the link that she assumes him to make between the origin of autonomy in a process of subjection to disciplinary power and his presumptively negative normative assessment of the value of autonomy itself. Her objection is thus that Foucault draws an inappropriate conclusion as to the nefarious nature of autonomous subjectivity on the basis of a historical story about its objectionable origins.

As I suggested a moment ago, an initial response to Fraser would be to point out that she is wrong to assume that the point of Foucault's genealogical argument is to convince us that discipline and autonomy are bad and should therefore be rejected. Contra Fraser, Foucault is not against discipline (or the Enlightenment or even autonomy, for that matter). As he famously put it: "My point is not that everything is bad, but that everything is dangerous, which is not exactly the same as bad" (1997b: 256). The link between disciplinary subjection and autonomy is not bad, but dangerous, and the point of Foucault's work is to make us attentive to these dangers. On this reading, Foucault's aim is not to reject autonomy on the basis of its connection to disciplinary power but rather to *problematize* it, where this means to reveal both that autonomy is made up of contingent practices with a specific history, enabling us to see *that* it can be changed, and how it has been constituted, enabling us to see *how* it can be changed. This reading would enable one to argue that Foucault's use of genealogy is not vulnerable to the genetic fallacy objection – though other uses, such as Nietzsche's, may well be – on the grounds that he is not drawing straightforward normative conclusions from his genealogical arguments. The aim of genealogy is not to show that discipline and autonomy are bad or pernicious but rather to show that the connection between autonomy and discipline is dangerous and in need of problematization (Koopman, forthcoming).

One of the advantages of this approach is that it coheres well with those numerous instances in Foucault's late work where he, perhaps surprisingly from Fraser's point of view, *praises* autonomy. For example, when Foucault (1997c: 314) invokes the Enlightenment principle of "a critique and a permanent creation of ourselves in our autonomy" as a guide for his own philosophical project, it is clear that he is not rejecting autonomy at all. If his aim is not to reject autonomy but to problematize it, then the point of his account of subjection is to show how the emergence of autonomy at a specific historical moment, with the Enlightenment, is connected to disciplinary power relations. As he puts it: "The 'Enlightenment', which discovered the liberties, also invented the disciplines" (1977: 222). Enlightenment liberty – construed as Kantian autonomy – is inconceivable without discipline; it is produced by turning discipline into self-discipline. Nor is Foucault against the Enlightenment. Instead, he refuses what he calls "the 'blackmail' of the Enlightenment," insisting that one does not have to be either for or against the Enlightenment (1997c: 312–13); rather, one can acknowledge one's own rootedness in and dependence upon the Enlightenment while simultaneously engaging in a "permanent critique of ourselves" as products of the Enlightenment (ibid.: 313). Nor, finally, is Foucault against discipline. Rather, one could understand his late work as addressing the question of how self-discipline, understood in the broadest sense as a mode of work on oneself, can be turned to new and different ends, can be made to serve the "undefined work of freedom" (ibid.: 316).

As feminist Foucauldians Ladelle McWhorter (1999) and Cressida Heyes (2007) have emphasized, self-transformation for Foucault necessarily involves taking up in a transformative way the relations of disciplinary subjection that have made us who we are. However there is a lingering problem with this strategy of responding to Fraser's critique. After remarking that his point is not that everything is bad but that everything is dangerous, Foucault continues:

> I think that the ethico-political choice we have to make every day is to determine which is the main danger. Take as an example Robert Castel's analysis of the history of the antipsychiatry movement. I agree completely with what Castel says, but that does not mean, as some people suppose, that the mental hospitals were better than antipsychiatry; that does not mean that we were not right to criticize those mental hospitals. I think it was good to do that, because *they* were the danger. And now it's quite clear that the danger has changed. (1997b: 256)

The question that the initial response to Fraser outlined above leaves on the table is this: is not the claim that something is dangerous itself a normative claim that is supposed to be substantiated by Foucault's genealogy? Even if we admit, as Foucault surely would, that the identification of danger – let alone the main danger – is a highly fallibilistic and contextually sensitive judgment, since even our own ethico-political interventions can create new dangers to which we will need to be attentive, this is still a normative judgment. Even if we agree that something can be dangerous without being therefore bad (for example, taking certain kinds of drugs, engaging in sado-masochistic sexual practices, or even sky-diving or rock-climbing), we call something dangerous precisely because it may lead to something bad (for example, getting hurt or killed, or harming someone else). Saying that something is dangerous does not allow one to sidestep the issue of the normative implications of genealogy altogether, as the response to Fraser outlined above attempts to do. This means that we have yet to answer the genetic fallacy charge.

A second, and more promising, line of response to Fraser's criticism is to admit that Foucault's genealogical critique of the connection between autonomy and subjection is a genetic argument, one that seeks to draw normative conclusions about the dangers of our Enlightenment conception of autonomy, but to argue that it is nevertheless not fallacious. As has been argued with respect to some informal fallacies (see Groarke 2007), commentators have recently challenged the assumption that all arguments that take the form of the genetic fallacy are indeed fallacious. In some cases, it is widely accepted that features relevant to the origin of a belief, proposition, theory, or value can be shown to be relevant to the truth or legitimacy of the belief, proposition, theory or value (see Crouch 1993 and Klement 2002).[3] In order for genetic arguments to be used non-fallaciously, we must know the causal history of the belief or value in question and be able to identify the features of that history that are relevant to the assessment of that belief or value. This suggests that the best question to ask in response to Fraser's critique is this: is it actually inappropriate for Foucault to draw conclusions about the dangerous nature of autonomous subjectivity from a genealogical story about its connectedness to disciplinary power relations?

In order to address this question, it is helpful to distinguish between structural and historical accounts of autonomy (on this point, see Benson 1994). Most philosophical conceptions of autonomy understand it as a capacity to reflect critically on one's beliefs, desire, values, normative commitments, and so forth. Structural accounts focus solely on an individual's current capacities, not on how she came to have those capacities. The most prominent structural accounts construe autonomy as the proper relationship between an individual's higher order and lower order desires (see, for example, Dworkin 1988; Frankfurt 1987). Historical accounts, by contrast, focus not only on an individual's capacities for critical reflection, but also on the process by which the individual came to have the desires (motives, values, beliefs) that she has (see, for example, Christman 1991; 1993).

Although this distinction emerges in the very different context of the analytic philosophy literature on autonomy, it nevertheless maps nicely onto the strand of the Foucault/Habermas debate under discussion here. Habermas's account is plausibly construed as a structural one. He understands autonomy as the capacity to reflect critically on and, if need be, to provide reasons for the moral norms, ethical values, beliefs, traditions, and so on that one endorses. There is, no doubt, an important historical dimension to Habermas's account. Autonomous individuals are produced through a process of linguistic socialization into a post-conventional society; their autonomy consists in their growing independence in relation to the social structures into which that socialization process integrates them (Habermas 1992). However, for Habermas, that historical dimension is relevant only insofar as it generates the capacity for reflexivity that is central to his notion of autonomy; it is not relevant for assessing the degree to which an individual is autonomous. As we saw above, for Habermas, assuming that those capacities are in place and are exercised appropriately, the agent is autonomous, no matter how she came to have them.

Foucault's approach, by contrast, is plausibly construed as a historical one. He shares with other proponents of the historical approach the view that the structural capacity for reflection is not a sufficient condition for autonomy (see Christman 1991). Historical autonomy theorists maintain that certain kinds of autonomy violations become evident only when we take into account the causal history of how individuals came to have the desires and beliefs that they do have; think, for example, of a person who was brainwashed to have the set of beliefs and desires that they currently have. The interesting twist that Foucault introduces is to interrogate not only the historical processes whereby modern individuals come to have the values and desires that guide self-reflection, but also the historically and socially specific processes that give rise to the capacity for self-reflection itself. As he puts it, "what is at stake" in his project "is this: how can the growth of capabilities be disconnected from the intensification of power relations?" (1997c: 317). Under conditions of late Western modernity, capacities that are typically linked to autonomy are inculcated in individuals by means of normalizing, disciplinary power. Thus, while modern subjects may seem perfectly autonomous according to the structural account because they have acquired the capacity for critical reflection, Foucault's genealogical-historical account reveals such causal history of the acquisition of that capacity, and its intimate connections to relations of power.

But suppose we grant that the causal history of the process whereby individuals attain not only the desires, values, and forms of life on which they reflect autonomously, but also the very capacity for reflexivity itself is relevant for our assessments of autonomy, how are we to assess that process? On what grounds can we claim that the process by which autonomy is achieved is illegitimate? There are two strategies for answering this question. The first, which I'll call the internalist strategy, asks what the agent would think were she to reflect on that causal history, and whether she would resist it if/when it is presented to her. The second, which I'll call the externalist strategy, asks from a third-person, external perspective whether the process whereby one has attained the capacity for autonomy is legitimate. Each of these approaches has its dangers (see Anderson 2008). The danger of the internalist approach is that it fails to account for the fact that the agent's willingness to endorse the historical conditions may itself be the product of pernicious, autonomy-inhibiting influences. On the other hand, the danger of the externalist approach is that it is difficult, if not impossible, to specify from a perspective external to the agent the conditions that constrain autonomy without arbitrarily labeling as non-autonomous those whose beliefs, values, and forms of life with which we happen to disagree.

If I am right that Foucault's account of autonomy is plausibly construed as a historical one, the distinction between the internalist and externalist versions of the historical approach to autonomy presents us with two possibilities for interpreting his argument. On the internalist reading, Foucault's aim is to point out to his readers the historical conditions of their formation as autonomous subjects, specifically, their connection with disciplinary, normalizing, panoptical power relations. But he leaves it up to the reader to decide whether or not to endorse those historical conditions. We have already seen a version of this reading of Foucault, in the context of the first line of response to Fraser's genetic fallacy objection that I discussed above. Although this reading seems at first glance to offer Foucault a way out of genetic fallacy objection, as I argued above, it does not really get him out of the problem. Nor does it fit very comfortably with Foucault's overall tone, which certainly seems to imply that he thinks that the fully panoptical society is dangerous in itself, whatever his readers might think. Moreover, as the discussion of the internalist and externalist strategies has revealed, it leaves Foucault open to the charge that the reader might well endorse those historical conditions only because she has been so thoroughly disciplined by them.

On the externalist reading, by contrast, Foucault is arguing that, when measured by standards that are external to the perspective of individual agents, the crucial role that disciplinary power plays in the formation of subjects renders their putative autonomy suspect. What looks and perhaps even feels like individual autonomy in late modernity is actually, given the historical conditions that have conditioned its emergence, disciplinary subjection. This reading has the advantage of avoiding the problems with the internalist reading, but it leaves Foucault open to objections concerning the difficulties inherent in trying to establish agent-neutral criteria for autonomy that are neither arbitrary, capricious, nor ideological. As I shall discuss in the concluding section, I think Foucault's frank acknowledgment of the necessary entanglement of power and validity provides at least a partial solution to this problem.

So which is the better reading of Foucault? There is textual evidence on both sides of this question, and it may well be that Foucault did not have a consistent position on this point.[4] As is probably evident by now, I favor what I am calling the externalist reading, but I am less interested in debating this interpretive issue here than I am in making two important conceptual points. First, on *either* of these readings, the genetic fallacy charge misses the mark. There is no fallacy involved in considering the causal history by means of which individuals come to be autonomous. If Foucault's genealogies show us that an individual only comes to be autonomous as a result of a process of subjection to disciplinary power relations, then this is relevant to our assessments of autonomy. When we talk about assessments of autonomy, however, it is important to recall, as I argued above, that Foucault's point is not that autonomy is bad. Rather, his point is that what looks like autonomy may not really be autonomy, especially to the extent that it does not acknowledge or reflect upon its own connection to power relations. If this is right, then Foucault's use of a genetic argument is not fallacious. This does not mean, of course, that Foucault's genetic argument is convincing. One might agree that the historical conditions under which individuals develop the internal rational and psychological capacities for deliberation, reflection, and so on, are relevant for assessments of autonomy, and yet argue that Foucault has not properly specified the relevant historical conditions.[5] But this is very different from disqualifying from the outset any and all historical-genealogical arguments about the formation of autonomy, as Fraser's genetic fallacy objection suggests we do. The real question should be this: does Foucault make a convincing case for the connection between disciplinary subjection and the formation of autonomy in late modernity?

The second point is that, on either of these readings, Foucault's genealogical critique is perfectly compatible with his *endorsement* of a structural account of autonomy. After all, the historical account of autonomy presupposes the structural account; it simply introduces an additional constraint on assessments of autonomy (see Christman 1993; Mele 1993). On the historical account, in order to be autonomous, an agent has to have certain capacities (for reflection, deliberation, and so on) *and* to have acquired them in an acceptable way (however we determine what counts as acceptable in this context). On my reading of him, Foucault does endorse a structural conception of autonomy and he connects this conception to the historical constraint that emerges from his genealogical critique. As I have argued in more detail elsewhere (Allen 2008: ch. 3), Foucault's positive conception of autonomy is an inversion of the Kantian conception. Rather than understanding autonomy as freely binding oneself to the moral law, Foucault understands it as freely calling into question that which is presented to us as necessary, thus opening up the space for the transgression of those limits on our experience that turn out to be both contingent and linked to objectionable forms of constraint. Hence his characterization of his own philosophical project as "oriented toward the 'contemporary limits of the necessary', that is, toward what is not or is no longer indispensable for the constitution of ourselves as autonomous subjects" (1997c: 313). If, with Fraser, we assume that the point of Foucault's genealogical critique is to equate autonomy with domination and thereby reject it, then such invocations will seem to stand in complete contradiction to that project (see also McCarthy 1991). If, on the other hand, we interpret that critique as articulating a historical constraint on assessments of autonomy – a project that aims not at rejecting autonomy as an ideal but instead at offering a better account of it – then this apparent contradiction disappears.

Finally, this interpretation brings out the advantages that Foucault's account of autonomy has over Habermas's. The question of how to disconnect the growth of capabilities from the intensification of power relations is one that Habermas will have a difficult time asking, let alone answering (see Tully 1999). Foucault's historical account also makes his view more hospitable than Habermas's to concerns about the impact of oppressive socialization practices on members of subordinated groups. Habermas's lack of attention to the role that power plays in socialization processes makes it difficult for him to offer a satisfactory critical-theoretical account of some of the most pressing social problems of our time, including sexism and racism, which are reproduced and maintained, in large part, through oppressive socialization practices. This perhaps explains why Foucault's conception of subjection has been so much more attractive to feminist theorists than has Habermas's, and this despite the theoretical difficulties concerning autonomy and agency that it seems to generate.

Conclusion

In his essay on Nietzsche in *The Philosophical Discourse of Modernity*, Habermas makes it clear that he rejects the genealogical critique of autonomy precisely because it leads ineluctably to a problematic reduction of validity to power. The problem with this reduction is this: "Once all predicates concerning validity are devalued, once it is power and not validity claims that is expressed in value appraisals – by what criterion shall critique still be able to propose discriminations? It must at least be able to discriminate between a power that *deserves* to be esteemed and one that *deserves* to be devalued" (Habermas 1987b: 125). Whereas Nietzsche attempted to solve this problem by appeal to his distinction between active, life-affirming forces and reactive, life-negating ones, Foucault proposes no such criterion. Thus, as Habermas (ibid.: 276) sees it, in Foucauldian genealogy, "validity claims are functionistically reduced to the effects of power"; hence, for Foucault, "the meaning of validity claims consists in the power effects they have" (ibid.: 279). The problematic result of this methodological decision is that "this basic assumption of the theory of power is self-referential; if it is correct, it must destroy the foundations of the research inspired by it as well" (ibid.: 289). Habermas maintains that Foucault realizes this difficulty and in response ties genealogy as a counterscience to the fate of subjugated knowledges. However, in the end, Habermas maintains that this attempt to escape the self-referentiality of the reduction of validity to power falls short: "Genealogy only confirms that the validity claims of counterdiscourses count no more and no less than those of the discourses in power – they, too, *are* nothing more than the effects of power they unleash" (ibid.: 281).

However, here again Habermas misunderstands Foucault, whose aim is not to reduce validity to power but rather to think through their inescapable entanglement. For instance, Foucault insists that his aim in introducing the notion of power/knowledge regimes was never to reduce knowledge to power; rather, it was to consider power and knowledge in their inseparability. Similarly, his critique of the relationship between power and truth aims not at a reduction of truth to power but at the recognition that "truth is a thing of this world: it is produced only by virtue of multiple forms of constraint" (2000a: 131). Nor should his claim that freedom is not outside of power be taken to mean that freedom is reduced to power; rather, it simply means that power and freedom exist in a permanent "agonism" (2000b: 342).

Moreover, in keeping with the strategy I pursued above, one can also turn this claim about the reduction of validity to power around, and argue that Habermas's insistence on the context transcendence of validity claims, their ability both to be rooted in particular contexts and yet to burst every context asunder, opens Habermas (1987b) up to the charge of theoretical authoritarianism (Cooke 2006). As Judith Butler puts the point: "The recourse to a position – hypothetical, counterfactual, or imaginary – that places itself beyond the play of power, and which seeks to establish the metapolitical basis for a negotiation of power relations, is perhaps the most insidious ruse of power" (1995: 39). If we take this point seriously, then the principal insight Foucault offers the project of critical theory is this: *theoretical authoritarianism can be avoided only by adopting a more historically self-conscious and critically reflexive stance toward our own normative standards.* This would include, but not be limited to, the ways in which our conception of autonomy may be connected to disciplinary subjection. The point is not to avoid making normative judgments, and Foucault does not, in my view, attempt to do this. The point is, as he put it, to "give up hope of ever acceding to a point of view that could give us access to any complete and definite knowledge of what may constitute our historical limits" (1997c: 316). This does not mean giving up on the possibility of critique, but it does mean re-imagining the project of critical theory as a much more self-consciously contextualist project. And this means that there is always more for critique to do, and that we, as critical theorists, "are always in the position of beginning again" (ibid.: 317).

Notes

1   The next few paragraphs summarize an argument that I develop in more detail in chapter 5 of *The Politics of Our Selves* (Allen 2008).
2   I am very grateful to Colin Koopman for pointing this out to me, and for careful and illuminating comments on an earlier version of this paper.
3   One could argue, for example, that such a view underlies epistemological reliabilism and some versions of virtue epistemology. Thanks to Colin Koopman for this suggestion.
4   Nor should he really be expected to, since I am importing this distinction from a set of debates in analytic philosophy that took place several years after Foucault died.
5   Richard Rorty (1992) seems to be heading toward such a criticism.

References

Allen, A. (2000) "The Anti-Subjective Hypothesis: Michel Foucault and the Death of the Subject." *The Philosophical Forum* 31 (2): 113–30.
Allen, A. (2003) "Foucault and Enlightenment: A Critical Reappraisal." *Constellations* 10 (2): 180–98.
Allen, A. (2006) "Dependency, Subordination, and Recognition: On Judith Butler's Theory of Subjection." *Continental Philosophy Review* 38: 199–222.
Allen, A. (2008) *The Politics of Our Selves: Power, Autonomy and Gender in Contemporary Critical Theory.* New York: Columbia University Press.

Anderson, J. (2008) "Disputing Autonomy: Second-Order Desires and the Dynamics of Ascribing Autonomy." *Sats – Nordic Journal of Philosophy* 9 (1): 7–26.

Ashenden, S. and D. Owen, eds. (1999) *Foucault contra Habermas: Recasting the Dialogue between Genealogy and Critical Theory.* London: Sage Publications.

Benson, P. (1994) "Free Agency and Self-Worth." *Journal of Philosophy* 91 (12): 650–68.

Butler, J. (1995) "Contingent Foundations: Feminism and the Question of 'Postmodernism.'" In S. Benhabib, J. Butler, D. Cornell, and N. Fraser, eds., *Feminist Contentions: A Philosophical Exchange.* New York: Routledge.

Butler, J. (1997) *The Psychic Life of Power: Theories in Subjection.* Stanford, CA: Stanford University Press.

Christman, J. (1991) "Autonomy and Personal History." *Canadian Journal of Philosophy* 21 (1): 1–24.

Christman, J. (1993) "Defending Historical Autonomy: A Reply to Professor Mele." *Canadian Journal of Philosophy* 23 (2): 281–90.

Cohen, M. and E. Nagel (1934) *An Introduction to Logic and Scientific Method.* New York: Harcourt, Brace and Company

Cooke, M. (2006) *Re-Presenting the Good Society.* Cambridge, MA: MIT Press.

Crouch, M. (1993) "A 'Limited' Defense of the Genetic Fallacy." *Metaphilosophy* 24 (3): 227–40.

Davidson, A. (2003) "Introduction." In Michel Foucault, *"Society Must Be Defended": Lectures at the Collège de France, 1975–1976.* New York: Picador.

Dworkin, G. (1988) *The Theory and Practice of Autonomy.* Cambridge: Cambridge University Press.

Foucault, M. (1977) *Discipline and Punish: The Birth of the Prison,* trans. A. Sheridan. New York: Vintage.

Foucault, M. (1978) *The History of Sexuality,* vol. 1: *An Introduction,* trans. R. Hurley. New York: Vintage.

Foucault, M. (1997a) "The Ethics of a Concern for Self as a Practice of Freedom." In P. Rabinow, ed., *Ethics: Subjectivity and Truth: Essential Works of Michel Foucault,* vol. 1. New York: The New Press.

Foucault, M. (1997b) "On the Genealogy of Ethics: An Overview of Work in Progress." In P. Rabinow, ed., *Ethics: Subjectivity and Truth: Essential Works of Michel Foucault,* vol. 1. New York: The New Press.

Foucault, M. (1997c) "What is Enlightenment?" In P. Rabinow, ed., *Ethics: Subjectivity and Truth: Essential Works of Michel Foucault,* vol. 1. New York: The New Press.

Foucault, M. (2000a) "Truth and Power." In J. Faubion, ed., *Power: Essential Works of Michel Foucault,* vol. 3. New York: The New Press.

Foucault, M. (2000b) "The Subject and Power." In J. Faubion, ed., *Power: Essential Works of Michel Foucault,* vol. 3. New York: The New Press.

Frankfurt, H. (1987) "Freedom of the Will and the Concept of a Person." In H. Frankfurt, *The Importance of What We Care About*. Cambridge: Cambridge University Press.

Fraser, N. (1989) *Unruly Practices: Power, Discourse and Gender in Contemporary Social Theory*. Minneapolis: University of Minnesota Press.

Groarke, L. (2007) "Informal Logic." *Stanford Encyclopedia of Philosophy*. http://plato.stanford.edu/entries/logic-informal/. Accessed November 3, 2008.

Habermas, J. (1984) *The Theory of Communicative Action*, vol. 1: *Reason and the Rationalization of Society*, trans. T. McCarthy. Boston, MA: Beacon Press.

Habermas, J. (1987a) *The Theory of Communicative Action*, vol. 2: *Lifeworld and System: A Critique of Functionalist Reason*, trans. T. McCarthy. Boston, MA: Beacon Press.

Habermas, J. (1987b) *The Philosophical Discourse of Modernity: Twelve Lectures*, trans. F. G. Lawrence. Cambridge, MA: MIT Press.

Habermas, J. (1990) "Moral Consciousness and Communicative Action." In J. Habermas, *Moral Consciousness and Communicative Action*, trans. C. Lenhardt and S. Weber Nicholsen. Cambridge, MA: MIT Press.

Habermas, J. (1991) "A Reply." In A. Honneth and H. Jonas, eds., *Communicative Action: Essays on Habermas's Theory of Communicative Action*. Cambridge, MA: MIT Press.

Habermas, J. (1992) "Individuation through Socialization: On George Herbert Mead's Theory of Subjectivity." In J. Habermas, *Postmetaphysical Thinking: Philosophical Essays*, trans. W. M. Hohengarten. Cambridge, MA: MIT Press.

Habermas, J. (1994) "Taking Aim at the Heart of the Present." In M. Kelly, ed., *Critique and Power: Recasting the Foucault/Habermas Debate*. Cambridge, MA: MIT Press.

Habermas, J. (2001) "Reflections on Communicative Pathology." In J. Habermas, *On the Pragmatics of Social Interaction*, trans. B. Fultner. Cambridge, MA: MIT Press.

Habermas, J. (2003) *The Future of Human Nature*. Cambridge: Polity.

Heyes, C. (2007) *Self-Transformations: Foucault, Ethics, and Normalized Bodies*. Oxford: Oxford University Press.

Honneth, A. (1991) *The Critique of Power: Reflective Stages in a Critical Social Theory*, trans. K. Baynes. Cambridge, MA: MIT Press.

Klement, K. (2002) "When is Genetic Reasoning Not Fallacious?" *Argumentation* 16: 383–400.

Koopman, C. (forthcoming) *Genealogy as Problematization*.

McCarthy, T. (1991) "The Critique of Impure Reason: Foucault and the Frankfurt School." In T. McCarthy, *Ideals and Illusions: On Deconstruction and Reconstruction in Contemporary Critical Theory*. Cambridge, MA: MIT Press.

McWhorter, L. (1999) *Bodies and Pleasures: Foucault and the Politics of Sexual Normalization*. Bloomington: Indiana University Press.

Mele, A. (1993) "History and Personal Autonomy." *Canadian Journal of Philosophy* 23 (2): 271–80.
Rorty, R. (1992) "Moral Identity and Private Autonomy." In *Michel Foucault: Philosopher*, trans. T. J. Armstrong. New York: Routledge.
Tully, J. (1999) "To Think and Act Differently: Foucault's Four Reciprocal Objections to Habermas's Theory." In S. Ashenden and D. Owen, eds., *Foucault contra Habermas: Recasting the Dialogue between Genealogy and Critical Theory.* London: Sage Publications.

5

Foucault, Davidson, and Interpretation

C. G. Prado

It is hard to imagine two thinkers more disparate than Michel Foucault and Donald Davidson. Each typified a different canonical and methodological tradition, and it is unlikely that Davidson thought of Foucault's work as philosophy or Foucault of Davidson's as of much interest. Nonetheless, aspects of their thought actually are complementary. No doubt surprisingly to many, Foucault's understanding of subject formation complements Davidson's account of linguistic interpretation. My aim in describing this complementarity is to show how Foucault's work was of a depth and importance that makes it transcend canons and entrenched methodologies.

For a decade my project has been to interest analytic philosophers in Michel Foucault's work (Prado 2000; 2003a; 2003b; 2006). This paper was prompted by the opportunity to contribute to the present volume commemorating the 25th anniversary of Foucault's death. To combine my project and this commemorative objective, I discuss how some of Foucault's ideas, a continental thinker and postmodernist, apply to Davidson's work, one of the analytic tradition's most prominent exponents and the least likely to be linked with Foucault (Ramberg 1989; Lepore and Ludwig 2005).

My inclination was to expand on what I have written elsewhere about Foucault and John Searle; however unlikely a pair Foucault and Searle may seem, there were connections between them (Prado 2006). They knew one another in Berkeley. Foucault referred to Searle in print; in "What Is an Author?" Foucault refers to "Searle's analyses" in discussing proper names and compares his own use of "speech activity" with Searle's use of "speech acts" (Rabinow 1984: 105; Foucault 2001: 13). Searle taught a course on Foucault's *The Order of Things* and they shared an interest in Velasquez's *Las Meninas* (Searle 1980; Foucault 1973: 3–16). In addition, there are a few limited comparative treatments of the two, most notably Hubert Dreyfus and Paul Rabinow's comparison of Foucault and Searle on statements and speech acts (1983: 45–8).

Contrary to Foucault and Searle, as far as I have been able to determine Foucault and Davidson did not comment on each other's views. When Davidson read his "A Nice Derangement of Epitaphs" at Queen's University, in Kingston, Ontario, in September 1984, I commented on the paper and drew parallels with Gadamer and Foucault but got little uptake from Davidson on Gadamer and none on Foucault (Davidson 1986; Ramberg 2003). Davidson and Foucault apparently never met. The likeliest venue for them to have encountered one another was Berkeley, where Foucault and Searle met, but Foucault had left Berkeley by the time Davidson arrived there in 1981.

For my purposes, the lack of contact between Foucault and Davidson is an advantage because it underscores that despite each having achieved a standing that made their respective writings exemplary instances of two different canonical and methodological traditions, a conception basic to Foucault's thinking complements and in a way completes an account equally basic to Davidson's thought.

My point of departure is a remark by a reviewer of my *A House Divided* (Prado 2003a). Commenting on a parallel I draw between Foucault and Davidson, the reviewer agrees that Foucault and Davidson "are useful mutual supplements," adding that it would be a "great project to supplement Davidson's austere account of interpretation" with Foucault's insights (Prado 2003b; Wheeler 2004: 5). What follows is a start on that project.

I begin with acknowledgment that complementing Davidson's account of interpretation with anything Foucault had to say is impeded by an unfortunate attitude, an irreducible difference in level of technicality, and an obstructive misperception. The unfortunate attitude is the widespread dismissal by analytic philosophers of Foucault, whose work is "completely ignored by most American philosophers" despite its huge influence (Eribon 1991: 313). Foucault is described as having "nothing to say [about] philosophical theories of truth and knowledge" and Richard Rorty tells us that "a distinguished analytic philosopher said that 'intellectual hygiene' requires one not to read … Foucault" (Nola 1994: 3; Rorty 1982: 224). Contrary to this view, I think to write off Foucault "is a disservice … to the important ideas that he can bring to North American philosophy" (Prado 2000: 145).

The irreducible difference has to do with how Davidson's philosophizing focuses on fundamental logico-linguistic issues, whereas Foucault's consideration of linguistic communication and of what he calls "discourses" is at the level of what most analytic philosophers would consider linguistic pragmatics. Foucault's interest in language is in institutional discourses: the idioms of the hospital, the prison, the asylum, and of the learned disciplines. I make no attempt in what follows to diminish this difference between Davidson and Foucault; my aim is only to show how Foucault's conception of subject formation complements Davidson's account of interpretation.

The obstructive misperception is an entrenched belief that Foucault's relativism regarding truth entails irrealism – specifically, linguistic idealism. This misperception is the most serious in the present context because, if Foucault were a linguistic idealist, it would preclude complementing Davidson's views with his. To proceed, I first deal with the obstructive misperception of Foucault as a linguistic idealist; I next outline the aspect of Davidson's account to which Foucault's ideas are most relevant; I then offer my proposal about how Foucault's conception of subject formation complements Davidson's account of interpretation.

The Misperception

Foucault's is a relativistic conception of truth. He maintains that statements are only true or false when they meet the requirements of a particular discursive "regime of truth." Every society has "types of discourse which it accepts … as true" as well as "mechanisms … which enable one to distinguish true and false statements." Each also has those "who are charged with saying what counts as true" (Foucault 1980a: 131).

Foucault's relativization of truth follows on his understanding of truth as entirely linguistic: a property of sentences rather than a relation that some sentences bear to something beyond themselves. Truth is *currency in discourse*, not a mirroring of states of affairs. Foucault's conception of truth loosens "the embrace, apparently so tight, of words and things" (1972: 49). He separates truth from the disposition of the world by making *being true* a status granted to sentences in discursive formations rather than those sentences corresponding to states of affairs.

Foucault's relativization of truth is the reason why he is seen as a linguistic idealist, and his being so would preclude application of his ideas to Davidson's account of interpretation because Davidson's account presupposes realism. The trouble is, Foucault's understanding of truth as a property that is practice-bestowed rather than world-bestowed looks to many to entail denial of the world. This is wrong; there are no ontological implications in Foucault's relativism putting him at odds with Davidson on realism (Prado 2000; 2006). Foucault explicitly rejects linguistic idealism or the view that there cannot be objects and relations between them independent of language in which those objects are named and the relations between them described. He insists his relativization of truth "does not mean that there is nothing there and that everything comes out of somebody's head" (1984: 17).

But linguistic idealism is ambiguous between an ontological interpretation that holds objects do not exist without language, and an epistemological interpretation that holds only that objects cannot be objects of thought or belief if there is no language in which they are named and referred to. Foucault holds the epistemological position despite his impatient dismissal of linguistic idealism. And perhaps because of that impatience, he provides no textual acknowledgment that I have found of the difference between the ontological and epistemological versions of linguistic idealism.

Foucault's rejection of linguistic idealism is rooted in his repudiation of the implications of his archaeological work, which did have ontological linguistic-idealist implications because it was structuralist in character, notwithstanding Foucault's claim that he used "none of the methods, concepts, or key terms that characterise structural analysis" (1973: xiv). Structuralism made discourse the autonomous determinant of practice, so gave discourse ontological priority. Foucault eventually rejected structuralism and the ontological implications in his archaeology by ceasing "to treat language as autonomous and as constitutive of reality," thus ridding himself of the irrealism that "lurk[s] in the structuralist suggestion that discourse organizes ... all social practices" (Hoy 1986: 4).

Rejection of structuralism and linguistic idealism turned on Foucault's abandonment of the "variants of a strict analysis of discourse" used in his earlier books. This rejection was effected by his introduction of the notion of power or power relations which "had not been previously thematized" in his work (Dreyfus and Rabinow 1983: 104). Foucault explains that his earlier work missed "the problem of ... the effects of power" on discourse (1980a: 105). What is important about this rethinking is that acknowledgment of the effects of power on discourse acknowledges the influence of the nonlinguistic on the linguistic, thus negating the structuralist priority of the linguistic. However, things are different with genealogy. While archaeology had evident ontological implications, genealogy does not, despite integral relativization of truth. Foucault's denial of linguistic idealism regarding genealogy does not have to do with the existence of nonlinguistic reality, but rather its lack of an epistemic role in the establishment of the truth of statements.

"We are subjected to the production of truth through power" (Foucault 1980a: 93). By understanding truth as a product of power, Foucault denies only that nonlinguistic reality is what makes beliefs and statements true. Perhaps surprisingly, he agrees with Wilfrid Sellars that attributions of truth "do not assert relations between linguistic and nonlinguistic items" and both disagree with Searle, for whom "[s]tatements are made true by how things are in the world" (Sellars 1968: 82; Searle 1995: 219). Rorty concurs with Foucault and Sellars, maintaining that there is "no way of transferring nonlinguistic brutality ... to the truth of sentences" (Rorty 1991: 81). Davidson essentially shares this view, maintaining that "[n]othing ... no thing, makes sentences ... true: not experience ... not the world, can make a sentence true" (1985: 194). Reality is "dumb," silent; it is the cause of beliefs expressed in statements, not what makes those statements true (Foucault 1972: 49).

A bar to understanding truth as wholly linguistic is accepting that sentences about our physical environment are not true in virtue of corresponding to how things are in that environment. The difficulty is complicated by Foucault sometimes sounding as if he accepts truth as accurate representation of reality in some cases. The ambiguity is due to his critical focus being disciplines like economics and psychiatry: forms of inquiry "which try to give themselves the status of sciences" by presenting their theoretical conclusions as accurately portraying objective natures and processes (Foucault 1983a: 208). This focus makes it appear as if truth is power-produced in the social sciences and other institutionalized discourses, but not in the physical sciences. That this is a mistake is clear in a question Foucault raises when discussing the relation between power and knowledge:

> [I]f, concerning a science like theoretical physics or organic chemistry, one poses the problem of its relations with the political and economic structures of society, isn't one posing an excessively complicated question? ... [O]n the other hand, if one takes a form of knowledge like psychiatry, won't the question be much easier to resolve[?] ... Couldn't the interweaving of effects of power and knowledge be grasped with greater certainty in the case of a science as "dubious" as psychiatry? (Foucault 1980a: 109)

Foucault understands *all* truth as linguistic and power-produced. Any apparent ambiguity is due to how showing that power produces truth in the physical sciences is a very difficult matter and not one he undertakes. He explicitly rejected interpretation of his position as distinguishing between hard truth about physical reality and what passes for truth in other contexts, joking that when he asserts power produces truth, many say "'Ah good! Then it is not the truth'" (Foucault 1984: 17). Power-produced truth is all the truth there is.

Many find the two-truth interpretation of Foucault's claims compelling because they fail to understand how the truth of a sentence like "Water expands when it freezes" can be a product of power. They may grant that whether "freezes" means "loses caloric fluid" or "loses mean kinetic energy" is a product of power, but few are prepared to grant that the truth of the sentence is not a function of water expanding when it freezes. A second difficulty is that Foucault employs four different senses of truth, including one which is only partly linguistic, without distinguishing clearly among them (Prado 2000). The first sense is the *criterial* and is evident in Foucault's claim that every society "has its regime of truth" (ibid.: 118; Foucault 1980a: 131). The criterial use is a version of cultural relativism in being about what counts as true in particular discourses, whether they be those of diverse cultures or the idioms of different learned disciplines.

The second and textually most prevalent sense is the *constructivist*, in which the truth of sentences is a function of power's making them true in discourses by preferential and supported employment of those sentences and their logical equivalents (Prado 2000: 119). Power makes sentences true by sanctioning and promoting their use. This is how we are constantly "subjected to the production of truth through power" and how truth is currency in discourse (Foucault 1980a: 93).

The third or *perspectivist* sense of truth derives from Nietzsche's view that truth is not the linguistic mirroring of states of affairs and that there are "only interpretations" (Prado 2000: 122; Nietzsche 1968: 267). But what Foucault takes from Nietzsche is not denial of the objective world. Alexander Nehamas' (1985) understanding of Nietzschean perspectivism applies to Foucault in that, for Foucault, perspectivism is denial of the possibility of descriptive completeness. Foucauldian perspectivism is understanding that there cannot be a holistic description of the world within which diverse perspectives can be rationalized as so many true but incomplete points of view.

The fourth sense of truth is the *experiential*, which distinguishes between truth learned through investigation (*l'enquête*) and "truth" realized in experience (*l'épreuve*) (Prado 2000: 128). The latter results when cognitive elements rearrange themselves because of provocative experiences and we come to see something differently. What we achieve in "limit experiences" is truth that "does not belong to the order of that which is, but rather of that which happens: it is an event" (Miller 1993: 271). Experiential truth is "repugnant to both science and philosophy" because it is not propositional (ibid.: 270). Experiential truth is about change or realignment of attitudes and beliefs.

It is the first two senses that concern us, and, with them in mind, what needs clarification is captured in a passage where Foucault explains that in speaking about truth, he does not mean "the ensemble of truths which are to be discovered and accepted," but rather means "the ensemble of rules according to which the true and the false are separated and specific effects of power attached to the true" (Foucault 1980a: 132). Unfortunately, Foucault muddles things with bad phrasing, supporting the misperception that he is ambiguous about truth and nonlinguistic reality. Foucault ought not to speak of *truths* in the first clause of this passage, but rather of *factuality*.

Dreyfus and Rabinow render the passage more perspicaciously, translating it as Foucault saying he is not concerned with "those true *things* which are waiting to be discovered" (Dreyfus and Rabinow 1983: 117). Their translation underscores that what Foucault is setting aside are not truths but nonlinguistic states of affairs, which, being things, events, and states of physical reality, are neither true nor false.

Rorty puts the point clearly when he acknowledges "brute physical resistance" in defending the pragmatic account of truth against charges of irrealism: brute reality does not play an epistemic role regarding the truth of sentences (Rorty 1991: 81). Despite his lack of clarity, this is Foucault's position. Unlike Foucault, Rorty explains the intuitive connection between linguistic truth and brute reality, saying that we have the capacity to "pair off bits of the language with bits of what one takes the world to be," as when we "rap out routine ... reports like 'This is water,' 'That's red'" (Rorty 1982: 162). What ties some sentences to physical reality is *our* doing, not some elusive correspondence. Sentences, then, are not *made* true by how things are in the world; they are only *related to* how things are in the world by us. Rorty grants that the pairing of sentences with states of affairs is "messy ... [o]nce one gets to negative universal hypotheticals, and the like," but neither messiness nor Foucault's unwillingness to tackle how power produces the truths of physics and chemistry suffice to make him a linguistic idealist (ibid.).

Consideration of how Foucault uses and deals with truth makes clear that his conception of truth as linguistic is not denial of the objective world. Denying that objective reality has an epistemic role in truth-making is not ontological denial of reality. We are not precluded, then, from applying Foucault's ideas to Davidson's account of interpretation.

Davidson on Interpretation

Turning to Davidson's account of interpretation, what is central is that he rejects the traditional understanding of language as conventional. He does not think that language users communicate by following conventional rules about the meaning and interpretation of statements. This is why he finds the idea of "a language" suspect. Davidson rejects language as conventional "for the simple reason that communication *does* succeed without the kind of regularity in the use of language that the conventional account presupposes" (Ramberg 1989: 101). This is the point made in "A Nice Derangement of Epitaphs" (Davidson 1986).

Davidson explains successful linguistic communication without recourse to linguistic conventions by focusing on language users' expectations regarding utterance meanings. He calls users' expectations *prior* and *passing* theories, speaking of "theories" basically because the expectations are recursive. Davidson contends that a language user "has, at any moment of a speech transaction," an operant theory enabling bi-directional interpretation. Language users have expectations regarding what to make of other speakers' statements and what listeners should make of their own statements. Prior and passing theories are described in this way:

> For the hearer, the prior theory expresses how he is prepared in advance to interpret an utterance of the speaker, while the passing theory is how he *does* interpret the utterance. For the speaker, the prior theory is what he *believes* the interpreter's prior theory to be, while his passing theory is the theory he *intends* the interpreter to use. (Davidson 1986: 442)

Hearers enter "speech transactions" with expectations regarding the utterances they anticipate hearing, but in particular circumstances they may understand what they hear other than as expected for contextual reasons. Speakers enter speech transactions with expectations regarding how hearers will understand their utterances, but in particular circumstances they may mean hearers to understand their utterances differently for contextual reasons.

An example illustrates the difference between prior and passing theories. Jules has invited Jim to his home. Jim arrives and Jules greets him at the door. Jules and Jim enter a speech transaction as Jules utters the sentence: "Glad you could come." Jules intends Jim to interpret this sentence as his being welcome, and Jim is prepared to hear some such utterance and to interpret it as meaning he is welcome. However, Jules adds: "Julia dropped by." Ordinarily, Jules would intend this to be interpreted by Jim merely as information regarding Julia's presence, and usually Jim would so interpret the utterance. But Jules and Jim both know that Julia is Jim's ex-wife and that there is animosity between them. This shared knowledge changes the situation and different interpretations come into play. Jules intends that Jim interpret his utterance, "Julia dropped by," not just as information that Julia is there, but as "Perhaps you'd best not come in," and Jim so interprets the utterance.

If language is conceived of as conventional, there is no difficulty about the intended and interpreted meaning of "Glad you could come," but there is a problem about intending and interpreting "Julia dropped by" as "Perhaps you'd best not come in." The problem is explaining Jules's utterance's idiosyncratic success. It would be a reduction to absurdity of the conventional account to introduce ad hoc conventions to explain how "Julia dropped by" is intended and successfully interpreted as "Perhaps you'd best not come in." Consider that if Jules and Jim shared different knowledge, Jules's statement could have been intended and correctly interpreted by Jim as "Now you can meet Julia."

Reference to knowledge shared by Jules and Jim indicates how Davidson's account of interpretation presupposes two conditional elements that enable successful linguistic communication. Both are enabling conditions in the sense that, rather like transcendental principles, they make effective interpretation possible. The first element is *realism*, which enables communication by excluding obstructive skepticism. Communication cannot proceed if some individuals take their interlocutors and/or the environment they share with them as possibly subjective or in some other way problematic.

The second element is *the principle of charity* or presupposition that interlocutors share mainly true beliefs about their common environment. This principle enables communication by excluding reflective or unreflective attribution to hearers of gross systematic error and/or conceptual incommensurability. Communication cannot proceed if individuals take their interlocutors as mostly wrong about everything they believe or as conceptualizing their awareness in unimaginably alien ways.

Skepticism about interlocutors' beliefs, conceptualizations, existence, and the common environment would preclude successful communication, but there is more involved beyond these conditional factors. There are questions about how prior and passing theories are acquired and how they are stimulated in the sense of why one or another is applied. Davidson offers little regarding the acquisition and application of prior and passing theories, saying only that language users apply their prior and passing theories on the basis of "knowledge of the character, dress, roles, sex, of the speaker, and whatever else has been gained by observing the speaker's behavior, linguistic or otherwise" (Davidson 1986: 441).

Davidson, working at a high level of abstraction, is justified in not detailing how prior and passing theories are acquired or what determines their application on particular occasions. Nonetheless, his account is certainly "austere" in referring only to language users' knowledge about their interlocutors. This minimal reference glosses a large number of factors and says nothing about how roles, for instance, are recognized in the first place. The austerity of Davidson's account brings us to Foucault.

The Proposal

Given that linguistic idealism does not bar doing so, application of Foucault's ideas to Davidson's account of interpretation goes as follows. I begin by noting the nature of Foucault's interest in language. Referring to how Foucault surprisingly overlooks the identity of statements and speech acts when considering Searle's work, Dreyfus and Rabinow explain that the reason for the oversight is because Foucault's interest is "entirely different from ... Searle's. He is not concerned with *everyday* speech acts. ... Rather, Foucault is interested in just those types of speech acts which ... gain their autonomy by passing some sort of institutional test" (1983: 47–8).

Foucault's interest is in institutionalized discourses: the idioms of institutions like hospitals and prisons and of institutionalized practices like medicine, psychiatry, and the social sciences. Unlike Searle and Davidson, he is not concerned with what enables successful language use in the first instance. But what matters here is not the focus of his interest but his underlying conception of how individuals come to use language as they do. Though Foucault does not pursue the matter of how everyday speech acts work, his treatment of institutional discourses presupposes a particular understanding of how language is used, and that understanding centers on a thoroughly anti-Cartesian conception of the subject.

For Foucault, subjects are not essence-defined entities who pre-exist the conduct-determining beliefs they acquire and the acts they perform. Subjects are emergent; they supervene on trainable *bodies* as products of what bodies *do* (1983a: 208). Foucault tells us that "[d]iscipline 'makes' individuals"; that "discipline creates out of the bodies it controls … individuality" (1979: 170, 167). This is why his genealogical analytics are concerned not only with investigating what "conditions, limits, and institutionalizes discursive formations," but with tracing "the different modes by which … human beings are made subjects" (Dreyfus and Rabinow 1983: 104; Foucault 1983a: 208).

The fundamental idea in Foucault's understanding of how subjects are formed is as old as Aristotle's *Nicomachean Ethics*: "A state [of character] arises from [the repetition of] similar activities" (Aristotle 1985: 35). What Foucault adds to Aristotle's idea is that the forming of subjects has two inseparable aspects: planned and deliberate influences on individuals – the effects of discipline; and happenstance influences resulting from the actions of others and contextual factors. The latter condition the former, often rendering discipline's results problematic.

The disciplining of bodies, and so the forming of subjects, is best exemplified by the governance of inmates of prisons and asylums. How discipline works is considered in detail in *Discipline and Punish* (Foucault 1979). Foucault then applies his methodology in the first volume of *The History of Sexuality* to broader societal discipline by considering social governance of sexual practices and the forming of sexual subjects (Foucault 1980b).

The relevance of the formation of subjects, and the core of my proposal, is that how language users interpret what is said to them and how they intend what they say should be interpreted are functions of their being the subjects they are made to be. In Davidsonian terms, the prior and passing theories language users employ are products of what made and makes them the subjects they are. The disciplined and happenchance behavior that forms subjects instills interpretive inclinations as integral parts of inculcated perspectives and attitudes.

To understand how interpretive inclinations are instilled in individuals, it helps to look at the purest cases of learning to interpret a speaker, and the most relevant are found in Davidson's (2001) discussion of *radical interpretation* or learning to understand speakers with whom one does not share a language. Individuals engaging in radical interpretation are attempting to instill in themselves the interpretive inclinations that would otherwise be imposed on them in familial, educational, and social contexts.

Similarly to W. V. O. Quine's radical translation, Davidson's radical interpretation centers on attending to speakers' utterances and actions, and the apparent stimulants of the utterances and actions. Quine's best-known example of radical translation involves a speaker uttering "gavagai" and gesturing when a rabbit runs by and the radical translator hypothesizing that "gavagai" means "rabbit" in the speaker's language. The translator works only with the utterance, the speaker's actions, and the apparently most relevant thing or event in the immediate environment. Davidson goes a little further than Quine, being concerned not only with what "gavagai" means in the speaker's language, but also what the speaker intends by saying "gavagai" as the rabbit runs by.

Davidson adds the two crucial elements referred to above in his account of radical interpretation: interpreting the utterances of speakers with whom no language is shared requires assuming shared, mostly true beliefs about the common environment – the principle of charity; and radical interpretation proceeds on the assumption that the mostly true beliefs speakers and interpreters share are about an objective environment – realism.

Only given these assumptions can radical interpretation proceed as a relating of speakers' utterances to what is taken as stimulating those utterances. As noted above, skepticism about the objective reality of interlocutors' shared environment hinders or precludes interpretation, and allowing the possibility of conceptual incommensurability also hinders or precludes interpretation. Objects of common awareness could not be taken as utterance-prompts or referents if speakers' conceptualization of awareness is thought possibly to differ significantly from that of interpreters or if the independent reality of those objects is thought systematically problematic.

Aside from bringing out the importance of charity and realism, radical interpretation also brings out more clearly than normal cases how the first part of "[w]hat matters to successful linguistic communication is the intention of the speaker to be interpreted in a certain way" (Davidson 2005: 51). Speakers' intentions are what radical interpreters are trying to establish by observing the connections between speakers' utterances and actions and the things and events in the shared environment. Generally, radical interpreters are trying to form prior theories with respect to speakers they are trying to understand so as to be "prepared in advance to interpret an utterance" (Davidson 1986: 442). More particularly, they are trying to form passing theories to achieve "the actual interpretation of the speaker's words along the intended lines through the interpreter's recognition of the speaker's intention" (Davidson 2005: 51).

Assuming that what radical interpreters do when they communicate successfully with speakers of a language previously unknown to them is not best understood as their learning new linguistic conventions, how should we understand their acquisition of new prior and passing theories? Moreover, how are prior and passing theories applied, and how may passing theories override prior theories in particular exchanges? Something more than what Davidson offers is needed.

Complementing Davidson's account of interpretation with Foucault's ideas centers on understanding acquisition of interpretive inclinations or prior and passing theories as changes in subjects. If language were conventional in the way Davidson rejects, the acquisition of interpretive inclinations as learned linguistic conventions would be the acquisition of behavior-determining beliefs. For Foucault, the acquisition of interpretive inclinations is integral to the forming of subjects. He explains this in terms of how discipline and power relations work, but John Dewey puts the same basic point more simply in terms of *habit*. Dewey tells us that "habits … constitute the self" (1930: 25). In a remark that could easily have been made by Foucault, Dewey contends that "[w]ere it not for the continued operation of all habits … no such thing as character could exist"; he adds that "[c]haracter is the interpenetration of habits" (ibid.: 38).

In a further instance of a kind of intellectual synchronicity with Foucault, Dewey remarks that "[t]he basic characteristic of habit is that every experience enacted and undergone modifies the one who acts and undergoes [it]," adding that "this modification affects, whether we wish it or not, the quality of subsequent experiences." This is because "it is a somewhat different person who enters into them"; it is a somewhat different subject who has those subsequent experiences (Dewey 1988: 18). This is exactly Foucault's understanding of subject formation: governed actions instill habits, and habits cumulatively make subjects.

What Foucault offers to complement Davidson's account of interpretation, then, has to do with how we can conceive the acquisition of prior and passing theories. The key idea is that their acquisition is changes *in* the subject, as opposed to only acquisition of beliefs *by* the subject. Acquisition of prior and passing theories is not the learning of conventions, as Davidson rightly contends, but instead is modification of subjects through habit-formation.

Use of Foucault's ideas about subject formation does more than provide a clearer way of understanding how prior and passing theories are acquired; it also provides a clearer way of understanding everything Davidson glosses as what language users know about their interlocutors. What they know or have is not so many beliefs, so much information; rather, it is interpretive and behavioral dispositions that are the elements of the complex, integrated wholes that constitute them as subjects.

To proceed, it is important to recall that Foucauldian subjects are emergent; that the body is "the locus of a dissociated self," a dissociated self that has "the illusion of [being] a substantial unity" (Foucault 1971: 83). The body supports a constructed subject that does not recognize itself as constructed and takes itself to be an essence-defined singularity existent prior to the habit-inculcating effects of socialization and education. Lack of recognition of the constructed nature of the self results in misguided efforts to understand behavioral and interpretive dispositions as intentional states, which in turn raises questions about their acquisition and application. When it is understood that behavioral and interpretive dispositions are constitutive elements of subjects, rather than intentional states that subjects acquire, their acquisition can be understood as inculcation of habit and their application as basically the only interpretive and behavioral responses open to subjects in various situations. Of course, new practices may be deliberately engaged in, as in the case of radical translation, but that is a matter of modifying or adding to subjects' constitutive dispositions.

A problem that arises in applying Foucault's constructivist conception of the subject to Davidson's account of interpretation has to do with the implicit nature of the philosophical import of Foucault's contentions. He speaks of the need to develop what he calls "ontologies":

> [First,] an historical ontology of ourselves in relation to truth through which we constitute ourselves as subjects of knowledge; second, an historical ontology of ourselves in relation to a field of power through which we constitute ourselves as subjects acting on others; third, an historical ontology in relation to ethics through which we constitute ourselves as moral agents. (Foucault 1983b: 237)

But despite his calling these genealogical analyses "ontologies," what Foucault offers is anthropological and historical treatment of subject formation; he leaves philosophical content mostly implicit. There is need, then, to flesh out a key aspect of that implicit content, and to do so I borrow from Searle.

What Searle (1987) offers that is of use is his description of how by coping with the world around us, many of the intentional activities that we engage in become and are retained as nonintentional capacities. This description enables understanding of how behavioral and interpretive dispositions – specifically, prior and passing theories – are acquired and employed by subjects as capacities without subjects intentionally (consciously or unconsciously) exercising these capacities. The core of Searle's description is the same Aristotelian idea referred to above, which is that recurring deliberate engagement in an action makes that action habitual. This also is the core of Foucault's – and Dewey's – understanding of subject formation (Prado, forthcoming).

Searle's practice-inculcated nonintentional capacities provide a way of understanding Foucault's subject-determining constituents and of explaining how elements introduced by disciplined action persist as dispositions of formed subjects. Searlean nonintentional capacities begin as intentional – as deliberate or reflective – behavior, and with repetition become established nonintentional capacities. In the case of radical interpreters, initial interpretive efforts are deliberate and reflective, and with communicative success those efforts at understanding speakers of unknown languages eventually become established as nonintentional capacities to understand the speakers. This is how prior and passing theories are acquired. Moreover, the question about how prior and passing theories are applied ceases to be pressing when we appreciate that what Davidson glosses as what hearers know about speakers is so many nonintentional capacities that are exercised by subjects, not intentionally, but as automatic responses to the sorts of situations that led to their establishment.

The proposal, then, is that we construe the subjects that are constructed by inculcation of habits as complexes of dispositions consisting of practice-instilled nonintentional capacities. This construal enables understanding of Davidson's account of interpretation as exercise of nonintentional capacities, exercise prompted by occurrences like those responsible for the inculcation of those capacities. The case of the radical interpreter serves to illustrate in a pointed way how intentional interpretive activity establishes the conglomerations of interpretive dispositions Davidson calls prior and passing theories. Thanks to Searle, we then can understand the exercise of those dispositions as establishing long-term nonintentional capacities.

Of course, the establishment of interpretive dispositions and inculcation of nonintentional capacities are not only additive; new capacities and dispositions modify and are conditioned by previously established ones. This is a crucial point, because the complexes of nonintentional capacities and the dispositions they support are integral elements of subjectivities and so define the individuals who exhibit the attitudinal and behavioral consistency that is necessary for subjects to be the same individuals over time.

What emerges is that Foucault's conception of subject formation, augmented with Searle's account of nonintentional capacities, enables understanding of prior and passing theories as exercise of particular dispositions in particular contexts due to particular prompts similar to those operant in the initial establishment of the dispositions. This means there is no epistemological or ontological mystery about how language users retain and employ the interpretive theories they employ. There certainly are empirical questions needing answers, but there is no need to flesh out Davidson's account of interpretation by postulating something like a perplexing unconscious selection and application process.

My conclusion is that if we understand Foucauldian subjects as complexes of dispositional – and other – states, we better comprehend Davidson's account of interpretation as being that prior and passing theories are nonintentional state-based interpretive dispositions acquired through initially intentional or reflective interpretive activity. Activation of these dispositions on given occasions then is understood in terms of recurrence of the same or similar factors as were operant in their initial acquisition.

It likely is worth stressing that initial habit-inculcating interpretive success occurs in contexts rich with various sorts of cues and features. This means that Davidson's apparently blithe reference to language-users' "knowledge of the character, dress, roles, sex, of the speaker, and whatever else has been gained by observing the speaker's behavior, linguistic or otherwise" is not as unproductively general a gloss as it first appears (1986: 441). The remark can be read as referring to all of the factors that prompt successful interpretation in the initial disposition-establishing cases. In fact, so understood, establishment of interpretive dispositions also explains misinterpretation as mainly a function of undue reliance on what is taken as known about interlocutors: the inclination to stereotypical thinking about their meanings.

I close by noting that whether or not Davidson would endorse my suggested application of Foucault's conception of subject formation to his account of interpretation is not to the point. Nor, for that matter, is whether Davidson would have accepted the enabling use of Searle's account of nonintentional capacities. What matters here is not whether Davidson would accept my proposal about complementing his account, but that by availing ourselves of Foucault's ideas, the ideas of a thinker canonically and methodologically distant from Davidson, we can put together a more cogent picture than we find in Davidson's own work on how language users intend the meanings they intend and understand the meanings their interlocutors intend them to understand. That seems more than sufficient to show the importance of Foucault's thought to a philosophical tradition quite different from his own.

References

Aristotle (1985) *Nicomachean Ethics*, trans. T. Irwin. Indianapolis: Hackett Publications.

Davidson, D. (1985) *Inquiries into Truth and Interpretation*. Oxford: Clarendon Press.

Davidson, D. (1986) "A Nice Derangement of Epitaphs." In E. Lepore, ed., *Truth and Interpretation*. Oxford: Blackwell, pp. 433–46.

Davidson, D. (2001) "Radical Interpretation." In *Inquiries into Truth and Interpretation*, 2nd edn. Oxford: Clarendon Press, pp. 125–40.

Davidson, D. (2005) *Truth and Predication*. Cambridge, MA: The Belknap Press of Harvard University Press.

Dewey, J. (1930) *Human Nature and Conduct: An Introduction to Social Psychology* (with new introduction by Dewey). New York: The Modern Library.

Dewey, J. (1988) "Experience and Education." In J. A. Boydston, ed., *John Dewey: The Later Works, 1925–1953*, vol. 13. Carbondale and Edwardsville: Southern Illinois University Press, pp. 1–62.

Dreyfus, H. and P. Rabinow (1983) *Michel Foucault: Beyond Structuralism and Hermeneutics*, 2nd edn., with an Afterword by Foucault and an interview with Foucault. Chicago: University of Chicago Press.

Eribon, D. (1991) *Michel Foucault*, trans. B. Wing. Cambridge, MA: Harvard University Press.

Foucault, M. (1971) "Nietzsche, Genealogy, History." Repr. in P. Rabinow, ed., *The Foucault Reader*. New York: Pantheon Books, 1984, pp. 76–100.

Foucault, M. (1972) *The Archaeology of Knowledge* (including *The Discourse on Language*), trans. A. M. Sheridan Smith. New York: Harper and Row.

Foucault, M. (1973) *The Order of Things: An Archaeology of the Human Sciences*. New York: Vintage.

Foucault, M. (1979) *Discipline and Punish: The Birth of the Prison*, trans. A. Sheridan. New York: Pantheon.

Foucault, M. (1980a) *Power/Knowledge: Selected Interviews and Other Writings*, ed. C. Gordon. New York: Pantheon.

Foucault, M. (1980b) *The History of Sexuality*, vol. 1, trans. R. Hurley. New York: Vintage.

Foucault, M. (1983a) "The Subject and Power." In H. Dreyfus and P. Rabinow, *Michel Foucault: Beyond Structuralism and Hermeneutics*. Chicago: University of Chicago Press, pp. 208–26.

Foucault, M. (1983b) "On the Genealogy of Ethics." In H. Dreyfus and P. Rabinow, *Michel Foucault: Beyond Structuralism and Hermeneutics*. Chicago: University of Chicago Press, pp. 229–52.

Foucault, M. (1984) "The Ethics of Care for the Self as a Practice of Freedom." In J. W. Bernauer and D. Rasmussen, eds., *The Final Foucault*. Cambridge, MA: MIT Press, 1988, pp. 1–20.

Foucault, M. (2001) *Fearless Speech*. Los Angeles, CA: Semiotext(e).

Hoy, D. C., ed. (1986) *Foucault: A Critical Reader*. Oxford: Basil Blackwell.

Lepore, E. and K. Ludwig (2005) *Davidson: Meaning, Truth, Language, and Reality*. Oxford and New York: Oxford University Press.

Miller, J. (1993) *The Passion of Michel Foucault*. New York: Simon and Schuster.

Nehamas, A. (1985) *Nietzsche: Life as Literature*. Cambridge, MA: Harvard University Press.

Nietzsche, F. (1968) *The Will to Power*, ed. Walter Kaufman; trans. W. Kaufman and R. J. Hollingdale. New York: Vintage Books.

Nola, R. (1994) "Post-Modernism, A French Cultural Chernobyl: Foucault on Power/Knowledge." *Inquiry* 37 (1): 3–43.

Prado, C. G. (2000) *Starting With Foucault: An Introduction to Genealogy*, 2nd edn. Boulder, CO and San Francisco, CA: Westview Press.

Prado, C. G. (2003a) *A House Divided: Comparing Analytic and Continental Philosophy*. Amherst, NY: Humanity Books.

Prado, C. G. (2003b) "Correspondism, Constructivism, and Realism: The Case of Searle and Foucault." In *A House Divided: Comparing Analytic and Continental Philosophy*. Amherst, NY: Humanity Books, pp. 185–212.

Prado, C. G. (2006) *Searle and Foucault on Truth*. Cambridge and New York: Cambridge University Press.

Prado, C. G. (forthcoming) "Educating the Self: Dewey and Foucault."

Rabinow, P., ed. (1984) *The Foucault Reader*. New York: Pantheon Books.

Ramberg, B. (2003) "Illuminating Language: Interpretation and Understanding in Gadamer and Davidson." In *A House Divided: Comparing Analytic and Continental Philosophy*. Amherst, NY: Humanity Books, pp. 213–34.

Ramberg, B. (1989) *Donald Davidson's Philosophy of Language: An Introduction*. Oxford: Blackwell.

Rorty, R. (1982) *Consequences of Pragmatism*. Minneapolis: University of Minnesota.

Rorty, R. (1991) *Objectivity, Relativism, and Truth: Philosophical Papers*, vol. 1. New York: Cambridge University Press.

Searle, J. (1980) "'Las Meninas' and the Paradoxes of Pictorial Representation." *Critical Inquiry* 6 (3): 477–88.
Searle, J. (1987) *Intentionality: An Essay in the Philosophy of Mind.* Cambridge: Cambridge University Press.
Searle, J. (1995) *The Construction of Social Reality.* New York: The Free Press.
Sellars, W. (1968) *Science and Metaphysics.* New York: Humanities Press.
Wheeler, S. (2004) "Notre Dame Philosophical Reviews." At http://ndpr.icaap.org/content/archives/2004/6/wheeler-prado.html.

6

The "Death of Man":
Foucault and Anti-Humanism

Béatrice Han-Pile

Like many of the "-ism" words criticized by Heidegger, humanism is a concept which is as widely used as it is indeterminate. Both its extension and its value are subject to significant variations. In the English-speaking world, it is often associated with an optimistic and secular view of the world which asserts the privilege of human beings over non-organic (or organic but nonhuman) entities, defending the rights of human beings to happiness and to the development of their individual potential. Yet on the continent, and in particular in France and Germany, at the time of the "death of man," humanism was seen by many as a dirty word, partly because of its implied anthropocentrism and partly due to some dubious political associations (Foucault 1999). After the postwar enthusiasm for existentialism, a wave of anti-humanism arose, led in Germany by Heidegger's *Letter on Humanism*, which denounced the understanding of the essence of man presupposed by humanism as metaphysical. In France, the controversy about humanism was closely associated with the debates surrounding structuralism and with four main figures: Lévi-Strauss, Lacan, Althusser, and Foucault himself. In Foucault's case, much of the controversy focused on his provocative statements about man being a "recent invention" promised to an imminent "death" and threatened with erasure like a "face drawn in the sand at the edge of the sea" (1994e: 386, 387). Yet it would be mistaken to think that there was much uniformity in the anti-humanist camp, or that there was agreement on a positive definition of an alternative model to humanism.

Other players in the field of anti-humanism were literary theorists such as Maurice Blanchot, who emphasized the self-generating character of language over the role of the writer in the production of literary pieces, or historians from the École des Annales like Fernand Braudel. Although these thinkers differed widely in their disciplines, assumptions, and conclusions, they all denied the primacy of man, be it as an epistemological starting point (the subject as the foundation of all possible knowledge, as in Husserlian phenomenology) or as a practical agent (freedom as the main operator and focus of historical development as in Hegelian history). Correlatively, they emphasized the part played by unconscious structures in the determination of thought and behavior: the "author" was redefined by Foucault (1998: 205–22) as a "function" of the texts rather than their source; Althusser redescribed human agents as "bearers" (*Träger*) of historical determination, not as the actors of history (Althusser and Balibar 1970: 180). Braudel (1982) introduced the idea of multiple durations at work in history, of which "eventful" (*événementielle*) human history was only the most superficial. Thus French anti-humanism entailed, generally speaking, a denunciation both of foundationalism and of an Enlightenment-inspired, progressivist view of history as the result of the actions of autonomous agents.

Foucault (1990: chs. 1 and 5) categorically denied that he was a structuralist; he claimed to differ from Lévi-Strauss because of his interest in actual, not virtual, systems. Unlike Althusser, Foucault (1994a: 656) did not believe that our historical development is dependent solely on causal determination. Yet (as illustrated by the above distinctions) he was often keener on defining his position *a contrario* than on providing a positive set of criteria. Furthermore, polemical context led him and others to publish occasionally excessive statements which in retrospect stand out more by virtue of their provocative character than because of their intellectual perspicaciousness. In this paper, I shall try to avoid rhetorical heat, and will refrain from defending either humanism or anti-humanism. I am more interested in the debate itself. Controversial, often acerbic, dialogues between contemporaries are not rare in the history of philosophy – think Hegel–Schelling; Heidegger–Carnap; Rawls–Habermas. Yet the philosophical interest of such controversies often lies as much in what is presupposed by each of the interlocutors as in what is explicitly said. If one examines the assumptions of each proponent, such debates often appear to rest on mutual misunderstandings; and, unless these are identified, it is impossible for the external observer to take a stand on the issues in question or to discern whether the heat of the intellectual battle covers the possibility of a deeper agreement.

Thus I do not propose to enter the debate about the death of man but to bring to light its theoretical underpinnings. To my knowledge, this hasn't been done so far. Those who have written on Foucault's anti-humanism have tended to focus on its relation to Heidegger's critique of Cartesianism (Hoy 1981) and/or on the Foucault/Habermas controversy (Honneth 1991), as well as on enlisting Foucault's ideas in feminist critiques of humanism

(Sawicki 1991). N. Fraser (1994) distinguished between three possible grounds for Foucault's rejection of humanism: (a) "conceptual or philosophical" (humanism as too entangled in Western subject-focused metaphysics); (b) strategic (the appeal to humanist values as covering up strategies of domination); and (c) normative (humanism as being intrinsically objectionable, on the ground that subjection is per se a form of subjugation). These three possibilities are supposed to correspond to the three main stages of Foucault's philosophical development (archaeology, genealogy, and the history of subjectivity). With respect to this useful nomenclature, the reading I propose in this paper is, roughly speaking, conceptual: it argues that Foucault's rejection of humanism was motivated by his philosophical analyses of the *aporia* of the anthropological turn and the analytic of finitude, and that some of the bitterness of the "death of man" debate was due to the fact that such analyses were grievously misunderstood by his opponents. However my position differs from Fraser's in at least three respects: (a) it focuses mostly on Foucault's early work; (b) it does not argue from parallels between Foucault and Heidegger but seeks to identify internally the philosophical grounds for Foucault's rejection of humanism; and (c), contrary to Fraser, I suggest that the later Foucault's work, far from being a hardening of his early position (from a "merely conceptual," as she puts it, to a strongly normative but in her view untenable position), offers the possibility of a reconciliation by sketching out a position which, rather than rejecting *tout court* such values as freedom or self-creation, upholds them as ideals but seeks to construe them in non-metaphysical ways.

Let us first get an idea of the nature and tone of the debate. The extent of the indignation and misunderstandings generated by Foucault's somewhat conspicuous declarations about the death of man can be illustrated by the following passages, taken from two of the most vocal proponents of humanism: Garaudy, dubbed a "soft" Marxist (Foucault 1994a: 541), and Sartre, the "nineteenth-century philosopher" (ibid.: 542):

> When he tells us that man is a creation of the end of the 18th century, I would like Foucault to explain us where he is going to locate Augustine's *Confessions* or even the research of the Greek fathers who, from the notion of the divine person, and then from Christology, arrived at the notion of the human person. (Garaudy 1994: 380)

> "Man" does not exist, and Marx had rejected him long before Foucault or Lacan when he said: "I don't see any man, I only see workers, bourgeois,

intellectuals." If one persists in calling "subject" a sort of substantial I …
then the subject has been dead for a long time. But the initial decentering
which makes man disappear behind the structures implies in itself a form
of negativity, and man surges from this negation. There is a subject, or a
subjectivity if you prefer, as soon as there is an effort to overcome while
retaining a given situation. (Sartre 1994: 70)

While they are both opposed to Foucault's conclusions in *The Order of
Things*, it is doubtful that Garaudy and Sartre would have agreed as to why.
First, they each have something quite different in mind when they speak of
"man": Garaudy is referring to the religious notion of the human person as
a bearer of rights endowed with a special status (a conception further
developed by Kant's focus on the capacity of rational beings for self-
government and the moral worth that derives from it, by opposition to
"mere things" which have a price but no intrinsic value). By contrast, Sartre
rejects such moral abstractions and sees man in a secular way, as "surging
from negation." This "surge" alludes to *Being and Nothingness*'s definition
of consciousness as a nihilating power which separates itself from the
world through the very movement by which it projects itself into it. As
pure negation, consciousness cannot be identified with any of the contents
that are given to it (it has no essence);[1] nor can it be determined by them.
Thus, at a historical level, agents may be dependent on their socioeconom-
ical insertion (their "situation"), but the latter can be "overcome" through
practical engagement (Sartre 1994: 72). While there is possible overlap
between the two conceptions, it is clear that they do not coincide. Secondly,
the grounds of the two objections are different: Garaudy is accusing
Foucault of historical inaccuracy, while Sartre is defending the primacy of
freedom both as a causally determining principle and as a historical
explanatory category, thus rejecting the idea that agents may be unconsciously determined by structures which pre-exist them and on which they
have no power. But beyond these differences, the crucial issue is that both
critics miss the point of what Foucault means by "man": he does not refer
to the "human person," nor to any "substantial I," nor to free consciousness. To understand this, one needs to look at the complex account of the
connection between the appearance of "man," humanism, and anthropology proposed by *The Order of Things*.

The first thing to note is that for the early Foucault humanism has a
very specific, narrow referent. This is indicated by his rather surprising
historical reconstruction of its birth, which is referred to the Enlightenment

and not, as is more traditional, to the revival and reinterpretation of the Ciceronian notion of *humanitates* during the Renaissance: thus the first humanists on Foucault's list are not Rabelais, Montaigne, or Pico Della Mirandola, but Kant, Hegel, and Marx. "The Humanist movement," he tells us, "dates from the end of the 19th century. Secondly, when one looks a little closely at the cultures of the 16th, 17th and 18th centuries, one realises that man literally has no place in them. Culture is then preoccupied with God, the world and the resemblance of things" (1994a: 540). Garaudy would probably have thrown up his hands in the air in despair at this statement, which flies in the face of common sense and of the received view of the history of humanism. After all there were human beings on this planet long before the nineteenth century, and references about man abound in Renaissance and subsequent texts (and prior writings such as Genesis). To understand this paradox, one needs to locate Foucault's analyses at the appropriate level: "[A]t the archaeological level, which reveals the general, historical a priori of each of these branches of knowledge [the human sciences], modern man – that man assignable in his corporeal, labouring and speaking existence – is only possible as a configuration of finitude" (1994e: 317). As we shall see, the situation is complicated by the fact that the new understanding of finitude itself is referred to: man (ibid.). But for the moment, note that the shift to the archaeological level provides us with the key to understanding Foucault's provocative statements about the death of man: one must distinguish between surface understandings of man (for example as a living, working, speaking being) and man as the new historical a priori that underlies our comprehension of the first. Thus:

> [M]an's mode of being as constituted in modern thought enables it to play two roles: he is at the same time the foundation of all positivities and at the same time present in the element of empirical things. … It is not a matter of man's essence in general but simply of that historical a priori which, since the 19th century, has served as an almost self-evident ground for our thought. (Ibid.: 344)

Just as each épistémè makes possible the appearance of specific objects and theories, in the same way man in the archaeological sense is the condition of possibility of the current conceptions of man. Yet precisely for this reason, it is not synonymous with any of these understandings: "Renaissance 'humanism' and Classical 'rationalism' were indeed able to

> In one sense, man is governed by labour, life and language: his concrete existence finds its determinations in them. … [Yet] all those contents … have positivity within the space of knowledge … only because they are thoroughly imbued with finitude. For they would not be there … if man … was trapped in the mute … opening of animal life; but nor would they posit themselves in the acute angle that hides them from their own direction if man could traverse them without residuum in the lightning flash of an infinite understanding. That is to say that each of these forms in which man can learn that he is finite is given to him only against the background of his own finitude. Moreover, the latter is not the most completely purified essence of positivity, but that upon the basis of which it is possible for positivity to arise. At the foundation of all the empirical positivities … , we discover a finitude – which is in a sense the same … and yet is radically other. (Ibid.: 313–14)

The key to this difficult excerpt lies in distinguishing between two different senses of finitude (empirical and transcendental) and of determination (causal and epistemic[3]). The "governance" of life, labor, and language over our "concrete existence" gives us a hint about the nature of what I have called elsewhere empirical finitude (Han 2003). It refers to causal determinations and resides in the fact that human beings are determined by various processes in which they find themselves enmeshed from the day of their birth and over which they have little control. Each in their own way, such processes disclose various aspects of our empirical finitude: we cannot alter our biochemistry so as to become immune to illness or aging, nor can we use a private language. Thus labor, life, and language are the "forms in which man can learn that he is [empirically] finite." But such forms are also objects of knowledge (further refined in such disciplines as biology, economics, or linguistics). In this, they are dependent on the transcendental aspect of "man" which defines the conditions under which all empirical objects are epistemically determined. Life, language, and labor, which are part of the limitations that bear causally on empirical finitude, only "have positivity within the space of knowledge" because they are "thoroughly imbued with finitude"; yet, crucially, such finitude must now be conceived of at the transcendental level. Foucault refers it to our impossibility of "traversing [such contents] without residuum in the lightning flash of an infinite understanding." This is clearly an allusion to Kant's definition of the *intuitus originarius* as the sort of intellect which would not be dependent on the reception of sensory material and could by itself produce a fully spontaneous knowledge of its object. Such an intellect would be infinite ("the lightning flash of an infinite understanding") and acquire an immediate and perfect knowledge of its objects ("without residuum"). Yet while such intellectual intuition may be appropriate to characterize God's mode of knowing, it is not open to human beings. Thus transcendental finitude is no empirical matter (it is not the "completely purified essence of positivity"); it resides in the fact that we cannot form any empirical knowledge unless we receive some external input, usually through time and space, but at least through time: although we are capable of spontaneous activity (for example in synthesizing the manifold under the pure concepts of reason), the process whereby we acquire knowledge is not fully active. Yet precisely because it is thus limited, transcendental finitude provides the epistemic conditions ("that upon which it is possible for positivity to arise") which allow the contents that causally determine us as empirical beings to enter the space of knowledge. Note, crucially, that transcendental finitude differs from its empirical counterpart in that the limitation it entails can be analytically deduced from the very concept of the transcendental as a *standpoint* (which implies a specific perspective and thus limiting conditions, by opposition to a God's eye view which would not be limited in such a way). By contrast, empirical finitude can only be understood synthetically, from empirical observations about the nature of human beings as living or speaking entities.

Thus "at the very heart of empiricity, there is indicated the obligation to work backwards to an analytic of finitude, in which man's being will be able to provide a [transcendental] foundation … for all these forms that indicate to him that his is not [empirically] infinite" (Foucault 1994e: 315). The problem, however, is that the ambiguity of "man," which both separates and unites the empirical and the transcendental, causes the two forms of finitude to overlap by means of an implicit shift which makes epistemic determination ultimately dependent on its empirical, causal counterpart: the relation between transcendental and empirical finitude becomes a vicious circle. This shift is evoked, albeit somewhat obscurely, in the rest of the passage I originally quoted:

> And he, as soon as he thinks, merely unveils himself in the form of a being who is already, in a necessarily subjacent density, in an irreducible anteriority, a living being, and instrument of production, a vehicle for words which exist before him. All these contents … traverse him as if he were merely an object of nature. (Ibid.: 313)

Note the multiple temporal locutions at work in this quote ("as soon as he thinks," "already," "in an irreducible anteriority," "which exist before him").

It may be tempting to understand the anteriority they connote from a purely empirical point of view, in which case the passage would refer to the empirical genesis of thought. Thought itself would be seen in a naturalistic way, as causally determined by empirical conditions (for example neurochemical processes that are specific to man as an empirical being). Yet the passage also indicates that "man," although "traversed" by empirical contents, is not "merely an object of nature." As we saw, the reason for this lies in the possibility of considering "man" from a transcendental perspective. From such a standpoint, however, the temporal locutions acquire a new referent: they mark the opening of the epistemic field. By definition, such an opening should not itself be temporal – Foucault himself points out that in the *First Critique* representation has its "foundation *beyond all experience*, in the a priori that renders it possible" (ibid.: 242; my italics). In the "Transcendental Aesthetic," time is an a priori form of sensibility on which the possibility of conceiving chronological time depends; as a condition of possibility of experience, it cannot feature in the field that it determines. Yet the use of retrospective temporal locutions in the passage quoted cancels out this neat distinction by inscribing the opening of the epistemic field itself within the chronology of empirical time. Thus the analytic of finitude is characterized by a paradox of retrospection whereby transcendental finitude is disclosed as pre-existing itself in the form of empirical finitude (Han 2002: Pt I, ch. 1). Such pre-existence (which Derrida calls "primitivity" in the case of Husserl's phenomenology) invalidates "man's" ability to provide a universal and necessary foundation for knowledge. The empirical contents that were previously deemed causally determinant but epistemically determined acquire a "quasi-transcendental" function (Foucault 1994e: 244)[4] in that they are now viewed as chronologically primary and causally determinant *for epistemic conditions themselves*. Thus man as a transcendental subject "unveils himself as already there, as a living being" governed by the empirical laws of life, a speaking being using a language that pre-exists him. In other words, transcendental finitude and empirical finitude are superposed in such a way that the former, rather than being the analytic correlate of the notion of a transcendental standpoint, is now cashed out in terms of the synthetic, empirical limitations (life, language, labor) that bear causally on man. In Foucault's (1994e: 316) words: "[I]f man's knowledge is finite, it is because he is trapped, without possibility of liberation, within the positive contents of language, labour and life [which thus indirectly become epistemically determinant]." Consequently, this identification of transcendental and empirical finitude, of epistemic and causal determination, invalidates "man's" ability to provide a universal and necessary foundation for knowledge.

Thus anthropology as an "analytic of man" (ibid.: 340) has come to displace Kant's critique. In a well-known but obscure passage, Foucault refers to this anthropological doubling over of finitude over itself as the "Fold":

> By means of this question [*was ist der Mensch?*] a form of reflection was constituted which is mixed in its levels and characteristic of modern philosophy. … It concerns an empirico-transcendental duplication by means of which an attempt is made to make the man of nature, of exchange, or of discourse, serve as the [transcendental] foundation of his own finitude. (Ibid.: 341)

A large part of chapter 9 of *The Order of Things* is devoted to outlining the nefarious consequences of this "empirico-transcendental duplication" both for post-Kantians and contemporary philosophy. Yet it may be advisable to stop at this point. Recall that this long analysis of the analytic of finitude had two aims. First, to clarify what Foucault meant by "man" and thus to expose the misunderstandings underlying the debate about its death. Secondly, to help us understand how Foucault's denunciation of "man" may ground his rejection of humanism. While the first goal has (hopefully) been achieved, it is not clear that this is the case for the second: even if they accepted Foucault's indictment of anthropology and of the analytic of finitude, humanists could still question its relevance to their own position altogether. Foucault tells us that after "man" appeared as the "subject of all knowledge and object of a possible knowledge," "such an ambiguous situation characterise[d] what one could call the anthropologico-humanist structure of 19th century thought" (ibid.: 607; 1999: 93). Yet what is "humanist" about this structure? Just as the "death of man" did not refer to actual human beings, in the same way it is very doubtful that when Sartre or Garaudy – or other humanists attacked by Foucault, such as Teilhard de Chardin or Camus – spoke of man they meant the empirico-transcendental double. In the humanist literature, "man" is much more likely to connote the dignity of the human person as an end in itself, the primacy of the subject (or of consciousness) or human freedom (the list not being exclusive). For example, the last two themes are central to Sartre's own definition of "existentialist humanism": "[S]ince man is thus self-surpassing [a reference to man's freedom as a nihilating power] and can grasp objects only in relation to his self-surpassing, he is himself the heart and centre of his transcendence. There is no other universe except the human universe, the universe of human subjectivity" (1973: 55). So how (if at all) is Foucault's general denunciation of the "anthropological sleep" relevant to humanism?

This problem is illustrated by the well-known passage below, which starts from a consideration of anthropology in general and concludes with a vitriolic attack against various forms of humanism:

> Anthropology constitutes perhaps the fundamental arrangement that has governed and controlled the path of philosophical thought from Kant until our own day. This arrangement is essential, since it forms part of our history; but it is disintegrating before our eyes, since we are beginning to recognise and denounce in it, in a critical mode, both a forgetfulness of the opening that made it possible and a stubborn obstacle standing obstinately in the way of an imminent new form of thought. To all those who still wish to talk about man, about his reign or his liberation, to all those who still ask themselves questions about what man is in his essence, to all those who wish to take him as their starting point in their attempts to reach the truth, to all those who, on the other hand, refer all knowledge back to the truths of man himself … , to all these warped and twisted forms of reflection we can only answer with a philosophical laugh – which means, to a certain extent, a silent one. (Foucault 1994e: 342)

For all its rhetorical power (and the undeniable attraction of silent philosophical laughter), the passage looks like a non sequitur: *The Order of Things* has succeeded so well in narrowing the meaning of "man" to the empirico-transcendental double that the gap between "man" and its humanist incarnations seems fairly unbridgeable. Yet for Foucault's critique of anthropology to bite on humanism, such a gap needs to be bridged. So what ought we do? One possibility would be to give up on hermeneutic charity altogether and conclude that Foucault is just as guilty of misunderstanding his opponents' position as they were of misreading his. But this may be premature. Alternatively, one could attempt to show that, in fact, "man" and humanist man are synonymous – a dubious strategy in my view since so much of the thrust of Foucault's analyses of the analytic of finitude is precisely devoted to identifying a specific meaning for "man." Yet another, perhaps more promising, possibility may be to suggest that since the analytic of finitude is supposed to be the epistemic ground of all subsequent thought developments, somehow there must be a relation of entailment between "man" and man such that the second could be shown to be conceptually, or at least historically, dependent on the first. If this were the case, then Foucault's criticism of "man" would have genuine implications for theories that focus on human subjectivity, consciousness, or freedom.

As Foucault never addressed this question, it is difficult to do more than provide a few pointers for such a strategy. Let's start by taking stock of the extent of the task. As hinted at by the passage just quoted, Foucault's denunciation of the anthropological turn branches into attacks against two main sets of targets: on the one hand, practical theories grounded in the idea of a "reign of man" or alternatively announcing his "liberation," and, on the other, theoretical questions about the essence of man assorted with attempts to use the latter as the alpha (a "starting point in their attempts to reach the truth," e.g. a foundation for knowledge) or omega of knowledge ("refer all knowledge back to the truth of man himself"). With respect to this second group, note that such "referring back" is ambiguous: depending on whether "man" is understood from a transcendental or an empirical perspective, the expression can equally allude to the foundational logic of the Copernican turn (e.g. referring empirical contents to their a priori conditions of possibility) or to the circular dynamic of the analytic of finitude (e.g. referring epistemic conditions themselves to the causal determinations that bear on man as an empirical being). In the first case, "referring all knowledge back to the truth of man" becomes tantamount to "using him as a starting point to reach truth." In this regard, it would hardly be controversial to suggest that most of the post-Kantian developments that focused on the foundational role of the subject followed from the characterization of the transcendental in the *Critique of Pure Reason*. Certainly this is the way Foucault himself reads the rise – and, in his view, failure – of German idealism (in particular Fichte) and both the Husserlian and Sartrean branches of phenomenology (see Habermas 1987a; Han 2005). By contrast, if one construes the "truth of man himself" as referring to the empirical aspect of "man," then in this case too the proposed strategy can find purchase in that Foucault understands positivism to be doing just this, and consequently to be a naturalistic reduction of "man's transcendental side to its empirical aspect": thus "this true discourse finds its foundation and model in the empirical truth whose genesis in nature and in history it retraces, so that one has an analysis of the positivist type" (1994e: 320). As I have shown elsewhere (Han 2005), Foucault criticizes such an attempt for its essentialism, and for unduly turning "man" into a mere object of nature.

As for the other group, the practical theories that promote the idea of a "reign" or "liberation" of man, they too can be seen as an inheritance of the Kantian emphasis on transcendental finitude, historically and possibly conceptually. The early Foucault emphasizes the historical filiation and refers such theories to Hegel and Marx (1994a: 540). He targets the use of human freedom as the main hermeneutic category to understand historical development, first in Kant's *Idea for a History from a Cosmopolitan Point of View* and then in dialectical form by Hegel and Marx. This also underlies Foucault's attacks against more recent movements, such as the humanist readings of historical materialism (Soper 1986) and what he calls, by opposition to the École des Annales and the then new "*histoire sérielle*," "continuous history" (1990: 12). The link with the foundational logic of the analytic of finitude is particularly clear in the following passage:

> [C]ontinuous history is the indispensable correlate of the founding function of the subject: … the promise that one day the subject, – in the form of historical consciousness – will once again be able to appropriate [itself] … . In various forms, this theme has played a constant role since the 19th century: to preserve, against all decenterings, the sovereignty of the subject and the twin figures of anthropology and humanism. (Ibid.)

Foucault goes on to denunciate various historical surges of this "founding function of the subject" (1994a: 542) in the guise of the search for a total history (against Nietzschean genealogy), the anthropologization of Marx (against such nonhumanist readings as Althusser's) or the more recent "reactivation" of dialectical readings of historical development as the "hard work of freedom" (a thinly veiled allusion to Sartre). The central role attributed to human freedom is deemed doubly nefarious: it leads to the epistemological mistake which consists in ignoring the causal determinations that bear on human beings, and it generates fallacious normative ideals focused on the idea of authenticity as the return to man's true nature:

> [B]ecause it is a philosophy of history, … of human practice … , of alienation and of reconciliation … , dialectics promises human beings, so to speak, that they will become true and authentic men. It promises man to man, and insofar as it does this, it is not dissociable from a humanist moral. (Ibid.: 540)

I do not have the space in this paper to examine whether the strategy just outlined is valid. The above suggests that it is at least possible to conceive of the missing links that would show the dependency of the various humanist conceptions attacked by Foucault on "man." If such a derivation were indeed correct, and if one accepts Foucault's conclusions in *The Order of Things* about the pernicious character of the analytic of finitude, then there would be some weighty reasons to endorse his criticism of humanism. Yet such reasons are not provided directly by Foucault's analyses and require a large amount of reconstruction. Furthermore, there remain some significant difficulties with the reasons that *are* given. Let me point out three.

First, even if one leaves aside the issue of the missing link between "man" and humanist man, Foucault's negative pronouncements about the value and future of humanism ultimately rest on two factors: his identification of the theoretical flaws of the analytic of finitude, and his belief in the imminent erasure of "man" as an epistemic structure. Yet the status of the former is made ambivalent by the fact that Foucault moves implicitly from case studies illustrating the failures of the analytic of finitude to apodictic claims about such failures being necessary. This apodictic dimension is denoted by various statements such as the following:

> [A]nthropology as an analytic of man has certainly played a constitutive role in modern thought, since to a large extent we are still not free from it. It became *necessary* at the moment when representations lost the power to determine … the interplay of its syntheses and analyses. It was *necessary* for empirical syntheses to be performed elsewhere than within the sovereignty of the "I think." They *had to be* required … in man's finitude. (1994e: 340; my italics)

Yet nothing in *The Order of Things* shows that the anthropological turn was necessary, only (at best) that it did happen. As Foucault said himself, the *Critique* carried within itself "the *peril* of an anthropology" (my italics). That such peril did actualize itself does not mean that it *had to*: facts cannot ground apodictic claims. The most that has been shown is that the coexistence of the empirical and the transcendental within "man" did encourage the sort of slippage typical of the analytic of finitude, but not that it necessarily caused it. Thus there is a deep ambivalence in *The Order of Things*, which can be read either as a de facto narrative that shows the various ways in which the anthropological turn has been detrimental to contemporary thought, or as a de jure indictment of "man" as necessarily leading to the analytic of finitude. This leaves the possibility of rescuing humanism from anthropology: even if she or he were to accept Foucault's criticism of "man," the humanist could still retort that although it is unfortunate that the Copernican turn ended up in the analytic of finitude, there is no reason to think that the empirico-transcendental structure is intrinsically flawed. In other words, the way would still be open for a type of humanism more aware of the dangers of anthropology and keen to preserve the separation of the empirical and the transcendental. Sartre's early phenomenology, with its emphasis on the purely nihilating power of consciousness and the impossibility of identifying it with any empirical content whatsoever (in the "transcendence of the Ego"), could be read precisely as attempting this sort of theoretical move.

Secondly, similar modal difficulties arise in relation to another problem, namely that of the implicit normativity of Foucault's analyses of anthropology. As is well known, one of the principles of archaeology as a method lies in its neutrality (by opposition to optimistic narratives focused on progress); for example, in *The Order of Things* Foucault is very careful to avoid any value judgment that would give Buffon's natural history pre-eminence over Aldrovandi's mixed recordings of facts, hearsay, and myths about animals. Thus Foucault claimed to be an "ethnographer of our culture," a detached theorist retracing the genesis of the current épistémè and identifying the consequences of its being grounded in the "mode of being" of "man" (1994a: 605; 1999: 91). Yet for all his self-professed archaeological neutrality, there is also a strongly normative aspect to his analysis: "[T]he heaviest inheritance that comes to us from the 19th century – and from which it is time to get rid off – is humanism. … Humanism pretends to solve problems that it can't pose!" (1994a: 514). Correlatively, his avowed aim was to "announce the first deterioration in European history of the anthropological and humanist episode that we have known during the 19th century" (ibid.: 502; 1996: 16) and to "define a method of analysis purged of all anthropologism" (1990: 16). Just like those of the humanists he attacked, Foucault's views oscillate between descriptive and normative registers. Somewhat ironically, this oscillation is one of the reproaches he makes to Sartre: "Sartre wanted to show that everywhere there is *meaning* [*sens*]. But … this is both an observation and an order" (1994a: 514). Apart from the question of how such normative claims can be grounded (which takes us back to the previous issue of the assertoric/apodictic slippage), this exhibits a tension between the archaeologist's theoretical ideal of detached neutrality and his practice. It is one thing to diagnose the death of "man," and another to rejoice at – let alone try to precipitate – the demise of the patient. Thus humanists could argue that Foucault did not practice what he preached, and that his discourse was no less normative than theirs; furthermore, even if they accepted his indictment of the analytic of finitude, they could still weasel out of the archaeologist's clutches by slipping through the gap between the assertoric and the apodictic.

Yet there is a third set of difficulties. Foucault sought to bolster his attacks against humanism by pointing out that (regardless of whether it was intrinsically or only incidentally detrimental to thought) "man" as a structure was on its way out anyway: if this was the case, then all movements grounded in this épistémè (including humanism) were bound to sink with the empirico -transcendental ship. Thus:

> [A]s soon as one realised that all human knowledge, all human existence … are trapped within structures, i.e. within a formal system of elements which obey formal relations that anyone can describe, man so to speak ceases to be his own subject. … One discovers that what makes man possible is at the end of the day a set of structures, structures that he may be able to describe but of which he is not the subject or the sovereign consciousness. (1994a: 601ff; 1999, 87ff)

Thus the rise of structuralism and the displacement of humanist concepts were seen as indications that the analytic of finitude is loosening its grip on modernity and that we are on the brink of an epistemic shift which will bring into being a new historical a priori, that of the "return of language" (Foucault 1994e: 383–6). However, there are two problems with this argument. Firstly, it is somewhat circular: on the one hand, the withdrawal of "man" as an épistémè is used to predict the doom of humanist conceptions of man; on the other, the demise of such conceptions is seen as indicative of the imminent death of "man." What counts as a premise in the first part of the reasoning becomes a conclusion in the second, and vice versa. Secondly, if one takes seriously the characterization of "man" as the historical a priori which has formed the condition of possibility of knowledge since the end of the eighteenth century, then the logic which consists in using empirical observations to infer its disappearance is somewhat dubious: by definition, transcendental conditions are immune to empirical refutation. Of course, one could answer this objection by pointing out that "man" (like all épistémès) is not a purely transcendental structure but a *historical a priori*: by virtue of its historical dimension it is susceptible to being affected by empirical changes. Yet such a reply would come at a significant theoretical cost, namely the replication, at a meta-level, of the slippage between the empirical and the transcendental characteristic of the analytic of finitude itself: the only way in which empirical changes could affect the epistemic determination provided by "man" as a historical a priori would be if such determination turned out, at the end of the day, to be causally determined by empirical processes. These would thus have exactly the same "quasi-transcendental" function as that which Foucault attributes to the empirical contents which "release their conditions of possibility" in the analytic of finitude. In this case, the humanist could retort that, even on Foucault's own terms, his pessimistic pronouncements about the disappearance of "man" (and subsequent indictments of the humanist notions that are supposed to depend on this épistémè) ends up formally replicating the very structure of what it criticizes, and thus could be seen as a further development (rather than a way out) of the analytic of finitude (Han 2002: Pt I, ch. 2): "man" may have a greater life expectancy than anticipated.

So what are we to make of the whole debate? It seems clear from the analyses above that neither his opponents nor Foucault himself had any decisive arguments to offer for or against humanism. The failure of the first rests on a misunderstanding of the nature of archaeology as a method, and of Foucault's correlative characterization of "man" as the empirico-transcendental double and of the analytic of finitude as our most recent epistemic ground. The objections presented to him failed to hit their mark because they took his statements about the "death of man" at face value and read into them various conceptions of man (as a person or a free consciousness) which, for the archaeologist, were merely derivative of the appearance of "man" as the empirico-transcendental double; to use a metaphor dear to Foucault, the humanist objections pertained to the "surface" of history, whereas the archaeologist was concerned with its depths. Yet, conversely, Foucault's attacks on humanism did not fare much better, although for different reasons: while he presented a very interesting reconstruction of how the ambiguity of "man" as a double made it possible for the Copernican turn to evolve into the analytic of finitude, a process which resulted in the anthropological sleep, he did not provide any explicit account of how the various humanist conceptions of man are related to "man." The consequence is that while the reader may end up convinced that the anthropological turn was indeed nefarious for various branches of philosophy, the humanist can still argue that so long as this charting of the depths of history by the archaeologist is not explicitly connected to surface developments, its conclusions are no objection to humanist conceptions of man. Furthermore, the modality of Foucault's criticism of humanism oscillates between the apodictic and the assertoric, the normative and the descriptive: as we saw, he formulates no grounds (universal or otherwise) for such normativity, and the description as it stands does not suffice. At best, his indictment of humanism remains promissory.

Can we learn anything from this double impasse? Hopefully, yes. For one thing, it provides *a contrario* insight into the nature of real philosophical exchange. As we saw, the debate about the death of man was not a genuine dialog but rather a case of philosophers talking (voluntarily or not) at cross purposes. To a large extent, the reason for this is that they mostly relied on the ambiguity of the term "man" rather than trying to clarify their own use of the concept in relation to other possible uses (and in particular that of their opponents). In reality, the so-called debate was an exercise in solipsism. This can certainly be seen as a failure of communication and a striking illustration of what philosophical exchanges should *not* be – somewhat unsurprisingly, the controversy died down without having being resolved. However, on a more positive note the debate brought to light two important issues which were influential on Foucault's philosophical development and resurfaced in his later remarks about humanism. Importantly, they did so in ways which transformed the terms of the early debate by allowing for the possibility of a rapprochement, albeit not so much in terms of the conceptual contents involved as with respect to the values upheld. Thus the later Foucault's work on subjectivity and freedom, even though it is still explicitly cast in opposition to humanism, may be seen as an implicit attempt to retain what Habermas would call the latter's "emancipatory force," while forging a non-metaphysical content for its central concepts. Let me explain: as is well known, at the end of the 1970s Foucault decided to refocus his genealogical studies on the project of a "history of subjectivity" (1994d: 634; 1998: 461). Such a history focused on the dynamic tensions between problematizations of the self, relations of power and forms of knowledge. It involved a redefinition of the subject, not as a "substance" but as a "form which is neither mostly nor always identical to itself" (1994d: 718; 1997: 290). Such a definition was openly designed to avoid the foundationalist and essentialist aspects of humanism denounced in Foucault's early work:

> [O]ne must also skirt the philosophical approach which consists in going up, toward a constituting subject which must account for what any object of knowledge in general can be; on the contrary, one must go downwards, toward the study of the concrete practices whereby the subject is constituted in the immanence of a domain of knowledge. (1994d: 634; 1998: 462)

Consequently, the later work developed in a different, more genealogical direction and proposed a historical critique which focused on the mutual variability of subject/object relations, and which itself referred to changes in social practices.[5] "[M]y aim," Foucault now tells us, "will be to show you how social practices can come to generate domains of knowledge which make not only new objects, new concepts, new techniques appear, but also totally new forms of subjects and of subjects of knowledge" (1994b: 539; 2000: 2). Thus in "La vérité et les formes juridiques," Foucault (1994b: 630ff) looks at the transformations brought within the judicial domain by the simultaneous appearance of a new form of objectivity and a new type of subjectivity. The former lies in the idea that proofs can be established by gathering facts which will serve for the evaluation of the truth claims put forward by the parties in dispute, as opposed to such proofs being dependent on the word and social status of individuals vouching for either party. Correlatively, the latter resides in the idea of a detached, neutral observer occupying an "ideal point" (ibid.: 631). In both cases, the new social practice that proved historically determining is the inquiry (*enquête*).

However, the adoption of this new focal point and method signals an important change vis-à-vis the earlier position: like the humanists (and unlike his younger self), the later Foucault now acknowledges the importance of the notion of subjectivity to understand human practices. At the same time, starting from these practices and emphasizing the reciprocity and historical plasticity of subject/object relations allows him to develop a theory of the subject which transforms the notion and avoids the pitfalls denounced in the early work; it does not treat such a subject as an invariant starting point, nor as the ground of knowledge. Thus Foucault denounces the "very grave fault" which consists in "presupposing, at the end of the day, that the human subject, the subject of knowledge, and the forms of knowledge themselves are in a way already and definitely pre-given, and that economic, social and political conditions of existence only deposit and imprint themselves in that definitely given subject" (ibid.: 539; 2000: 2). As a consequence, the dangers of the empirico-transcendental replication specific to the analytic of finitude are much less likely to arise. Thus, by giving up on the essentialism and the foundational ambitions inherited from the Copernican turn, Foucault throws out the anthropological bathwater but retains the proverbial baby. In this sense, the notorious "return of the subject" does not contradict his early attacks against the dominance of the subject on the postwar philosophical scene. On the contrary, it puts forward a promising alternative to think of subjects in a non-metaphysical, non-essentialist way; moreover, by doing so, it opens up the possibility of identifying a new common ground between Foucault and humanists.

This is made apparent by his later reflections on the possibility and nature of free agency (which is so central to humanism). As we saw, at the time of the debate about the "death of man" Foucault simply seemed to deny the existence of freedom, arguing that individuals are unconsciously determined by various structures (social or linguistic, for example) over which they have no control. Yet the theme acquires a much greater importance in the later work and becomes central to the definitions of both power and subjectivity: thus, the crucial difference between power and violence is that the former can only act on free agents. It not only presupposes but requires the possibility of resistance. Correlatively, freedom is seen as an intrinsic property of human beings and is identified with our ability for self-problematization, effecting a "permanent creation of ourselves in our autonomy" (1994d: 572; 1997: 313). While this ability is constrained by specific historical conditions, it nevertheless involves the possibility of spontaneous action (in particular through the creative transformation of such practices). In Foucault's terms, "the [practices of the self] are not something that the individual invents himself. They are schemas that he finds in his culture and which are proposed, suggested, imposed by his culture, his society or his social group" (1994d: 718; 1997: 291); but it is still the case that "[t]he subject constitutes itself through practices of subjugation [*assujettissement*], or, in a more autonomous fashion, through practices of liberation, of freedom, as in Antiquity" (1994d: 733; 1996: 452). Just like his later definition of subjectivity, Foucault's new understanding of freedom as a plastic, creative ability is meant to avoid essentialism (in the sense that it is purely formal and does not identify such ability with any of its historical forms). Foucault explicitly contrasts it with the more substantive conceptions of freedom underlying humanist positions: "[W]hat frightens me, in humanism, is that it presents a certain form of our ethics as a universal model, valid for any type of freedom. I think that our future includes more secrets, more possible freedoms and inventions than humanism allows us to imagine" (1994d: 782; 1988: 15). Note, however, that the target of Foucault's criticism is not the (rather humanist) idea that freedom should be a central value to human development – the title of one of Foucault's last interventions ("The Care of the Self as A Practice of Freedom") attests to this – but, rather, the limited and morally constraining conception allegedly put forward by humanists. The disagreement about the nature of freedom should not conceal a certain communality of ideals.

In this respect, it may be useful to point out – last but not least – that Foucault's emphasis on the centrality of freedom and plasticity of human self-creation is not quite as original as it may seem. In fact, it was typical of the one kind of humanism that he never discussed, namely that of the Renaissance.[6] Following Blumenberg (1983) (and to a lesser extent Craig 1987), Cooper (2002: 25ff) reads the revival of the humanities from the fourteenth century onwards as a reaction against the crisis generated by Ockham's skepticism toward the Augustinian confidence in the power of human reason, which he replaced with a "fascination for God's absolute and unconstrained power" (Cooper 2002: 26). From this emerged, instead of the orderly Augustinian world of ideas, fully accessible to the powers of the human mind, the bleak picture of an opaque universe ruled by the iron will of an unintelligible God, in which man had no particular privilege or place. The main reaction to this desolate vision was the Renaissance's emphasis on "self assertion" (Blumenberg 1983), which answered the challenge posed by the displacement of man as a knowing agent by refocusing on the human potential for creativity. In this shift from contemplation to agency, what came to be seen as characteristic of man are his creative abilities, deemed to mirror God's own and not to be bound by any particular nature or limits. This is particularly visible in Pico Della Mirandola's reworking of the myth of Epimetheus in his *Oratio*, in which God addresses man as follows:

> [W]e have given to thee, Adam, no fixed seat, no form of thy own, no gift peculiarly thine, that thou mayest feel as thine own, have as thine own, possess as thine own, the seat, the form, the gifts which thou thyself shalt desire. A limited nature in other creatures is confined within the laws written down by Us. In conformity with thy free judgment, in whose hands I have placed thee, thou art confined by no bounds; and thou will fix the limits of nature for thyself.[7] I have placed thee at the centre of the world, that from there thou mayest more conveniently look around and see whatsoever is in the world. Neither heavenly nor earthly, neither mortal nor immortal have We made thee. Thou, like a judge appointed for being honourable, art the molder and maker of thyself. (Pico Della Mirandola 1965: 4–5)

While there are limits to the rapprochement, this address strikes incredibly close chords to Foucault's own rejection of essentialism ("we have given thee … no form of thy own") and emphasis on self-creation (using an aesthetic paradigm echoed by Foucault's analyses of dandyism, Pico concludes that "thou mayest sculpt thyself into whatever shape thou dost prefer"). Such closeness reinforces the suggestion that there may be much more of a common ground than is usually thought – and this time not just in terms of the values upheld but also of conceptual content – between Foucault's mature views and at least some forms of humanism.

Notes

1   Of course, the question is open of whether one can successfully refute the idea of an essence of man and yet provide a definition of man. That it doesn't pick out empirical features does not mean that no essential properties are assigned.

2   There is an additional reason for the confusion: while it would be natural, in English, to use the neutral pronoun "it" to refer to the structure, and the masculine "he" for man as an empirical agent, in French there is no neutral, except in very few cases (such as "*il pleut*" [it is raining] or "*il y a*" [there is]). Thus in Foucault's texts the same masculine pronoun is used to denote both the structure ("man") and the individual (man). At the risk of artificiality in translation, I shall try to disentangle this ambiguity inasmuch as possible by substituting the neutral for the masculine when appropriate.

3   A determination is causal if it refers to the action of a cause, in such a way that the existence of the effect depends on that of the cause and the cause must be chronologically prior to (or at least simultaneous with) the effect. By contrast, a determination is epistemic (in an Allisonian sense) if it refers to the application of an a priori condition to the representation of an object. Such determination has no efficacious power and does not occur in time (although they can be defined in isolation of any given empirical content, epistemic conditions do not pre-exist their objects but are instantiated in them); it is a condition of intelligibility, not of existence.

4   The English translation is somewhat unfortunate as it renders the French "quasi-transcendental" with "transcendental" (with quotation marks).

5   "It is 'practices,' understood as modes of acting and thinking at the same time, which provide the key to the intelligibility of the correlative constitution of the subject and the object" (Foucault 1994d: 635; 1998: 463).

6   In the whole corpus I could only find one very brief allusion to J. Burckhardt's interpretation of the Renaissance: "[D]uring the Renaissance one also sees … that the hero is his own work of art. The idea that one may turn one's life into a work of art is an idea which is incontestably foreign to the Middle Ages and which appeared with the Renaissance" (Foucault 1994d: 410; 1997: 278).

7   Compare with: "[F]or me, what must be produced is not man as nature would have designed him, or as his essence would prescribe; we must produce something which does not exist yet and of which we cannot know what it will be" (Foucault 1994d: 74; 2000: 275).

References

Allison, H. (1983) *Kant's Transcendental Idealism: An Interpretation and Defense.* New Haven, CT: Yale University Press.

Althusser, L. and E. Balibar (1970) *Reading Capital*, trans. B. Brewster. London: New Left Books.

Blumenberg, L. (1983) *The Legitimacy of the Modern Age*. Cambridge, MA: MIT Press.

Braudel, F. (1982) *On History*, trans. S. Matthews. Chicago, IL: University of Chicago Press.

Cooper, D. E. (2002) *The Measure of Things: Humanism, Humility and Mystery*. Oxford: Oxford University Press.

Craig, E. (1987) *The Mind of God and the Works of Man*. Oxford: Oxford University Press.

Foucault, M. (1988) *Technologies of the Self: A Seminar with Michel Foucault*, ed. L. H. Martin et al. Cambridge, MA: MIT Press.

Foucault, M. (1990) *The Archaeology of Knowledge*. London: Routledge.

Foucault, M. (1994a) *Dits et Ecrits: 1954–1988*, vol. 1. Paris: Gallimard.

Foucault, M. (1994b) *Dits et Ecrits: 1954–1988*, vol. 2. Paris: Gallimard.

Foucault, M. (1994c) *Dits et Ecrits: 1954–1988*, vol. 3. Paris: Gallimard.

Foucault, M. (1994d) *Dits et Ecrits: 1954–1988*, vol. 4. Paris: Gallimard.

Foucault, M. (1994e) *The Order of Things*. New York: Random House.

Foucault, M. (1996) *Foucault Live (Interviews, 1961–1984)*, ed. S. Lotringer. New York: Semiotext(e).

Foucault, M. (1997) *Ethics, Subjectivity and Truth: The Essential Works of Foucault*, vol. 1, ed. P. Rabinow. New York: The New Press.

Foucault, M. (1998) *Aesthetics, Method, and Epistemology: The Essential Works of Foucault*, vol. 2, ed. J. D. Faubion. New York: The New Press.

Foucault, M. (1999) *Religion and Culture*, ed. J. R. Carrette. New York: Routledge.

Foucault, M. (2000) *Power: The Essential Works of Foucault*, vol. 3, ed. C. Gordon. New York: The New Press.

Fraser, N. (1994) "Michel Foucault: A 'Young Conservative'?" In M. Kelly, ed., *Critique and Power*. Cambridge, MA: MIT Press, pp. 185–211.

Garaudy, G. (1994) "Structuralisme et mort de l'homme." In B. Smart, ed., *Michel Foucault: Critical Assessments*, vol. 1. London: Routledge.

Habermas, J. (1987a) "The Critique of Reason as an Unmasking of the Human Sciences: Michel Foucault." In *The Philosophical Discourse of Modernity: Twelve Lectures*. Cambridge: Polity, pp. 238–66.

Habermas, J. (1987b) "Questions Concerning the Theory of Power." In *The Philosophical Discourse of Modernity: Twelve Lectures*. Cambridge, MA: MIT Press.

Han, B. (2002) *Foucault's Critical Project: Between the Transcendental and the Historical*. Stanford, CA: Stanford University Press.

Han, B. (2003) "Heidegger and Foucault on Kant and Finitude." In A. Milchman, ed., *Critical Encounters: Heidegger/Foucault*. Indianapolis: Indiana University Press.

Han, B. (2005) "Analytic of Finitude and the History of Subjectivity." In G. Gutting, ed., *The Cambridge Companion to Foucault*. Cambridge: Cambridge University Press.

Honneth, A. (1991) *The Critique of Power: Reflective Stages in a Critical Social Theory*, trans. K. Baynes. Cambridge, MA: MIT Press.

Hoy, D. (1981) "Power, Repression, Progress: Foucault, Lukes and the Frankfurt School." *Triquarterly* 52: 43–63.

Pico Della Mirandola (1965) *On the Dignity of Man*. Indianapolis, IN: Hackett Publishing Company.

Sartre, J.-P. (1973) *Existentialism and Humanism*. London: Eyre Methuen.

Sartre, J.-P. (1994) "Jean-Paul Sartre répond." In B. Smart, ed., *Michel Foucault: Critical Assessments*, vol. 1. London: Routledge.

Sawicki, J. (1991) *Disciplining Foucault: Feminism, Power, and the Body*. London: Routledge.

Soper, K. (1986) *Humanism and Anti-Humanism*. London: Hutchinson and Co.

7

Foucault's Theory of Knowledge

Barry Allen

This chapter examines Foucault's ideas about knowledge. I compare his archaeology of knowledge to usual approaches in analytic epistemology, and consider the later genealogical arguments, as well as the idea of power/ knowledge. I also discuss Foucault's thought about knowledge in relation to the arguments of Nietzsche, American Pragmatism, and the new Pragmatism of Richard Rorty.

The major text for Foucault's ideas about knowledge is his chapter "Archaeology and the Sciences" in *The Archaeology of Knowledge*. He makes five main points.

1. Knowledge is to be identified with "discursive practice." Any "group of statements" formed "in a regular manner by a discursive practice … can be called *knowledge*. Knowledge is that of which one can speak in a discursive practice" (1972: 182).

What is a discursive practice? Foucault's explanation is in terms of statements and their system or rules. A discourse is "a single system for the formation of statements" (ibid.: 186); and "a complex, differentiated practice, governed by analysable rules and transformations" (ibid.: 211). The inquiry he calls the "archaeology of knowledge" analyses "the rules proper to the different discursive practices." It sifts epistemic statements from the mass of things said, and "tries to establish rules of formation" (ibid.: 207), the syntax of the knowledge of a time.

A "statement" (*énoncé*) is not merely a logical proposition or a grammatical sentence or even a speech act. It is a specialized speech act, in which what is said (the statement) is a serious candidate for the truth about an object of knowledge. Foucault's idea of *énoncé* is glossed by Hubert Dreyfus and Paul Rabinow as "serious speech act," meaning a serious candidate for evaluation in terms of true and false (1983: 48). Ian Hacking (2002) calls such statements *truth-candidates*. Truth as such is less important to this status than truth-*value* (being either true or false), and more important than truth-value is the "seriousness" of the statement, which means that it appeals to those who receive it as a serious contribution to a discourse of knowledge.

Here are three statements from the *Malleus Maleficarum* (Kramer and Sprenger 1971), a fifteenth-century treatise on witchcraft:[1]

- human children can be generated by incubi and succubi demons;
- witches are more common than in the time of the Bible;
- women are more likely than men to practice witchcraft.

Grammatically, each is a well-formed sentence. Logically, each admits of evaluation as true or false. We may want to dismiss them as "obviously false," but they have the interesting quality of being lost knowledge, formerly serious truth-candidates that are now excluded from the locutionary content of speech acts, and in the Western countries at least cannot be used for statements that others can be expected to take seriously.

So Foucault's thought is that knowledge is discursive practice, which is to say a historical economy of serious speech acts. This is a paradox for Western thought. Statements circulating in discursive practice may be false; they may contain mistakes, errors, or inaccuracies. But knowledge cannot be mistaken, cannot be error, cannot be false. So how can Foucault seriously equate knowledge with discursive practice? The answer comes with the second point about knowledge, which is to distinguish *connaissance* and *savoir*.

2.   "By *connaissance* I mean the relation of the subject to the object and the formal rules that govern it. *Savoir* refers to the conditions that are necessary in a particular period for this or that type of object to be given to *connaissance* and for this or that enunciation to be formulated" (1972: 15). Foucault mentions the emergence of clinical medicine in the early nineteenth century as an example of the difference. This was a new medicine, "the result of a recasting at the level of epistemic knowledge (*savoir*) itself, and not at the level of accumulated, refined, deepened, adjusted knowledge (*connaissances*)" (Foucault 1975: 168–9). In other words, not the same old stuff done better and better, but something altogether new. The knowledgeable *connaissance* that physicians master "is not formed in the same way and according to the same

rules" as earlier medical training. "It is not a matter of the same game, somewhat improved, but of a quite different game" (ibid.: 137).

The knowledge statements that people make, the statements they actually put out into circulation, amount to *connaissance*, and not the "knowledge" that Foucault identifies with discursive practice. *Savoir* is the grid, the generative rules, the historical episteme by reference to which a difference between coherent or incoherent propositions, or more or less exact descriptions, can be established (see Machlup 1980). The first meaning of "knowledge" in Foucault's theory is not the epistemic surface-phenomena, what statements are made, what arguments and what evidence. The primary "knowledge" is a silent play of rules that generate the phenomenal surface (*connaissance*). These rules are changeable, historical, in something like the way that languages are. Foucault's perspective is resolutely historical. Knowledge is a historical economy of statements, period. He acknowledges no distinction between knowledge and what passes for known. What is or is not knowledge is as arbitrary as the color of a banknote or the sound of a word.

3.   Foucault's most extensive statement about knowledge appears in a dense paragraph of the *Archaeology* (1972: 182–3). To summarize, knowledge is said to be:

(a)   "That of which one can speak in a discursive practice."
(b)   "The space in which the subject may take a position and speak of the objects with which he deals in his discourse."
(c)   "The field of coordination and subordination of statements in which concepts appear, and are defined, applied, and transformed."
(d)   "The possibilities of use and appropriation offered by discourse."

Each point merits a comment:

(a)   "That of which one can speak in a discursive practice."
The statements that actually circulate, all of them, errors and falsehoods included, are the "knowledge" (*connaissance*) of a historical period. Errors and falsehoods are included because they are generated or "made possible" by the same *savoir* as governs the true, accurate, justified, and demonstrated.

Foucault seems as indifferent to *techne* as Plato was. His idea of knowledge includes the false and mistaken, but it *excludes* anything that is not a statement and any action that is not a speech act. Knowledge is carefully restricted to the order of logos. There is no place for knowing (*connaissance*) that cannot be summed up in a statement, no knowledge that isn't a proposition taken for true (or the rules that generate it). Hence, there is no "knowledge" in an engineering diagram, a bridge, an aircraft, a surgical operation, or a musical performance.

(b)   "The space in which the subject may take a position and speak of the objects with which he deals in his discourse."
Foucault seems never to miss an opportunity to disparage subjectivity and the expectations with which philosophers invested this concept from Descartes and Hegel to Husserl and Sartre. Such great things were expected of it! There was something heroic in a foundational subjectivity "grounding" this and "making possible" that. No, Foucault says. "The subject" is hollow, its unity a façade, its epistemic prowess a fable. A subject can't "ground" anything, because it is not a primitive unity. That was Nietzsche's argument (1966: §16). There's no *substance* to a subject, no durable unity. A subject is a series of effects. It cannot make things possible, because it is itself a function of the language it speaks and the discipline of its body. Foucault finds his own way to the same conclusion, first by reducing "the subject" to an artifact of discursive formation, which then allows him to stand Descartes on his head: knowledge is an external regularity in which subjectivity is inscribed.

(c)   "The field of coordination and subordination of statements in which concepts appear, and are defined, applied, and transformed."
Where, exactly, in the profuse detail of discursive practice should we look to find "knowledge"? We are to look at statements, look at their coordination and subordination, watch as concepts appear, are defined, applied, and transformed, seeking the rules and regulations, the epistemic syntax of this knowledge.

(d)   "The possibilities of use and appropriation offered by discourse."
Here, "possibilities of use" means opportunities when one subject's statement and not another's passes for true. These opportunities are supposedly governed by rules of discursive practice. That I can speak and have my statement carry the day, accepted as knowledge, as the truth, is not testimony to my epistemic virtue. It is sheer historical contingency, as improbable and arbitrary as the price of pearls in Babylon.

4. To return to my reading of Foucault's chapter "Archaeology and the Sciences," the fourth point he makes is that the historicity of knowledge extends to the objects of knowledge, the "things" knowledge is about. The objects of knowledge, the objectivities knowledge is concerned with, are not substances; they are nodal points of intersection among relations actualized in discourse. "What, in short, we wish to do," he says, "is to dispense with 'things'" – meaning beings ontologically prior to the historical contingency of the language that names them. He forsakes "the enigmatic treasure of 'things' anterior to discourse" for "the regular formation of objects that emerge only in discourse," objects defined "without reference to the *ground*, the foundation of things, but by relating them to the body of rules that enable them to form as objects of a discourse and thus constitutes the conditions of their historical appearance" (1972: 47–8).

Here is a place for a word about "episteme." We have to distinguish Foucault's word from the *epistemē* of ancient thought, which named the most philosophical idea of knowledge – contemplative, disinterested, logical knowledge of truth; not merely true but self-certifying, indubitable, a foundation on which to build science (Allen 2005b). Clearly, that's not Foucault's idea, which seems instead to be that of an epistemological field and a discursive formation:

> What I am attempting to bring to light is the epistemological field, the *episteme* in which knowledge, envisaged apart from all criteria having reference to its rational value or to its objective forms, grounds its positivity and thereby manifests a history not of growing perfection, but rather of its own conditions of possibility. (1973: xxi–xxii)

In a dense passage (1972: 191–2), Foucault elaborates on what his concept of the episteme is supposed to do:

- gather into a unified field all the discursive practices that give rise to the epistemological figures, sciences, and formal systems of an epoch;
- dictate which discursive practices consolidate into the formal positivity of a science, in what sequence, and with what obstacles;
- dictate relations among the sciences – for instance, reducibility (e.g., chemistry to physics) or relative autonomy (e.g., physics to economics);
- constantly change, being a historical entity like an economy or a war, rather than a timeless structure of transcendental logic.

The episteme seems to be an entire historical economy of knowledge, incorporating all the discursive practices, every positivity, all the sciences and semi-sciences of a period. Foucault calls it "the totality of relations that can be discovered, for a given period, between the sciences when one analyses them at the level of discursive regularities" (ibid.: 191). The relations are "discursive." They determine what discourse must establish "in order to speak of this or that object, in order to deal with them, name them, analyze them, classify them, explain them, etc." Yet these discursive relations are also ontological, "constituting the objects of discourse from within that practice" (ibid.: 46).

The picture of "objects" composed not of material substance but merely a "totality of relations" to other equally insubstantial entities recalls Heidegger's existential analysis in *Being and Time*. Heidegger described knowledge as an intentional relation to an entity, something that occurs as a moment in a global matrix of such relations – Dasein's "being-in-the-world" (Dreyfus 1991). For Heidegger, the knowledge discovered by inquiry is made possible by a greater, profoundly *given* revelation of the world, a primordial openness (*Entbergen*) of beings that defines the underlying orientation of our every thought and action. I see nothing of this "phenomenological" orientation in Foucault. His picture seems instead to be of a hapless subject without intrinsic unity lurching through history from one contingent episteme to another, without an underlying ontological structure. History is resolutely ontic, one damn thing after another.

5.   If knowledge is as Foucault says, what about the sciences, the most prominent instance of knowledge? A science is, as it were, congealed from the use of language, its more disciplined language game emerging in the midst of shaggier, less disciplined discourse. "The sciences … appear in the element of a discursive formation and against the background of knowledge" (1972: 184). The image of back- and foreground alternates with one of territory and domain: a science is said to be a "scientific domain" located within the boundaries of a larger "archaeological territory" (ibid.: 183). Foucault explains the geographic image with the example of Denis Diderot's *Dream of D'Alembert* (1769) (see Crocker 1959). The work is a dazzling display of natural-historical knowledge. Daring hypotheses seem to anticipate later ideas of Goethe, Cuvier, Lamarck, even Darwin. Yet the text remained unpublished, forgotten by its author in a drawer, found only by accident a century later. It therefore did not participate in the exchanges of eighteenth-century natural history. It was, as Foucault explains, part of the

territory of that knowledge, a masterpiece of its discourse, but not part of the natural history *domain*. It shows us something of *what* was known, but not *how* knowledge is established in scientific discourse, in which it did not participate.

The genealogy of a science begins when the chaos of unregulated discourse passes a threshold of *positivity*. A system of rules emerges for the formation of statements. To speak of "positivity" means the formation has the solidity (one might say "substance," though it is not substantial) to last a certain time and characterize a moment in the history of knowledge. "The positivity of a discourse characterizes its unity throughout time" (1972: 126). The discourse may or may not cross a further threshold of *epistemologization*. This is the point at which one delimited, specialized group of statements emerges, claiming to validate the norms of verification and coherence operating in the wider discursive formation of which they are a part. This epistemologized positivity may finally pass the threshold of scientificity, if and when the system of rules (1) comes to exercise authority as model, critique, or verification; (2) acquires powers of domination in relation to other, less prestigious discourse; and (3) satisfies what Foucault blandly refers to as the "formal criteria" of a science, as if we knew all about that.

His example of discourse crossing the threshold of science is the nineteenth-century emergence of psychiatry. This was of course the subject of his research in *The History of Madness*. He makes three points about this emerging science:

1 What makes the new discourse possible is a set of relations, connecting hospitals, prisons, industry and labor, jurisprudence, and morality. These are connected economically, in "discursive practice," and enable the formulation and circulation of statements in a conversation the emerging science sought to monopolize.

2 The discursive practice appears as a new medical science, but its discourse, its statements, its authority to say what is true and known reappear in other fields – legal decisions, literature, philosophy, government policy, everyday opinions.

3 The birth of psychiatry was not a progressive development in the theory and practice of a medicine of madness. What went before psychiatry was different. It was not trying and failing to be what psychiatry became. Rather than completing the older practice, the new psychiatry struggles with it for territory, struggling to define its domain in the

epistemological field. If we are to take this example as exemplary, the lesson seems to be one of incommensurable discourse. Discourses are narcissistic; they only talk to themselves, about themselves. Any apparent use of similar concepts is a historical fallacy of equivocation. Copernicus can't converse with Ptolemy. As Thomas Kuhn (1970: 117) said, they live in different worlds.

For Foucault, these are worlds of discourse, not ontological worlds of "beings." The primary sense of knowledge for archaeology is, as we saw, the practical, discursive presuppositions of the statement, rather than the body of statements that constitute a theory or science. This knowledge is not "made true" by the being of things. What makes it true is an "ensemble of rules according to which the true and the false are separated and specific effects of power attached to the true" (Foucault 1980: 132). There may be more to the world than discourse, but not to knowledge. It's all talk. Rule-governed, but still talk, statements and their regularities, and not, for instance, machines or non-discursive actions. He does say that discourse is situated in a field of "non-discursive practices." These "are not disturbing elements which … suppress its true voice and emit in its place a travestied discourse, but, on the contrary, [are among] its formative elements" (1972: 68). Yet discourse is the glue that binds them, the energy that mobilizes them, the thread that weaves "institutions, techniques, social groups, [and] perceptual organizations" (ibid.: 72) into a coherent *discursive* formation. Non-discursive things or relations belong to knowledge only insofar as they contribute to a statement.

One might wonder whether this one-sided discursivism is peculiar to Foucault's work before the later "genealogical" studies. What the later work calls "disciplinary knowledge," for instance, is a good deal more than just talk. He discusses the use of architecture in creating "disciplinary space," and the invention of timetables, alarm clocks, and the artificial nipple to induce the "docility" of disciplinary subjectivity. Some of the techniques and technologies he discusses belong to discourse. Confession, for instance, is described as "a ritual of discourse" (1978: 61). The techniques of "examination" – "small techniques of notation, of registration, of constituting files, of arranging facts in columns and tables" – are "procedures of writing that made it possible to integrate individual data into cumulative systems," which makes them "scriptuary and documentary" and therefore discursive, and they are credited with the construction of individuals and populations as objects of knowledge. Other, less obviously discursive artifacts, like factory whistles, alarm clocks, and artificial nipples, seem to find their point in the new statements they make possible; for instance, making it possible to say something scientific about an individual (delinquent, schizophrenic, dangerous offender), and to make scientific statements about "collective facts, the calculation of the gaps between individuals, their distribution in a given 'population'" (1979: 190–1). My point, then, is not that Foucault fails to take the non-discursive into account; it is his idea of what taking it into account requires. He acknowledges the non-discursive only to subordinate it to the arbitrary rules of discourse. It is the discursive accomplishment of a statement that dignifies non-discursive artifacts as *knowledge,* making the practices that mobilize them *knowledge*-practices, their associated institutions *knowledge*-institutions. The only *non*-discursive that matters to knowledge is *pre*discursive, on its way to language, and "the prediscursive is still discursive … One remains within the dimensions of discourse" (1972: 76).

Suppose we have contradictory statements, each with evidence and arguments, both having currency in some historical economy of knowledge. Logically, one alone can be true. For Foucault, both are knowledge. The fact that only one is true and the other false apparently makes no difference, though we remember that he's thinking of *savoir.* Contradictory statements are products of the same syntax of knowledge, defining the epistemic economy in which those statements have currency. That is plausible. If you can take seriously the statement that there are more witches than in biblical times, you must take seriously the contrary statement that there are about the same or fewer witches.

Contradictory statements may both belong to *savoir.* Can both be *connaissance*-knowledge, the "knowledge-that" which actually circulates among speakers? Apparently so. Both statements have their arguments, their evidence, their advocates, and should therefore count as *connaissance.* So contradictory statements can belong to *savoir* (historical rules of epistemic syntax), and to *connaissance,* the statements that actually circulate with the authority of knowledge.

This observation highlights Foucault's indifference to what might be called a normative concept of knowledge, distinguishing knowledge from what is claimed, believed, or said to be known (what *passes* for knowledge). Should one question this indifference? Foucault may think a normative concept of knowledge is naive given Nietzsche's critique of epistemology. He also seems to consider the concept an obstacle to due appreciation of the political side of truth, which concentrates on what passes for true and doesn't worry about truth "itself."

It is of course the most insistent argument of Foucault's work after *The Archaeology of Knowledge* to connect knowledge and truth with disciplinary power. Tradition held these apart in the West. One had to make a choice: withdraw into contemplative disinterest and dedicate your life to knowledge; or live in public, contesting for power, where appearance is everything and truth a matter of indifference. Knowledge is truly knowledge when it is answerable only to truth; power is not truly power when subject to the authority of knowledge, the armature of Plato's argument for philosopher-kings. Naturally, Foucault has no use for that, and here he follows Nietzsche. He goes beyond Nietzsche in at least two ways. First, he focuses on verifiable historical differences of social power, and doesn't let "power" become a metaphysical mystery, as Nietzsche sometimes does. Second, he pushed past current limits in social analysis with the most important rethinking of the historical-sociological concept of power since Max Weber (Allen 1998).

The way truth-values are distributed over statements – what is acknowledged as true, discredited as false, and so on – lines up with the major lines of social power, especially in modern Western societies. Foucault makes this argument many times. In the English-language collection *Power/Knowledge*, he put it in terms of the questions, "What rights are created by the power/truth nexus, that is, the power of those who can say what is true, and the truth produced by the exercise of power? What kind of power can produce and be exercised by a discovery with the value of truth?" (1980: 78–108). Maybe everything that circulates in the economy of statements is knowledge, but clearly not everything is *true*. It is at the interface of social power and disciplinary knowledge, through the distinction and distribution of truth-values (*true/false*), that the placid surface of the episteme is divided and made mobile. A statement may belong to knowledge even if everybody knows it is false. But precisely because everybody knows it is false, it is not a statement anyone can make, because no one who matters will take it seriously.

According to Foucault, knowledge acquired a new priority with the movement he describes from medieval juridical sovereignty to early modern government. More and more of life is reduced for administrative purposes to a problem of expertise and "what is true." Wisdom is a traditional virtue of rulers, but when wisdom is interpreted in terms of empirical knowledge for the management of things, knowledge acquires a new political valency. The question, "What must a ruler know?" takes a new form, motivating a set of "analyses and forms of knowledge, which began to develop in the late sixteenth century and grew in importance during the seventeenth." These all had "essentially to do with knowledge of the state, in all its different elements, dimensions, and factors of power, questions which were termed precisely 'statistics,' meaning the science of the state," constructing "a *savoir* of state that could be used as a tactic of government" (1991: 96, 97–8).

To an analytic or neo-Kantian epistemologist Foucault may seem not to "believe" in truth. But you cannot say he is indifferent to whether his statements are true or false. No one can be. Taken seriously, the attitude is fatal. Professional historians who read Foucault may sometimes find his arguments overbold, but none thinks he was just incompetent (Goldstein 1994). To understand this much truthfulness does not require the metaphysics of Truth. Foucault's scholarly truthfulness is tactical, pragmatic, not strategic or teleological. He wants to be effective, to be taken seriously, and must therefore conduct his discourse appropriately, which means conforming to disciplinary standards of truthfulness, which is exactly what he does. This much care for truth can be understood as caring for what passes for true or can be made to pass for true in a discourse; for instance, European historical research in the latter twentieth century. Put in that context, assessed by that standard, Foucault's work shows a healthy respect for truth, without presupposing any real difference between truth and what passes.

Here then is the respect in which Foucault does *not* "believe" in truth. His professional attitude toward knowledge is indifference to the difference between *passing for true* and "really being true." Never does he distinguish knowledge from something that merely happens to pass for known. His perspective resolutely suspends these epistemological standards. Epistemology cannot be expected to welcome the concept of "passing for true." Without distinguishing what is true from what merely passes, there is no point to inquiry concerning the criteria of truth (*real* truth); no point in making truth a condition of knowledge (*real* knowledge); and no normative difference between knowledge and what merely passes for true and known – all textbook examples of epistemological problems.

Foucault seems to take Nietzsche to have shown that normative epistemology is a deeply compromised project, pursued in earnest only by those equally compromised in self-knowledge. Be that as it may, epistemology is useless for investigating the political power-effect of truth. Whether a prestigious statement is "really true" or "really knowledge" makes no difference to its currency as a statement, or its disciplinary effect on docile bodies. Rather than asking what in the "knowledge" of a time is really true, Foucault for once raises a question about how the "knowledge" of a time is always also a *not*-knowledge, an *exclusion* of otherwise acceptable statements from actual discourse (*connaissance*). Such statements are reduced to silence by the same rules that enable other statements to circulate. There are two forms of this exclusion:

1　Subjugated knowledge. This refers to statements belonging to a given epistemological field and therefore classified as knowledge, yet excluded from scientific domains as incompetent, unqualified, absurd, or irrelevant. Foucault discussed this exclusion in his "Two Lectures" in *Power/Knowledge*. Examples he mentions include the "knowledge" of psychiatric patients or nurses: knowledge about the institutions that diagnose them, the abnormalities they register, and the treatment they administer. Yet what a psychiatric nurse or patient knows typically has no credit, no currency, no candidacy for truth in psychiatric discourse, where it may enter only robed in quotation marks and under the care of a psychiatrist.

2　Lost knowledge. Subjugated knowledge is a synchronic phenomenon – knowledge excluded from the sciences (or any formal system, for instance, psychoanalysis) by the same rules that make it possible as a statement. Lost knowledge is the diachronic counterpart – knowledge that is no longer known, that *cannot* be known, due to historical change in the syntax of knowledge. One example I have already mentioned is the demonological knowledge of the *Malleus Maleficarum*. Another example is what Christian desert fathers (for instance, John Cassian) "knew" about desire. Today we cannot see it as knowledge, though there was a time and place, a historical economy and discursive practice, when their statements were valuable knowledge about a difficult, vitally important subject. The knowledge is now lost. Archaeology can recover the fossils of this *savoir*, but nothing can overcome the exclusion of those statements from the epistemological field.

There is former knowledge, lost knowledge, and unprestigious, subjugated knowledge, but no serious statement is not knowledge, since all there is to "being knowledge" is serious truth-candidacy. That is Foucault's neo-Weberian "value-free" analysis, with his anti-epistemological indifference to normative concepts of knowledge and truth. This indifference makes archaeology hostile to epistemology. One can ask whether we really need an alternative to epistemology, and whether Foucault's archaeology is it. Do we need an alternative? I think so. Knowledge is too important not to think about, and that thinking needs orientation that usual approaches in neo-Kantian and analytic epistemology can no longer offer. Is Foucault's archaeology an improvement? Probably not.

Foucault's idea of knowledge can be summed up in the expression "prestigious discourse" (Allen 1999; 2004; 2005a). Knowledge is a status for statements. To "know" is to make pronouncements whose prestige predisposes people to take them seriously. Knowledge is what knowledge authorities take seriously. To "know" is to occupy a position (a prestige) in a historical episteme from which to speak in the name of knowledge. There is something positivistic about Foucault's procedure. Positivists let the methodological tail wag the philosophical dog. They are like the drunk looking for his keys under a lamppost, not because he lost them there but because the light is so good (McCloskey 1994). That seems to describe Foucault, too. He looks for knowledge in discursive practice because he has such a good theory of it. Arbitrary discourse is all he sees in knowledge because it is all that his methodology lets him admit he sees. I suppose he thinks it is delusional to believe in a difference between knowing and authoritative say-so. Certainly his archaeology has nothing to say about it. The question is whether that is a defect of his theory, or whether there is a reason to be indifferent to normative knowledge.

Foucault liked to talk about "rules." What distinguishes his theory from "structuralism" is that it is not binary oppositions but generative rules he is describing – unconscious, anonymous rules. He is closer to Noam Chomsky than to Ferdinand de Saussure. Discursive formations (and therefore knowledge and truth-value) "are, strictly speaking, groups of statements" (1972: 115). With rules, lots of rules:

- rules for how a discursive practice groups objects, forms concepts, and enunciates statements;
- rules determining what statements are coherent or incoherent, and when they are verified or identified as errors.
- a rule-governed system of reference by which a series of signs acquires relation to a domain of objects;
- a rule-governed distribution of subject positions defining which signs from which mouths shall count as serious statements;
- a rule-governed system of associated fields;
- a rule-governed system defining the ways statements are institutionalized, received, used, re-used, combined together, or appropriated into a strategy. (1972: 108, 115, 122, 181–2)

The proof of these putative rules remained an unfulfilled promise. Foucault never produced a single example of such rules, or explained how they would "generate" a historical statement. The metaphors of game and rule, depth and surface, grammar and archaeology seem to do no work. Regarding *connaissance* as the superficial effect of a "depth knowledge" (*savoir*) of the rules that generate it is no help to explain why certain statements enjoy their prestige; for it does nothing to explain why those rules and no others generate statements that historical people take seriously. Any question about "surface" knowledge – historical questions, such as why it appeared when and where it did, or philosophical questions about its validity or presuppositions – seems bound to arise again, and in no more tractable form, as a question about the hypothetical depth knowledge. Also, there is no evidence of these hypothetical rules apart from the prestigious statements they are invoked to explain. They are not independent discoveries that explain the value or credibility of statements. They are simply read back into the archive from which they were abstracted, as an imaginary generative episteme.

Foucault's two-tiered, surface-depth theory retains Western philosophy's logocentric, propositional bias (Allen 2004). Any question one might have about knowledge is essentially a question about statements, and is to be answered from the order of discourse. Knowledge is a matter of statements made, rather than of nonlinguistic actions performed or non-discursive technical capacities. Foucault arbitrarily limits "knowledge" to *liberal* knowledges, excluding the mechanical or more broadly technical. Despite disbelief in normative ideas of knowledge and truth, he confirms the classical position that useful, practical, technical, mechanical artifacts are not properly denominated "knowledge," at any rate not the best knowledge, or the knowledge most worth philosophical attention. *That* knowledge has to be *true*, or at least to *pass for true*.

Foucault reaffirms the ancient assumption that knowledge has to be true, even as he overturns the oldest idea of what "being true" is, the idea of ontological adequacy. The cause of a statement's truth-candidacy is in the language game, the discursive formation, not the being of a being. A statement's "truth" is merely its currency, a matter of arbitrary syntax and no less arbitrary social power. To ask whether a statement is really true is like asking whether a US dollar is really money ("I understand that it circulates, but *should* it? Is it *really* money?"). Both questions assume that there is more to these values than currency, an assumption that Foucault rejects. It's not clear why he does so. He may assume that a normative difference in knowledge presupposes a metaphysical concept of truth, though that's not necessarily so. American Pragmatism is an alternative to both Plato and Nietzsche. A pragmatic philosopher like William James or John Dewey can agree with everything Nietzsche implied in his statement "God is dead," without following him in his nihilism.

What made Pragmatism at once disreputable and seductive was how it took truth off the mantel, urging that the value of knowledge and science was not theoretical truth but powerful instruments of action. To these Pragmatists, the subversion of Platonic-Christian assumptions about "the Truth" provoked not a crisis of nihilism but a feeling of relief, motivating a critique of metaphysics and epistemology parallel to Nietzsche though independently inspired – and inspired it is, even hopeful. Their hope is not the rationalistic optimism Nietzsche criticized in Platonism, which makes the triumph of the Good a foregone conclusion. Pragmatism is a vision of the world as an evolving, unfinished place, "a wide open universe," John Dewey said, "without bounds in space or time, without final limits of origin or destiny, a universe with the lid off." William James said the same thing, and so did Nietzsche (Dewey 1993: 74; James 1978: 20, 123–4; Nietzsche 1967: §1065). These Pragmatists can also agree with Foucault that knowledge and truth are instrumentalities of social power, while avoiding his antinomianism, by which I mean his grim refusal to acknowledge differences of value; for instance, by allowing that some "knowledge" is more properly knowledge and some "truths" not really true. Pragmatists work in terms as non-metaphysical as anything in Nietzsche or Foucault, yet they take pains to reconstruct the normative understanding of knowledge and truth, providing an alternative to Nietzsche and Foucault.

I mentioned James and Dewey, though the most prominent of American Pragmatists today is the late Richard Rorty. Where does he stand on this issue of a possible synthesis of Foucault and Pragmatism? Ironically, too close to Foucault. Rorty rewrote American Pragmatism in terms that emphasize its similarity to postmodern European thought. I don't think Rorty wants or feels that he needs a "normative" idea of knowledge any more than Foucault did. Instead of Pragmatism as an alternative to European postmodernism (as for instance in the work of Hilary Putnam), Rorty's is a postmodern Pragmatism (Allen 2008b).

As for the theory of knowledge, Rorty says the desire for such a theory "is a desire for constraint – a desire to find 'foundations' to which one might cling, frameworks beyond which one must not stray, objects which impose themselves, representations which cannot be gainsaid … the desire for confrontation and constraint." Epistemology involves a search "for the immutable structures within which knowledge, life, and culture must be contained – structures set by the privileged representations which it studies" (Rorty 1979: 163; see also Allen 2000). Rorty thinks this project is premised on the mistaken idea of knowledge as representation. Only if knowing is conceived as a mirror-like reflection of objectivities does the project arise of enhancing knowledge by learning more about the mental optics. If you are skeptical of a Platonic conception of knowledge, you should be skeptical of the point or value of epistemology.

The question raised by Rorty's argument is also insistent in Foucault's work. Should a normative idea of knowledge be as aggressively ignored as Rorty and Foucault do? Earlier I said that knowledge is too important not to think about. I meant real knowledge, not merely prestigious discourse, perhaps not prestigious (or discourse) at all. One reason for holding on to a normative idea of knowledge is because only then does the point of research like Foucault's become clear. There is only one way to counter the power of disciplinary expertise. It is no good citing Foucault against the experts and problematizing their governmentality. What you have to do is show that they are wrong, that they do not know, that there are unconsidered alternatives, that others know better. For that purpose it is counterproductive to say that there is, after all, no significant difference between knowing and not knowing, or even between true and false; or to say they are arbitrary differences in the social deployment of discursive power. Unless you take knowledge seriously enough to think there's a difference between the mere claim to it and the quality itself, why should you care that knowledge and truth may be mobilized by disciplinary power? What's the point of analyzing the truth/power nexus, if the results leave us immobilized when we see it in action?

How might we understand normative knowledge? It's a question that is obviously beyond this paper, though I would like to make one point. We saw that Foucault is as truthful as any competent scholar. I suggested that this concern for truth is motivated by the desire to be effective in one's statements, to be taken seriously. It is a tactical, not strategic, truthfulness, and reveals no lingering metaphysical presupposition. Isn't *effectiveness* the idea we need to understand the difference between normative knowledge and its prestigious simulacra? Effectiveness is a quality not just of statements but of artifacts broadly conceived. That includes tools, technological devices, and any other technically mediated intervention. Discourse is but a region, a domain if you will, in the territory of knowledge, which lies in the land of artifacts and the realm of art (Allen 2004; 2008a).

Is there a difference between effectiveness and what prestigious authorities regard as effective? Is there an independent respect in which a statement, or any artifact, can be evaluated for effectiveness; independent, that is, of merely conventional authorities and their say-so? The answer again seems to lie with the artifacts. Whether an artifact exemplifies (normative) knowledge depends on the work, how it is put together, its performance, and not solely on what people say about it. Works are related not just to us and our words but to other works too. The genealogy of an artifact always refers to earlier artifacts, and the performance of artifacts is evaluated in relation to that history, a relation to other artifacts. More than discursive authority matters to knowledge because knowledge begins not with discourse but artifacts. Mute though it is, the artifact does intervene and sets terms to its cooperation (Latour 2002; 2004).

Note

1   Kramer and Sprenger (1971) say:

1   The practice of witchcraft essentially involves four things, one of which is carnal lust with incubi and succubi (20b–21a), who perform sexual acts with human beings not for delectation but to pollute them body and soul (28a, 112a–b). The acts they perform are real carnal acts (not imaginary), and should they produce children, the children belong to the man whose semen the incubus stole (28a). Sexual intercourse with demons and the offering up of unbaptized babies to Satan are "certainly very common at the present day" (21a).

2   Long ago (in Job's time), there were no witches (15a). But since then, by a slow process, their numbers have increased until now there are a great many witches: "in this twilight and evening of the world, when sin is flourishing on every side and in every place, when charity is growing cold, the evil of witches and their iniquities superabound" (16a). Recently, the number of witches has greatly increased (20b, 45a), the reason being that the world is in decline (69b).

3   Women are especially prone to witchcraft because "all witchcraft comes from carnal lust which is in women insatiable" (47a).

For further discussion of this work, see Allen 1993.

References

Allen, B. (1993) "Demonology, Styles of Reasoning, and Truth." *International Journal of Moral and Social Studies* 8: 95–122.

Allen, B. (1998) "Foucault and Modern Political Philosophy." In J. Moss, *The Later Foucault: Philosophy and Politics*. London: Sage, pp. 164–98.

Allen, B. (1999) "Power/Knowledge." In K. Racevskis, ed., *Critical Essays on Michel Foucault*. New York: G. K. Hall, pp. 69–81.

Allen, B. (2000) "What Was Epistemology?" In R. Brandom, ed., *Rorty and his Critics*. Oxford: Blackwell, pp. 220–36.

Allen, B. (2004) *Knowledge and Civilization*. Boulder, CO: Westview Press.

Allen, B. (2005a) "Foucault's Nominalism." In S. Tremain, ed., *Foucault and the Government of Disability*. Ann Arbor: University of Michigan Press, pp. 93–107.

Allen, B. (2005b) "Knowledge." In M. C. Horowitz, ed., *New Dictionary of the History of Ideas*. Detroit, MI: Charles Scribner's Sons.

Allen, B. (2008a) *Artifice and Design: Art and Technology in Human Experience*. Ithaca, NY: Cornell University Press.

Allen, B. (2008b) "Postmodern Pragmatism." *Philosophical Topics* 36 (2).

Crocker, L. G. (1959) "Diderot and Eighteenth-Century French Transformism." In B. Glass, O. Tomkin, and W. L. Strauss, eds., *Forerunners of Darwin*. Baltimore, MD: Johns Hopkins University Press.

Dewey, J. (1993) *Political Writings*, ed. D. Morris and I. Shapiro. Indianapolis, IN: Hackett.

Dreyfus, H. (1991) *Being-in-the-World: A Commentary on Heidegger's "Being and Time," Division I*. Cambridge, MA: MIT Press.

Dreyfus, H. and P. Rabinow (1983) *Michel Foucault: Beyond Hermeneutics and Structuralism*. Chicago, IL: University of Chicago Press.

Foucault, M. (1972) *The Archaeology of Knowledge*, trans. A. M. Sheridan Smith. New York: Pantheon.

Foucault, M. (1973) *The Order of Things: An Archaeology of the Human Sciences*. New York: Vintage.

Foucault, M. (1975) *The Birth of the Clinic: An Archaeology of Medical Perception*, trans. A. M. Sheridan Smith. New York: Vintage.

Foucault, M. (1978) *The History of Sexuality*, vol. 1: *Introduction*, trans. R. Hurley. New York: Vintage.

Foucault, M. (1979) *Discipline and Punish*, trans. A. Sheridan. New York: Vintage.

Foucault, M. (1980) *Power/Knowledge: Selected Interviews and Other Writings 1972–1977*, ed. C. Gorden. New York: Pantheon.

Foucault, M. (1991) "Governmentality." In G. Burchell et al., eds., *The Foucault Effect: Studies in Governmentality*. Chicago, IL: University of Chicago Press.

Goldstein, J., ed. (1994) *Foucault and the Writing of History*. Oxford: Blackwell.

Hacking, I. (2002) *Historical Ontology*. Cambridge, MA: Harvard University Press.

James, William (1978) *Pragmatism*. Cambridge, MA: Harvard University Press.

Kuhn, T. S. (1970) *The Structure of Scientific Revolutions*. Chicago, IL: University of Chicago Press.

Kramer, H. and J. Sprenger (1971 [1486]) *Malleus Maleficarum*, ed. and trans. M. Summers. New York: Dover Publications.

Latour, B. (2002) "Morality and Technology: The End of the Means." *Theory, Culture & Society* 19: 247–60.

Latour, B. (2004) *Politics of Nature: How to Bring the Sciences into Democracy*, trans. C. Porter. Cambridge, MA: Harvard University Press.

Machlup, F. (1980) *Knowledge: Its Creation, Distribution, and Economic Significance*, vol. 1: *Knowledge and Knowledge Production*. Princeton, NJ: Princeton University Press.

McCloskey, D. M. (1994) *Knowledge and Persuasion in Economics*. Cambridge: Cambridge University Press.

Nietzsche, F. (1966) *Beyond Good and Evil: Prelude to a Philosophy of the Future*, trans. W. Kaufmann. New York: Vintage.

Nietzsche, F. (1967) *The Will to Power*, trans. W. Kaufmann, and R. J. Hollingdale. New York: Vintage.

Rorty, R. (1979) *Philosophy and the Mirror of Nature*. Princeton, NJ: Princeton University Press.

8

Rethinking Experience with Foucault

Timothy O'Leary

At the end of Joyce's *A Portrait of the Artist as a Young Man*, the central protagonist, Stephen Dedalus, writes in his diary that he goes "to encounter for the millionth time the reality of experience" (Joyce 1992: 275). This formulation captures an important feature of, let us say, our experience of experience. That is, there is a sense in which experience is always something new, something that impresses us with its "reality," but it is also something that, since it occurs a million times, has always happened before. In its first aspect, it is something that a young man who is about to leave his family and his nation would find exhilarating and perhaps terrifying; in its other aspect, it seems to promise a repetition and familiarity that could lead to either boredom or wisdom. The tendency to think about experience as coming in two quite different, and perhaps contradictory, forms is common to many twentieth-century philosophers. Dewey, for example, makes a distinction between the general flow of undifferentiated, inchoate experience and the kind of experience that stands out against this background as "*an* experience" – which may be a fine meal, a game of chess, or a reading of a poem (Dewey 1980: 35).[1] Gadamer (2003), for his part, draws on a long tradition in German-language philosophy to make a distinction between experience as *Erlebnis* (approximately, immediate or lived experience) and as *Erfahrung* (approximately, accumulated experience).[2] And Foucault, as I will argue here, makes a distinction between the everyday experience of a given historical period and the transformative experiences that are made possible by, among other things, certain works of literature and philosophy.

In general, these distinctions seem to be made possible by a fundamental feature of the way we talk about experience.[3] On the one hand, we use the word experience as a count noun: we might speak of the experience of reading a book, the experience of winning a race, or the experience of witnessing a car crash. In all these cases, we use the word to designate things, incidents, events, that occur at a particular moment to a particular person; they are specifiable and countable. On the other hand, we use the word as a mass noun: we might speak of employing a person who has experience, of the wisdom that comes with experience, or of the migrant experience, the university experience, and so on. In these cases, we refer to something that is largely indeterminate in terms of place and time, something that is difficult to pin down and define; here, experience is, in some sense, an inchoate mass. It would be convenient if we could say that experience in the latter sense is made up of, or based upon, experience in the former sense. In that case, our particular, individual experiences would accumulate to form a long-term amalgamation that would be a kind of summing up of the individual parts, leading to maturity. However, this would be to ignore the fact that this formative influence also works in the opposite direction. That is, our accumulated experience also influences and colors the particular experiences that we can have in any given present. We know, for example, that we can never experience anything "for the first time" more than once. This is, no doubt, an obvious point, but it raises a fundamental philosophical question about the nature of experience: how, and to what extent, does experience have a history?

I want to address this question here, using the resources that Foucault's thought makes available.[4] In a 1979 interview, Foucault makes the following surprising assertion: "[A]n experience is always a fiction: it's something that one fabricates oneself, that doesn't exist before and will exist afterward" (2000: 243). What I want to do here is investigate the grounds on which Foucault bases this claim. The value of exploring these grounds is the insight it will give us into the extent to which Foucault can be read as a philosopher of experience and, more than that, as a philosopher of the historical transformation of experience. I will argue that one of Foucault's major concerns is to develop an account of experience in which the subject, the conscious subject, loses primacy in the constitution of experience. Foucault wishes to acknowledge and investigate the ways in which our experience exceeds our own private interactions with the world. However, he is interested not only in what we could call the shared a priori of our experience, but also in the historical transformations which those a priori undergo. And, ultimately, he is interested not only in the large-scale, anonymous contours of those shifts, but also in the possibility that certain experimental and critical practices can bring about significant changes at a micro-level. Therefore, what he finally demands of an account of experience is, first, the ability to link up the privacy of individual (or shared) experiences with large-scale historical phenomena and shifts. And, secondly, the ability to both account for and facilitate the transformation of experience through deliberate intervention.

In order to get a clear idea of what is at stake here, I want to present a vignette of a street experience, in which I invite the reader to be the protagonist. Consider the experience of seeing a homeless, psychotic person in the street. Imagine that you go out to buy a newspaper on a bright sunny morning, when you see ahead of you, sitting in a doorway, a man dressed in ragged, dirty clothes with a sleeping bag rolled up in the corner behind him. As you get closer you can hear him speaking and waving one hand as if he's arguing with somebody. You think about crossing over to the other side of the street, but you decide that would be silly – and even, perhaps, cruel. When you come level with the man you can see the empty beer bottles beside his sleeping bag as he begins to ask you for money for food. You wonder if you should give him anything, as you suspect he will use the money for his morning drink. You start to veer away from him, unable to decide what to do, when suddenly his tone changes to one of aggression as he realizes you're not going to give him anything. You quicken your pace as he shouts after you and you take refuge in a nearby shop. Later, sitting at home reading the newspaper, you see an article about how the government has cut funding for out-patient psychiatric care in your city. You begin to wonder if you should have handled the situation differently.

This is the kind of experience that could happen to any of us who live in a modern city, and it is an experience of the kind that we might report to somebody in the form of "Something happened when I went out to get the newspaper this morning. ..." But, what is it that happened? The first point to make is that, for Foucault, it is not sufficient to focus on the inner workings of our own psyche in order to explain this occurrence. Such an approach could never adequately explain, or even describe, an experience like this. This is not just because Foucault might be opposed to its psychologizing tendency, but, more importantly, because it fails to consider the extent to which this private experience is made possible by larger social, political, and ethical structures. For Foucault, this is a weakness in some approaches to experience that applies especially to phenomenology – or at least, to phenomenology as it was practiced in France during his formative years.[5] So, how would Foucault himself go about building an account of such an experience?

My suggestion is that we can read Foucault's work, almost in its entirety, as an attempt – admittedly comprising revisions and dead-ends – to provide the conceptual tools both for understanding an experience such as I described and for helping us to transform it through an engaged and experimental practice. I am not, however, arguing that Foucault, from the beginning, had set this as his project. I am simply suggesting that, seen from the perspective of his late work, or, more properly, seen from our perspective today, one of the most fruitful ways of using his work is as a set of tools that help us to understand, and potentially transform, our experience of the worlds in which we live. Hence, the reading of Foucault that I am proposing here is motivated by the same question with which Foucault approached Nietzsche: "What is the maximum of philosophical intensity, and what are the current philosophical effects to be found in these texts?" (1998: 447). And the answer I will give is that this intensity and these effects arise from the concept of experience and the idea of its historicity.

Two Concepts of Experience

Foucault's use of this concept, however, is not quite as consistent and univocal as some readers might wish. In fact, the many ways in which Foucault uses the term experience in his writings and interviews may appear to be bewildering in their range and apparent incoherence. He talks, for example, about the foundational "limit-experiences" of a culture (2006b: xxix); the "classical experience of madness" (2006a: 15); a possible "experience of the outside" and of "transgression" (1998: 77, 154); a "history of sexuality as experience" (1984a: 4); and, the idea that he wants to write "experience-books" rather than "truth-books" (2000: 246). One preliminary way to begin to make sense of these uses of the term is to divide them, as I have done elsewhere (O'Leary 2009: ch. 5), into two general categories. These two categories can be mapped, more or less loosely, onto the distinction we can make between "experience" as a mass noun and as a count noun.

On the one hand, the term is used to indicate the general forms of thought, perception, and practice that characterize a particular area of human life during a particular historical period. Hence, we have "all the major experiences of the Renaissance" (2006a: 8, modified), the "experience of order" between the sixteenth and nineteenth centuries (2001: 45), and even a contrast between the Christian and the modern experience of philosophy.[6] This concept of experience points, we could say, to the general background forms and structures that, in a general sense, determine, or at least set the parameters for, the everyday experience of people who live in a given period. So, it includes both these forms themselves and the range of actual experiences that individuals may have. In this sense, the term is used predominantly as a mass noun. Let's call this "everyday experience." On the other hand, the term is used to indicate an exceptional occurrence in the life of an individual (or, sometimes, a culture) which changes the way that individual (or culture) approaches a given area of human life. Hence, we have the idea that the division between reason and madness was a "limit-experience" in which Western culture excluded that which would function as its outside (2006b: xxix); and also the idea of a "limit-experience" as an individual experience of transgression that "wrenches the subject from itself" (2000: 241). And, most memorably in this vein, we have the idea that Foucault wants his own books to be read as "experience books," that is as books that would prevent us from "always being the same" (ibid.: 246). In this use of the term, Foucault makes full use of the fact that the French word *expérience* means both experience and experiment. "I am an experimenter," he says, "in the sense that I write in order to change myself and in order to no longer think the same thing as before" (ibid.: 240, modified). So, this is a concept of experience as an exceptional, perhaps unexpected, occurrence from which one emerges in some way changed. It is a kind of experience that can be specified in place and time and has a certain unrepeatable uniqueness. Let's call this "transformative experience."

The first point to be made about these two concepts is that while they are both present in the first and the last phases of Foucault's work, we will see that they are almost completely absent from his middle works (let's say, for the sake of convenience, the decade from 1966 to 1976). The second point to be made is that these two forms of experience have a very important, perhaps problematic, relation to each other. This is the fact, mentioned earlier, that these two kinds of experience are continuously influencing and modifying each other. Hence, Foucault will say that while our everyday experience is largely determined by general background structures, there is one kind of experience (transformative experience) which is capable of intervening in and modifying this everyday experience. As a result, one might raise questions about the coherence of using "experience" to indicate both an overall framework and one of the elements that occur within that framework (see Han 2002: 152–8). However, there isn't really any difficulty in accepting that, for example, a particular experience in the present can both rule out and make more likely a range of other experiences in the future. This seems to be at the basis of the approaches taken by Dewey and Gadamer, for example, not to mention the tiresome refrain from film trailers that somebody's life will be "changed forever." In other words, both philosophical and everyday language seem to recognize the coherence of using "experience" both to indicate a general background or framework that makes possible our common, everyday experiences and to indicate the rare events by which we are transformed.

Now I want to give an overview of "experience" as it appears in Foucault's works, from the earliest to the latest. We can read Foucault's first major work, *History of Madness* (2006a), which was originally published in 1961, as an investigation of madness that is structured around the relation between two forms of experience. On the one hand, it is an exploration of the "limit-experience" (2006b: xxix) which instituted the formal division between madness and reason, and an attempt (soon to be renounced by Foucault) to go back to the "zero degree" before this division was enacted (ibid.: xxvii). In this use of the term, Foucault is indicating a watershed moment in a culture in which a division (both theoretical and practical) is instigated and imposed, such that the experience of that time is fundamentally changed. This idea of a limit-experience is one that reappears, although in a rather different form, in Foucault's many essays on literature in the early to mid-1960s. In the literary essays, it is as if the fact that our culture has installed certain limits and divisions now gives us the opportunity to experience those limits in a probing, transgressive play. In his essay on Bataille, for example, Foucault presents transgression not as a brute denial of the limit, but as a "testing of the limit" (1998: 74).[7] These experiences are valuable for Foucault precisely because they make possible a transformation of the subject – they are transformative experiences.

On the other hand, and as a way of understanding the institution of this limit, the book investigates and describes in great detail what is called "the classical experience of madness" (2006a: 15). This is experience in the sense that I call everyday experience. While Foucault gives no explicit definition of this concept of experience, it is possible to piece together a sense of what it involves. First of all, it is a matter of the way that certain objects are seen and felt within a particular culture. Foucault talks about this, variously, as a matter of "feeling," "sensibility," and "perception" (ibid.: 27, 54). He wants to investigate the "mode of perception" that made possible the Great Confinement and gave birth to the classical age's "form of sensibility to madness"; that is, "the mode in which madness was perceived, and lived, by the classical age" (ibid.: 54, 55). But, even in this early work, experience is by no means simply a matter of perception and sensibility; it is not a purely individual phenomenon. The classical experience of madness also comprises, and is made possible by, shifting modes of knowledge and of practices such as exclusion, division, and control. Foucault makes this point clearly in an interview from the same time: "Madness only exists in a society, it does not exist outside the forms of sensibility which isolate it and the forms of repulsion which exclude or capture it" (1996: 8). On the one hand, then, there are forms of sensibility that isolate; on the other, there are forms of repulsion that both exclude and capture. Reading this through the lens of Foucault's later work, we could say that this is an early attempt to identify the forms of power/knowledge that partition, control, and examine the newly emerging object of madness. What we see here is a first sketch of an understanding of ordinary, everyday experience as something that is made possible by a complex web of sensibilities, forms of knowledge, and coercive practices. As Foucault later puts it, the book tried to describe a certain locus of experience, and to give an account of "the genesis of a system of thought, as the material of possible experiences" (1997: 202, modified).

Foucault himself, however, was by no means happy with the way experience was conceptualized in this book. This was partly due to his very early rejection of the idea of an original experience of madness that existed before the classical age – an idea which he had at least entertained in the original preface (2006b). But it was also, presumably, because the concept itself, even in what I have been calling its "everyday" sense, is very much undertheorized in this book. In fact, he was later to admit that his use of the concept there had been "very inconstant" (*très flottant*) (1997: 202). More generally, however, we can assume that his dissatisfaction, which led to the concept more or less disappearing from his works after the mid-1960s, arose at least in part from his hostility toward phenomenology. Whether or not Foucault was unfair in his characterizations of phenomenology (Gutting 2002: 81), there is no doubt that once he had adopted his archaeo-genealogical method he had to distance himself from what he took to be its prioritization of the subject as giver of meaning and foundation of experience. In an interview in 1978, for example, he says that his interest all along was not in the "lived experience" (*le vécu*) that is favored by phenomenologists, but in the "unlivable" experience that is explored by thinkers such as Nietzsche, Bataille, and Blanchot (2000: 241).

Hence, from *The Order of Things* (1966) up to the first volume of *The History of Sexuality* (1976), the concept almost completely disappears from his writing. But is it really so easy to dismiss the idea of a "lived experience" from Foucault's work? We need to remember that, as readers of Foucault today, we are by no means obliged to accept statements that appear to be closely connected to distant intellectual battles and by what

Gutting calls Foucault's own "anxiety of influence" (2002: 84). In fact, I would suggest that it is quite plausible to see Foucault's work in the decade 1966–76 as in fact laying the groundwork for a much more sophisticated account of something that we could call "lived experience" (or "everyday experience") – more sophisticated than he had achieved in *The History of Madness*, and also more sophisticated than he could have achieved using the tools of phenomenology. Indeed, as Rayner points out (2007: 66), one doesn't need an explicitly formulated theory of experience in order to pursue a philosophy of experience; and that, arguably, is precisely what Foucault was pursuing. Taking this approach, we would say that by pursuing his archaeological and genealogical histories, Foucault not only avoided the perceived pitfalls of the phenomenological philosophy of experience, but he himself finally acquired the means to give a fuller account of experience. Thus, it was in the late 1970s that he once again began speaking in terms of experience; both the old idea of a transformative experience and a newly refined idea of the conditions of possibility of the "lived" (although he didn't use this term). And, what is even more important, he began to be able to connect these two forms of experience in the idea of experimental, transformative practices.

The Matrix of Experience

In an extensive interview and in a cluster of texts, from the late 1970s and early 1980s, Foucault engaged in a final set of reformulations of the general direction and significance of his lifetime's intellectual project. Apart from the interview (2000: 239–97), the important texts here are the several versions of the Preface to the second volume of *History of Sexuality* (1984a), a dictionary entry that he wrote under a pseudonym, the first lecture of his Collège de France course of 1982–3, and an essay on Georges Canguilhem.[8] The interview is one of the best sources for Foucault's later understanding of his youthful valorization of limit-experiences. As such, it gives us an important formulation of one aspect of what I have called "transformative experience" – that is, the possibility that our subjectivity, as grounded in a certain relation to self, can be profoundly realigned through an experience of being torn away from the self (Foucault 2000: 241). However, it also presents Foucault's understanding of the role that works such as his own can play in similar processes of de-subjectivation and transformation. Before we can fully appreciate this potential, however, we need to consider the way that Foucault's understanding of "everyday experience" had deepened and changed over the course of almost two decades.

In a return to the theme of experience, which may have been surprising to many of his readers in the early 1980s, Foucault now presented his work as no less than an investigation of "the very historicity of forms of experience" (1997: 200). I will present this investigation as having two, related, aspects: first, a synchronic aspect involving a way of understanding the forms themselves, as they exist at a given time; second, a diachronic aspect involving a way of accounting for their modification across time. This is, however, an artificial division, since really these two aspects are constantly mutually imbricated. The synchronic model proposed by Foucault brings together the theoretical possibilities of the three major phases through which his work had passed. According to this model, experience arises out of the interplay between three elements: a domain of knowledge, a type of normativity, and a form of relation to self. Foucault considers that he is now able to give a more satisfactory account of experience because he has developed the means for analyzing and understanding these three aspects of human life. But, what exactly does it mean to say that experience arises out of an interplay between these elements?

Three key formulations are provided by Foucault. First, it is said that treating sexuality as something that is "historically singular" means to treat it as "the correlation" of the three elements mentioned above (1984a: 4; 1997: 200). He goes on to specify that this "complex experience is constituted from and around certain forms of behaviour"; it is an experience that "conjoins" a field of knowledge, a set of rules, and a form of self-relation (1997: 200). The second formulation employs the metaphor of a matrix, which we can understand both as a nurturing source within which something originates, and as a grid or network of overlapping strands. In this version, Foucault tells us that in the final volumes of *The History of Sexuality*, he chose to focus on the forms of self-relation which are "the third axis constitutive of every matrix of experience" (1997: 204, modified). In the third formulation, which he gives at the beginning of the first lecture of his 1982–3 course at the Collège de France, he is once again reframing his entire intellectual output in terms of the history of thought – or, what appears to be the same thing, the history of experience. What is interesting in this formulation, however, is the use of the French word *foyer* to indicate the complex set of practices and discourses that constitute an experience.

Hence, we read that a history of thought consists of "an analysis of what one could call *foyers* of experience" in which three axes are articulated.

These axes are: "the forms of a possible knowledge [*savoir*] ... the normative matrices of behaviour ... virtual modes of existence for possible subjects" (2008: 4–5). Foucault goes on to say that his *History of Madness* had tried to treat all three axes simultaneously, while his later works had focused on each axis individually. In its first phase, he had tried to "study experience as a matrix for the formation of knowledges [*savoirs*]"; in the second phase, he had investigated "the normative matrices of comportment"; while in the third phase, he wanted to analyze "the axis of constitution of the mode of being of the subject." To be precise, he had wanted to "analyze the different forms by which the individual is led to constitute himself as subject ... as moral subject of his sexual conduct" (ibid.: 6). But, what is the relation between these axes and this thing that Foucault calls, for example, the experience of madness? Is it the case that something called an "experience of madness" makes possible the phenomena that occur along these three axes (forms of knowledge, normativity, subjectivity)? Or, is it the case that, given the three axes or domains, and given the way that they interlock and correlate with one another, we can speak of something arising out of that as an "experience of madness" – or a series of possible experiences of madness? In other words, how terminologically imprecise is Foucault in these formulations?

Foucault's use of the term *foyer* here might help us to answer these questions. At first, he says that it is the articulation of the three axes that one could call "a *foyer* of experience" (ibid.: 5); and it is the history of these *foyers* that he wished to study. He wanted, he said, to "outline the possibility of a history of what one could call 'experiences.' Experience of madness, experience of illness, experience of criminality and experience of sexuality, so many *foyers* of experience which are, I believe, important in our culture" (ibid.: 7). But, what is a *foyer*? Is it the location in which something happens, or is it the source from which something emerges? The word is sometimes translated, in Foucault's work, as "locus," which in this case would imply that Foucault wants to study those places in which the experience of madness occurs. However, the term itself is rather ambiguous in French, with a range of meanings from hearth, home, and place of abode, to refuge, source, and even "hotbed." My suggestion is that Foucault is using this term, and the term "matrix," primarily to indicate the conditions that make possible a whole range of experiences (of both the everyday and the "limit" varieties). A *foyer* of experience would, therefore, be a complex set of conditions that make possible the experiences that occur, for example, around madness, sexuality, and so on. It is a source of those possible experiences, both making them possible for us and giving us the means with which to understand and interpret them when they occur.

In a sense, in fact, we could say that the idea of a *"foyer* of experience" functions in Foucault's late work rather like the term *dispositif* (apparatus, regime, deployment) had done a little earlier, and with the same fruitful ambiguity.

> What I'm trying to pick out with this term [*dispositif*] is, firstly, a thoroughly heterogenous ensemble consisting of discourses, institutions, architectural forms, regulatory decisions, laws, administrative measures, scientific statements, philosophical, moral and philanthropic propositions – in short, the said as much as the unsaid. Such are the elements of the apparatus [*dispositif*]. The apparatus [*dispositif*] itself is the system of relations that can be established between these elements. (Foucault 1977a: 194)

Note the similarity between the last sentence and the following, from the lecture we have been discussing: "[I]t is these three things, or rather it is the articulation of these three things which one can call, I believe, a *'foyer* of experience'" (2008: 5). In trying to comprehend Foucault's use of the concept of experience, therefore, it might help if we occasionally substitute the phrase *dispositif* for *foyer* of experience. And, in that case, we might think of a *foyer d'expérience* not as a "locus of experience" but as an "apparatus of experience."

While we can readily admit, therefore, that there is a certain terminological inconsistency in these many discussions of experience, it is also clear that the kernel of what Foucault is trying to achieve is to give a historical account of the complex, heterogenous elements that make possible something as simple as the experience of an encounter with a homeless man. And this account would seem to imply that any such experience is made possible by an apparatus comprising a complex web of practices and behaviors that can be analyzed along three fundamental axes: knowledge, normativity, and modes of subjectivity.

But, it may still be difficult to see how speaking of sexuality as a correlation of these three axes, or as emerging from a matrix of their interrelations, actually relates to anything that we might recognize as, say, an experience of sexuality. It has been pointed out by Han (2002: 152–8), for example, that these formulations of experience are far from achieving unambiguous clarity. In particular, Han argues that there is an ambivalence in the concept of experience insofar as it seems to incorporate both "objective" elements such as forms of knowledge and power, and "subjective" elements such as forms of self-consciousness (ibid.: 155).[9] However, I don't think it is necessary to follow Han in holding that Foucault is presenting two, contradictory, concepts of experience in these texts. I would suggest that the key to understanding these formulations lies in grasping the way that Foucault wants to bring together particular, everyday lived experiences with the larger epistemic, political, and ethical structures that make them possible. Taking the example of the classical Greek "experience of sexuality," Foucault is interested in knowing what makes possible, for example, the fact that aristocratic Greek men suffered concern and anxiety in their relations with boys – given that there were almost no legal restrictions on their pursuit of bodily pleasures. His question (1984a: 24) is why, and how, did these relatively free men come to question and try to limit their "everyday experiences" relating to the pleasures of Aphrodite.

In order to answer this question, Foucault follows a certain number of methodological principles that he had formulated in the very earliest version of the Preface to the second volume of the *History of Sexuality* (1998: 459–63). The first of these is particularly relevant here: he will reject, or at least practice a systematic skepticism toward, any purported universals about human desire and sexual behavior (ibid.: 461). Instead, he hopes to show how these supposed universals are themselves constituted. Hence, in the study of "sexuality" in classical Greece, the behavior of these men cannot be understood in terms of a universal, original, polymorphous sexual desire, or even in terms of a universal human need for austerity and control. In other words, their experience does not arise primarily within the insulated, private realm of their own mind and body. Rather, their experience of sexuality is constituted and made possible by the socially mandated practices (both discursive and non-discursive) through which they engage in the three domains of knowledge, normativity, and relation to self.

What this means is that in order to give an adequate account of, for example, the classical Greek, male experience of sexuality it is necessary to treat experience in both what could be called its objective and its subjective dimensions. And, moreover, it is necessary to insist that these subjective dimensions in large part depend on the objective dimensions. Foucault, therefore, seems to wish to address the very kind of subjective experience on which phenomenology focused. In fact, we could say that Foucault's entire interest in investigating experience is motivated by the wish to understand the complex connections between these two levels. In one particularly candid interview, for example, he reflects on the sense of danger and instability that pervaded his own childhood experience during World War II. This sense of a threatened private life, he says, may explain "the reason why I am fascinated by history and the relationship between personal experience and those events of which we are a part. I think that is the nucleus of my theoretical desires" (1997: 124).

In the case of sexuality, then, we can say that Foucault wants to be able to explain the ways in which even our most intimate and personal experiences are conditioned and made possible by large-scale historical events of which we are only dimly aware. And his claim is that in order to do this we need to consider the three axes that we have already discussed. Depending on the type of experience being considered, and on the period under scrutiny, we will be required to focus on one or other of these axes. So, while in the modern period, as described in the first volume of *The History of Sexuality*, the experience of sexuality is heavily determined by practices in the domains of knowledge and normativity, Foucault argues that in classical Greece it was the domain of relations to self that tended to take precedence in constituting an experience of sexuality. But, the basic principle is that all three axes have to be taken into consideration, since no one axis is sufficient on its own to explain a possible experience. As he points out in his last interview, "these three domains of experience can only be understood one in relation to the others and cannot be understood one without the others" (1984c: 243). Perhaps we can now see more clearly why experience is said to be a correlation between three axes, and why the intricate web of these axes is the matrix of any possible experience. The human being's experience of the world is never a matter of an isolated subject interacting with external objects upon which it bestows meaning. Rather, it is something that is made possible by historically sedimented systems of knowledge, sets of rules and norms, and ways of relating to self. It is in this sense that we can say that all our experiences are created, or "fabricated" (Foucault 2000: 243); on the proviso that we recognize that this creation is by no means a subjective choice, but is largely a product of a long, collective history.

This brings us back to the question of historical change. Earlier, I said that we can distinguish between a synchronic and a diachronic aspect of Foucault's account of experience, and now it is time to turn to that second aspect. Because, for Foucault, it is not only undesirable but impossible to treat of one without the other.

The Work of Thought

Foucault's return to a serious consideration of experience is announced, as we saw, in the statement in which he redefined his work as investigating "the very historicity of forms of experience" (1997: 200).[10] There are two related senses in which Foucault understands his work as an investigation of this historicity. And these senses correspond to the two core versions of the concept of experience that we identified above: everyday and transformative experience. First, it is a matter of trying to understand the large-scale changes that can be identified in, for example, the experience of sexuality, criminality, and so on. In other words, what account can be given of the shift from the early Christian constitution of sexuality in terms of the "flesh" to the nineteenth-century experience of it in terms of science and models of normal behavior? Second, it is a matter of trying to account for the role that deliberate human practices can play in bringing about these changes. In other words, moving beyond the idea that large-scale structures follow their own historical trajectory independently of human actions, or the idea that rigid power relations fully determine the field of possibilities for human action, Foucault is now concerned to allow a space for what he comes to call "a patient labour giving form to our impatience for liberty" (ibid.: 319). And this task is seen, as it had been at an earlier stage of his work, as one of transforming our experience, so that we no longer remain the same as before. These two elements, however, cannot be separated, because it is precisely the investigation of the historicity of experience in the first sense that makes possible its historicity in the second sense. Foucault insists:

> The experience through which we manage to grasp the intelligibility of certain mechanisms (for example imprisonment, punishment, etc.) and the way in which we manage to detach ourselves from them by perceiving them otherwise, should be one and the same thing. This is really the heart of what I am doing. (2000: 244, modified)

Let's look in more detail now at these two elements of historicity.

First, in order to understand any historical change, we have to take into consideration what Foucault calls "thought" (1997: 201). One of the methodological principles that Foucault enunciates in his late work is "the principle of irreducibility of thought," by which he means that forms of thought must always be considered as *one* of the elements that determine

                    Timothy O'Leary

historically singular forms of experience. While he recognizes that forms of experience may well comprise "universal structures" and may also be partly determined by concrete social arrangements, he insists that these two factors on their own are insufficient to explain experience; for that, we need to add "thought" (ibid.). While this is a theme that was already clearly announced in the title Foucault chose in 1969 for his Chair at the Collège de France ("The History of Systems of Thought"), it now takes on an added complexity:

> By "thought," [first] I mean that which institutes, in diverse possible forms, the game of truth and falsehood and which, consequently, constitutes the human being as a subject of knowledge; [second] that which founds the acceptance or the refusal of the rule and constitutes the human being as a social and juridical subject; [third] that which institutes the relation to self and to others, and constitutes the human being as ethical subject. (Ibid.: 200, modified)

Hence, thought is that through which the human being is constituted as a subject, in the three essential or fundamental areas of knowledge, normativity, and the relation to self.

However, this newly formulated understanding of thought really only makes a significant contribution to understanding historical change when we combine it with another important concept that Foucault adds to his discourse in the early 1980s: "problematization." This is a concept that, in effect, allows him to give an account of historical change in terms of thought. In other words, it makes it possible to explain large-scale shifts as, at least partially, the products of responses to "problems" that emerge to face a culture at a particular time as a result of social, political, or economic factors. So, for example, in classical Greece a problem emerged for aristocratic men in their relations with boys because of an isomorphism between their understanding of both sex and politics in terms of power and domination. One of these difficulties was the concern that allowing a boy to be dominated in a sex act by an adult male would render that boy unfit to assume authority in the city in his own adulthood. Once such a problem emerges, according to Foucault, we see a process of "problematization" in which the practices that had governed lives become uncertain and unstable; hence, they are subjected to questioning and reappraisal in the search for new (ultimately temporary) solutions. This task, of responding to difficulties in accepted forms of behavior, of defining them in terms of problems, and of proposing solutions, is what Foucault calls "problematization"; that is, the "specific work of thought" (ibid.: 118). Thought, in this sense, is "freedom in relation to what one does, the motion by which one detaches oneself from it, establishes it as an object, and reflects on it as a problem" (ibid.: 117).

If that is the work of thought, then the work of the history of thought is different: it is to rediscover at the root of these problems and solutions the "general form of problematization that made them possible"; to understand how "a given" is turned into a "question," how a group of "obstacles and difficulties" is turned into "problems" and solutions (ibid.: 118). Therefore, insofar as he wishes to carry out a "history of thought," Foucault focuses on these moments of rupture in an effort to understand the conditions that define and delimit the newly proposed solutions. How, for instance, were new objects constituted (the flesh, madness, hysteria, and so on)? How did concrete social and political arrangements feed into this objectivation? What new forms of self-relation were developed? How did these forms of self-relation interact with the forms of objectivation?

On the one hand, then, we can say that problematization is the historical phenomenon that Foucault takes as the object of his research. In the second volume of *The History of Sexuality*, for example, he explains that his concern is to analyze problematizations and the practices from which they emerge (1984a: 11). Reiterating a constant theme of his work at this time, he points out that he already had the means to understand the forms of knowledge that were in question (archaeology), and the changes they underwent as a result of their grounding in practices (genealogy), and that now he simply needed to develop a way of understanding the role of practices of the self in these problematizations. And this, precisely, is the project he carries out in the final volumes of the *History of Sexuality*.

On the other hand, however, problematization is not only the object of his research, it is also the objective of his research. In other words, Foucault's aim is not just to write a history of thought, but to write a critical history of thought. That is, the history of thought must also be a critical history of thought in the sense of a history that encourages, or even provokes, "a perpetual reproblematization" in the present (1994: 612).[11] So, in *Discipline and Punish* (1977b), for example, Foucault investigates the ways in which punishment was problematized at the turn of the nineteenth century and the way that certain proposed solutions (such as the prison) emerged from a complex web of social, economic, and political conditions. However, insofar as the work is a critical history, it aims also to provoke a reproblematization in the present. This doesn't mean looking for new solutions that would be defined in terms of the old problems, but trying to bring about a radical questioning of the very form of problematization itself. It is for this reason that Foucault always differentiated his position on the prisons from a reformist agenda. In effect, the task of a critical history of thought is to rethink our forms of problematization "from the root" and to "render problematic everything that is solid" (1994: 612).

This brings us back to the idea of an "experience book." Such a book, if it is a work of critical history, will explore the historical aspects of a field of problematization, but will do so in relation to a present situation which is also undergoing a process of problematization. The book, however, will not just describe an historical context and draw connections with a present context; it will also, and most importantly, attempt to provoke on the part of its readers a renewed work of thought in their own engagement with this complex of problems. And, it is on this basis that Foucault is finally able to link his work as an intellectual with the lived experience of three different key groups: first, Foucault himself, the author; second, those who lived in the period under study; and third, those who may suffer from related practices in the present.

One notable example of the first type of connection is Foucault's own experience of unease when he was working as a psychology intern in L'Hôpital Sainte Anne, a psychiatric hospital in Paris, in the early 1950s. It wasn't until a few years later, he says, when he began working on the history of psychiatry, that "this malaise, this personal experience, took the form of a historical criticism or a structural analysis" (1997: 123). It was a personal experience, therefore, which fed into, motivated, and was modified by his own theoretical work. An example of the second type of connection is the interest Foucault consistently showed in the lives of those who suffered at the hands of the systems of power and knowledge that he investigated. Hence, the experiences of Herculine Barbin, Pierre Rivière, and the victims of the "*lettres de cachet*" of pre-revolutionary France are extracted from archives and presented to the public with a mixture of awe and terror (Foucault 1977c; 1978; 1980). We might even suggest that Foucault's book on Raymond Roussel is at least in part motivated by similar concerns (2006c). An example of the third type of connection is the reception that *Discipline and Punish* received among those who worked in and around the prisons in the mid-1970s. Foucault recalls that the book was charged with being "paralyzing," in the sense that it seemed to condemn current practices but offered no new solutions. His response is that this is precisely what an "experience book" should do; it reverberates with the experience of a certain group of readers and forces them to engage in a work of reproblematization of their own practices (2000: 245–6).

What we see, then is a trajectory that leads from the personal experience of the author, through an investigation of the traces of the historical experience of certain groups of people, up to the experience of an undefined group in the present for whom this historical experience reverberates strongly. Thus, in trying to answer the question of how individual and collective experiences, in the past and the present, arise from historically singular forms of thought, Foucault contributes to the future formation of what he calls a "we" that can be the basis for a (partial and temporary) "community of action" (1997: 115). The task of such a community would be to engage in a "historico-practical test of the limits that we may go beyond" (ibid.: 316). And this, we could say, is the practical task of transforming our experience in the present.

Re-Making Experience

So, let's return now to the street experience that I described earlier. Based on our reading of Foucault as a philosopher of experience, what account can we give of this encounter? First of all, considering it purely from a synchronic point of view, we can identify three key aspects that make the experience possible. The first aspect, that of forms of knowledge, comprises everything that we know, and think we know, about mental illness, alcohol addiction, the causes of homelessness in a contemporary society, and so on. In other words, even for the ordinary individual, the experience is in some way determined by highly specialized systems of knowledge, both medical-scientific and sociological, that have filtered through the society in which they live. If, in this encounter, we hesitate about giving money to the man, this may be because we are oscillating between thinking of mental illness as a tragedy that befalls a person, and thus deserving of our sympathy, but alcohol dependence as an addiction for which they are themselves responsible.

Any reflection, or even "intuitive" reaction on these issues, however, has already begun to involve the second aspect, that of normativity and power relations. From the point of view of this aspect, the first point to be made is that underlying the entire experience is the fact that the man is asking us for money; he is begging. What kind of relation does this set up between us? And to what extent might our hesitation emerge from our not wanting to accept this "alms-giving" relation? After all, we might say, an affluent modern society should never allow this situation to arise. But, more generally, it is clear that the very fact that the man is homeless is itself a product of a complex web of power relations and social norms prevailing in the society in which we live. Furthermore, the way that he approaches us, first supplicating, perhaps mentioning food, and then more aggressively, is also a product of his own willingness to play with, and potentially transgress, the prevalent social norms.

From the point of view of the third aspect, our own mode of self-relation will also contribute to the formation of the experience. We may, for example, see ourselves as a kind and generous individual who always responds to pleas for help from others. Or, we may see ourselves as a politically progressive individual who doesn't engage in acts of more or less random charity, but expends effort (and perhaps money) to change social policy instead. In that case, we might refuse to give money, but still have a strong sense of our own enlightened philanthropy. Or, again, we may have come from another country, or from a rural area, where such encounters rarely happen; and we may be in the process of trying to decide what is the best way to respond to them and what kind of person we want to become in our new surroundings. In any case, these factors not only help to determine the actual outcome (whether or not we give money), but more fundamentally they determine our experience of the encounter: as welcome opportunity to dispense charity; as object lesson in the ills of our society; as challenge to a newly emerging self-constitution as ethical subject, and so on.

Using the Foucauldian threefold analysis of experience, then, we can see that an everyday occurrence such as I described owes a great deal to factors which can be considered from an "objective" point of view. The experience is not a simple confrontation between a perceiving subject and a world of objects. Rather, the forms of the subjective experience are to a large degree made possible by elements in the surrounding culture and society. Indeed, one might argue that there is not even any subject existing independently of these elements and preceding the experience itself. The subject is not the ground of possibility of the experience; rather, the form of subjectivity emerges in response to the occurrence of a whole range of experiences. And these experiences, with their concomitant forms of subjectivity, have their own historicity.

The historicity of the experience, in this sense, becomes quite clear if we consider that the nuances of the occurrence I described could not have happened, say, in the eighteenth century. If we had made a visit to Bethlehem

Hospital on one of the first Tuesdays of the month when entry was free, armed, as was the custom, with a long stick for provoking the inmates, there is no doubt that this experience would not only have been radically different from the experience I described, but is one that would be impossible to recreate today. And the reason, as Foucault demonstrates, is because of the massive shifts that have occurred along the three axes of knowledge, normativity and relation to self. One way of describing this historical change, therefore, would be to say that the "experience of madness" has undergone a transformation, in fact a series of ongoing transformations, since the eighteenth century. Gutting (2002: 77) is no doubt right to say that Foucault generally takes the phrase the "experience of madness" as an objective, rather than a subjective, genitive. That is, In *The History of Madness*, he addresses the experience of madness from the point of view of the "sane" rather than the "mad." While this is true of that work, however, it is not necessarily entailed by Foucault's method; and, as we have seen, it is by no means true of all Foucault's work. In addition to the examples already given (Herculine Barbin, Pierre Rivière, etc.) we can point to Foucault's comment, in relation to criminality, that he hopes to show how "a certain 'consciousness' of criminality could be formed (including the image that they might have of themselves, and the representation of criminals which the rest of us might entertain)" (1997: 204). Therefore, one can trace these historical transformations of experience in both the "subjective" and the "objective" mode – providing that a textual trace remains in the present.

In his archaeo-genealogical works, then, combined with his later investigation of modes of relation to self, Foucault has given us a way of understanding these changes along all three axes. But he also gives us, as we have seen, a way of conceptualizing, and promoting, the possibility of contributing to such transformations through the deliberate work of a critical history of thought. We could say, for example, that Foucault's own *History of Madness*, along with the work of R. D. Laing and David Cooper, was one catalyst in bringing about the set of conditions that made possible the contemporary experience I described. And, in the present, we could say that anybody who underwent that experience might, in the light of work such as that of Foucault, be provoked to undertake a critical reproblematization of the conditions that made the experience possible. What I have tried to show here is that Foucault's work, almost in its entirety, can be read as a contribution to a fully historicized philosophy of experience. In effect, Foucault gives us a way of thinking about experience as having a history that is subject both to long-term modifications and to individual changes that arise from our own engagement in work such as the critical history of thought. These individual, small-scale changes are the goal of an ethics in which we seek to distance ourselves from ourselves and to push beyond the limits that are imposed on our ways of thinking and acting. It is an ethics that strives to understand and surpass the ways of thinking and acting that make possible, for example, a certain everyday experience of seeing a homeless drunk in the street.

Notes

1   For a discussion of Foucault and Dewey in relation to the experience of literature, see O'Leary 2005.
2   For a discussion of Joyce's *A Portrait of the Artist as a Young Man*, in the light of Foucault's and Gadamer's accounts of experience, see O'Leary 2009: ch. 6.
3   My primary reference is, of course, to the English language, but the same point applies to French. Unfortunately I cannot say if the same also applies to German.
4   The possibility of reading Foucault as a "philosopher of experience" has been receiving growing attention from readers. See, for example: Han 2002; Gutting 2002; Oksala 2004; Flynn 2005; Rayner 2007; O'Leary 2009.
5   See discussions by, for example, Gutting 2002 and Flynn 2005: esp. ch. 9.
6   Lecture of March 28, 1984; unpublished, but recordings available at Fonds Michel Foucault, l'IMEC, Caen.
7   This "testing" is "*une épreuve*" and once again calls to mind the testing of an experience as experiment.
8   For the Prefaces, see Foucault 1984a and 1997: 199–205. The dictionary entry (1998: 459–63) is based on an early version of this Preface – see the introductory note in the French edition (1994: 631); the English translation of the note is incomplete. The lecture, not yet translated into English, is in Foucault 2008. For the essay on Canguilhem, see Foucault 1998: 465–78. I don't discuss this essay here, but Gutting (2002: 78) draws on it to differentiate Foucault's position from that of phenomenology.
9   It should be noted that Han makes much of a passage from Foucault (1984a: 4) in which we are told that sexuality will be treated as "an experience that caused individuals to recognize themselves as subjects of a 'sexuality'." This does indeed seem oddly ambiguous. How did this experience cause individuals to do this? However, a more accurate translation of the passage would be something like this – which, I think, loses the ambiguity: "an 'experience' was constituted, in such a way that individuals had to recognize themselves as subjects of a 'sexuality'."
10 The timeframe is not absolutely clear and it might be possible to interpret this passage as only referring to the last two volumes of *The History of Sexuality*,

but on balance I think it gives enough indications that Foucault had in mind his entire work, at least from the early 1960s.

11 Foucault makes this point in the revised version of "On the Genealogy of Ethics" (1997: 253–80) that he authorized for publication in French (1994).

References

Dewey, J. (1980) *Art as Experience*. New York: Perigee Books.

Flynn, T. R. (2005) *Sartre, Foucault, and Historical Reason*, vol. 2: *A Poststructuralist Mapping of History*. Chicago, IL: University of Chicago Press.

Foucault, M. (1976) *The History of Sexuality*, vol. 1: *An Introduction*, trans. R. Hurley. Harmondsworth: Penguin Books.

Foucault, M. (1977a) "The Confession of the Flesh." In *Power/Knowledge: Selected Interviews and Other Writings 1972–1977*, ed. C. Gordon. New York: Pantheon Books, 1980.

Foucault, M. (1977b) *Discipline and Punish: The Birth of the Prison*, trans. A. Sheridan. London: Allen Lane, Penguin

Foucault, M. (1977c) "Lives of Infamous Men." In *Essential Works of Foucault 1954–1984*, vol. 3: *Power*, ed. J. Faubion. New York: The New Press, 2000.

Foucault, M., ed. (1978) *I, Pierre Rivière, Having Slaughtered My Mother, My Sister and My Brother*. Harmondsworth: Peregrine Books.

Foucault, M., intro. (1980) *Herculine Barbin, Being the Recently Discovered Memoirs of a Nineteenth-Century French Hermaphrodite*. New York: Pantheon Books.

Foucault, M. (1984a) *The History of Sexuality*, vol. 2: *The Use of Pleasure*, trans. R. Hurley. Harmondsworth: Penguin Books, 1990.

Foucault, M. (1984b) *The History of Sexuality*, vol. 3: *The Care of the Self*, trans. R. Hurley. Harmondsworth: Penguin Books, 1990.

Foucault, M. (1984c) "The Return of Morality." In L. Kritzman, ed., *Michel Foucault: Politics, Philosophy, Culture; Interviews and Other Writings 1977–1984*, trans. A. Sheridan. New York: Routledge, 1990.

Foucault, M. (1994) *Dits et écrits 1954–1988*, vol. 4: *1980–1988*, ed. D. Defert and F. Ewald. Paris: Gallimard.

Foucault, M. (1996) *Foucault Live: Interviews, 1961–1984*, ed. S. Lotringer. New York: Semiotext(e).

Foucault, M. (1997) *Essential Works of Foucault, 1945–1984*, vol. 1: *Ethics: Subjectivity and Truth*, ed. P. Rabinow. New York: The New Press.

Foucault, M. (1998) *Essential Works of Foucault, 1945–1984*, vol. 2: *Aesthetics, Method, and Epistemology*, ed. J. Faubion. New York: The New Press.

Foucault, M. (2000) *Essential Works of Foucault, 1945–1984*, vol. 3: *Power*, ed. C. Gordon. New York: The New Press.

Foucault, M. (2001) *The Order of Things: An Archaeology of the Human Sciences.* London: Routledge.

Foucault, M. (2006a) *History of Madness*, trans. J. Murphy and J. Khalfa. London: Routledge.

Foucault, M. (2006b) "Preface to the 1961 edition." In *History of Madness*, trans. J. Murphy and J. Khalfa. London: Routledge.

Foucault, M. (2006c) *Death and the Labyrinth: The World of Raymond Roussel*, trans. C. Ruas. London: Continuum.

Foucault, M. (2008) *Le Gouvernement de soi et des autres: Cours au Collège de France (1982–1983)*, ed. F. Ewald, A. Fontana, and F. Gros. Paris: Seuil/Gallimard.

Gadamer, H.-G. (2003) *Truth and Method*, 2nd edn., trans. J. Weinsheimer and D. G. Marshall. New York: Continuum.

Gutting, G. (2002) "Foucault's Philosophy of Experience." *Boundary 2* 29 (2): 69–85.

Han, B. (2002) *Foucault's Critical Project: Between the Transcendental and the Historical*, trans. E. Pile. Stanford, CA: Stanford University Press.

Joyce, J. (1992) *A Portrait of the Artist as a Young Man.* London: Penguin Books.

Oksala, J. (2004) "Anarchic Bodies: Foucault and the Feminist Question of Experience." *Hypatia* 19 (4): 97–119.

O'Leary, T. (2005) "Foucault, Dewey And The Experience Of Literature." *New Literary History* 36 (4): 543–57.

O'Leary, T. (2009) *Foucault and Fiction: The Experience Book.* London: Continuum.

Rayner, T. (2007) *Foucault's Heidegger: Philosophy and Transformative Experience.* London: Continuum.

9

Foucault, Queer Theory, and the Discourse of Desire: Why Embrace an Ethics of Pleasures?

Jana Sawicki

"Each of my works is part of my own biography." (Foucault 1988a: 11)

"Acts are not very important, and pleasure – nobody knows what it is!" (Foucault 1984: 234)

Introduction

In a discussion about the later volumes of his history of sexuality, Foucault defends the philosophical nature of his genealogical inquiry into the desiring subject as follows:

> What is philosophy today – philosophical activity, I mean – if it is not the critical work that thought brings to bear on it? In what does it consist, if not in the endeavor to know how and to what extent it might be possible to think differently, instead of legitimating what is already known … to explore what might be changed, in its own thought, through the practice of a knowledge that is foreign to it. (1985: 8–9)

If the image of philosophy as thought thinking itself is not new, Foucault's willingness to embrace the personal and transformative dimension of this historico-philosophical practice represents an interesting twist. Ironically, the image of a practice involving an encounter with the past to address misery in the present bears some resemblance to psychoanalysis. Yet one of the central aims of Foucault's project was to release us from the centuries-long habit of understanding ourselves as "desiring subjects." If there is a resemblance between his philosophical practice and psychoanalytic technique, we should not expect it to be identical in function, meaning, or purpose to psychoanalytic theories and practices associated with the normalizing regime of sexuality and the discourse of "sex"-desire described in the first volume of *The History of Sexuality*.

Genealogy is closely aligned with Nietzschean perspectivism. Thus we should not be surprised that on several occasions Foucault indicated that his critical projects were related to personal experience. Yet most commentators fail to take his vantage point as a homosexual seriously. In failing to do so, they have overlooked a key dimension of the work. For one of Foucault's aims was to transform the experiences associated with being homosexual. Perhaps it would not be overstating the case to assert that insofar as homosexuality has regularly been associated with immorality, pathology, and criminality – all of which receive significant attention in his work – Foucault's social location as homosexual is the linchpin that links all of his genealogical writings.

In what follows I argue that in his genealogical inquiries into ancient Greco-Roman ethics, Foucault attempted to open the epistemological and cultural space for us to invent new truths about ourselves – to subject ourselves to new forms of self-understanding. Why? Because he believed that the cost associated with continuing to operate within the regime of sexual normalization was both too high and unnecessarily constraining. Consider as support for this claim Michael Warner's observation that "queerness has always been defined centrally by discourses of morality" (1993: xviii). The moral question concerning the homosexual has not been how to be a good one, but whether one should be one at all. Merely being a queer person can be enough to raise moral suspicion about one's character. No doubt we are all familiar with the tendency, despite recent progress, to represent and regard homosexuals and other queers as inherently immoral and sexually excessive – if not also criminal and pathological. Even Foucault's own personal sexual identity and practices – when they have not been ignored – have been used to discredit him (Shattuck 2000).

Foucault hoped that homosexuals could play an important role in moving beyond identity politics and creating new forms of sexual subjectivity. In late interviews with the gay press he described homosexuality as an eccentric standpoint in the social field from which particular problems might be illuminated and alternative forms of life and self-understanding might emerge. He viewed homosexuality as a "historical occasion to reopen affective and relational virtualities, not so much through intrinsic qualities of the homosexual, but because the ... diagonal lines he can lay out in the social fabric allow these virtualities to come to light" (1997: 138).

By virtue of his location as an outsider within society, Foucault implied, the homosexual is more likely to establish relationships that cut across the social field and produce relational possibilities beyond the strictures of the Oedipal frame as well as divisions of race, class, and gender. Foucault urged gays and lesbians not to be, but rather to become, homosexual – to realize the potential for altering the range of amorous relations and pleasurable experiences, and to invent new ways of living.

Although Foucault's remarks about homosexuals may strike us today as unoriginal and utopian, it is interesting to note that at this early juncture in the history of gay and lesbian rights activism, Foucault stressed the importance of thinking beyond identity politics and the demand for recognition. In this respect he anticipated the emergence of queer theory and its anti-identity politics. He asserted that even if legal and moral interdictions governing sexuality were attenuated, queer people would still confront the task of inventing new forms of ethical subjectivity. For he believed that the sexual liberation movements in the 1970s were not only theoretically impoverished insofar as they typically appealed to psychoanalytic theories of desire that he found problematic, but ethically impoverished as well. However, it is not obvious that the problems he identified in the early 1980s have changed significantly. Witness, for example, moves by many states in the US to bar same-sex marriage, the dominance of the minoritizing approach to seeking civil rights within lesbian, bisexual, gay, and transsexual (LBGT) groups, the intractability of heterosexist understandings of erotic and relational possibilities, the persistent desire to provide scientific accounts of sexual or transgender identity, and the ongoing stigmatization of sexual minorities. Thus turning to Foucault's late work on sexuality may still be of use in the project of enhancing sexual freedom.

Despite relative lack of interest in the queer angle on Foucault among a majority of scholars, his writings understandably have played a seminal role in the emergence of queer theory (Halperin 1995). Yet it is striking, perhaps even puzzling, that much of the queer reception of Foucault comes from within the camp of psychoanalytic theorists who draw on the very model of desire that he attempted to problematize. Leo Bersani, Judith Butler, Lee Edelman, and Timothy Dean are among the most obvious. Even more interesting is the attempt by some to reconcile Foucault and Freud. For example, both Bersani and Butler claim that the Freudian discourse of desire is indispensable for explaining how pleasures might resist power.

But I remain wary of the efforts by queer theorists to explain Foucault's account of resistant pleasures within a psychoanalytic framework. Rather than adopt the model of desire as a primordial lack, loss, or incompleteness at the heart of humanity, or as a necessary and futile striving for satisfaction and completeness, Foucault turned to pleasure as a potential source of creative and open-ended processes of self-transformation. Rather than appeal to psychoanalytic theory to explain the dynamics of power and pleasure, he appropriated key concepts within psychoanalytic theory in order to bend them to a new interpretive will. He certainly did not appeal to the discourse of sex-desire, even if he did appropriate elements of the apparatus of sexuality that he was problematizing.

Foucault and the Discourse of Sex-Desire

In *The Use of Pleasure* Foucault announced his intention to offer a genealogy of desiring man:

> [a genealogy of] the practices by which individuals were led to focus their attention on themselves, to decipher, recognize, and acknowledge themselves as subjects of desire, bring into play between themselves and themselves a certain relationship that allows them to discover, in desire, the truth of their being, be it natural or fallen. (1985: 5)

In this passage he identifies several problematic features of the discourse of desire: its emphasis on a hermeneutics of the self; the idea that in deciphering the self one discovers the truth of desire; and the possibility that the deep self discovered is one that may need to be renounced or repressed insofar as it is "fallen."

In some respects, the later volumes in *The History of Sexuality* continue the story he began in the first volume, despite their shift of focus from modernity to classical Greece. In the first volume, Foucault tells the following story about the dangers associated with the regime of sexuality and its discourse of sex-desire. As an object of the human sciences, a vehicle for administering the health, education, and welfare of the population, and a target for normalizing interventions in family and individual lives by medical, psychiatric, and legal authorities, the concept "sex" became a useful tool for controlling individuals and populations in the modern West. Foucault states: "The notion of 'sex' made it possible to group together, in an artificial unity, anatomical elements, biological functions, conducts, sensations, and pleasures, and it enabled one to make use of this fictitious unity as a causal principle, an omnipresent meaning, a secret to be discovered everywhere" (1978: 154–5).

As queer theorist David Halperin has aptly put it, the regime of sexuality psychologizes sex insofar as it "knits up desire, its objects, sexual behavior, gender identity, reproductive function, mental health, erotic sensibility, personal style, and degrees of normality or deviance into an individuating and sex normativizing feature of the personality called 'sexuality'" (2002: 29). Relying on earlier sexological classificatory schemes, psychoanalytic accounts of psychosexual development isolated the numerous ways in which desire might go astray. They established developmental norms, isolated multiple abnormal personages – the fetishist, the invert, and the hysteric, to name only a few – and devised new corrective techniques.

Hence, perversion was incorporated into the individual; and the "homosexual" emerged as a particular type. To be sure, the practice of sodomy predated the homosexual's arrival on the scene, and sexual morphologies as well as sexual subjectivities had previously been linked to sexual acts. But, as Halperin has argued, ancient and canonical codes did not link sodomy to "sexual identity" in the modern sense of the term (2002: 41–2). Foucault described our attachments to these new forms of sexual subjectivity, whether normal or abnormal, as part of an elaborate "government of individualization," a deployment of power that "applies itself to immediate everyday life which categorizes the individual, marks him by his own individuality, attaches him to his own identity, imposes a law of truth on him which he must recognize and which others have to recognize in him" (1983b: 212). Once again, the relation of power to sex is not principally repressive but productive. Individuals are repressed through an apparatus of sexuality that incites discourse about sex and produces knowledge, technologies, desires, and norms of psychosexual development as well as normalized sexual subjects prone to self-beratement and the desire to appear "normal." In effect, psychoanalysis represented the paradigm of a *scientia sexualis* – a corner stone of the regime of sexuality. It served a political rationality aimed at integrating individuals into society through a process of normalization – at increasing individualization through strategies of power linked to the emergence of the human sciences and the institutions and techniques associated with them. Among these institutions, of course, is the family. In a series of lecture given in Brazil in 1973, Foucault endorses Gilles Deleuze and Felix Guattari's position that "Oedipus is not a truth of nature, but an instrument of limitation and constraint that psychoanalysts, starting with Freud, use to contain desire and insert it within a family structure defined by our society at a particular moment" (2000: 16).

At the same time, however, there is evidence that Foucault was somewhat ambivalent about the value of psychoanalysis. Thus, in an intriguing move in the Brazil lectures, he suggests that there is an Oedipus complex in "our civilization" – one that "does not involve our unconscious and our desire, nor the relations between desire and the unconscious," but rather one that operates "not at the individual level but at the collective level ... in connection with power and knowledge" (ibid.: 17). Furthermore, whereas in *Discipline and Punish* he described the "psyche" (the modern disciplinary counterpart of the theological notion of the soul) as the "prison of the body," in an interview given at the time of its publication, he also suggested that one might be able to modify psychoanalysis's relationship to disciplinary power (1980: 71).

We might explain this ambivalence by noting that the aim of his genealogical critique was not to pronounce final judgment on the value of the psychoanalytic discourse, but to identify certain problems and dangers associated with an already problematic discourse, and to produce an experience in his readers that might spur the creation of new possibilities for work on the self in the present. Importantly, this would not involve creation *ex nihilo*, but rather transforming materials made available in our culture, bending them to a new will or deploying them within new strategy. So just as Nietzsche before him distinguished between the fixed (customs, practices, procedures) and fluid (meaning, aim) elements of punishment and endorsed the appropriation of procedures such as disciplinary techniques for new purposes, Foucault appreciated the possibilities of grouping elements of psychiatric practice and psychoanalytic theory with others in a new game of truth, deploying them within different strategies. For example, we find him using Freudian concepts and practices such as the unconscious (not individual, but historical), confession (not as expression, but as production or performance), and repression (again, not as prohibition, but incitement of desire), and, last but not least, pleasure, in new ways. Indeed, as I will now argue, producing an experience of the possibility of resignifying and redeploying "pleasure" is partly what he was up to in the second volume of *The History of Sexuality*.

Power and Pleasure

At the end of the first volume of *The History of Sexuality*, Foucault appealed to "bodies and pleasures" as a potential locus of resistance to the regime (*dispositif*) of sexuality (1978: 157). Not that power and pleasure are inherently opposed. This is the basic premise of the "repressive hypothesis" that Foucault famously challenged. Nor was he appealing to pleasures innocent of power. He was instead appealing to a pleasure that is less bound up with biopower and the *scientia sexualis* associated with it. For he clearly understood that power relations can be pleasurable. After all, throughout this first volume he drew attention to the pleasures associated with exercising power. He spoke of the "pleasure of analysis" bound up with the psychiatrist's will to know about sex; the pleasures associated with surveillance and control, or, as Suzanne Gearhart aptly expresses it: "The pleasure that comes of exercising a power that questions, monitors, watches, spies, searches out, palpates, brings to light; and on the other hand the pleasure that kindles at having to evade this power, flee from it, fool it, or travesty it" (1995: 389–90). There is also the pleasure attributed to the sense of empowerment produced by discipline. Disciplinary power not only renders subjects more docile; it also enhances their capacities.

Presumably, then, pleasures bound to the apparatus of sexuality are double-edged. They can be used in the service of problematic power relations; yet they can also be a source of their redirection, reversal, or diminution. Perhaps, Foucault surmised, appealing to pleasure is more likely to move individuals to change than the trope of desiring man. But what is the status of the pleasures that Foucault invokes? What is "pleasure"? And how might pleasures be enlisted in the service of undermining the regime of sexuality?

Reading Foucault on Pleasures

Foucault's enigmatic appeal to "bodies and pleasures" has invited many commentators to explain it. Arnold Davidson suggests that there is some inconsistency in his characterizations of pleasure insofar as Foucault also speaks of the pleasures associated with the voyeurism of *scientia sexualis*. This might indicate that pleasure is in fact bound up with the regime of sexuality. Other commentators (Butler, Bersani, Alcoff, Whitebook) conjecture that, despite his critique of the repressive hypothesis, Foucault ultimately invoked a pre-discursive and ahistorical force inherently resistant to any structure or constraint. Without this appeal, they argue, he could not explain how resistance to normalizing power is possible. Moreover, both Leo Bersani and Judith Butler, albeit in different ways, attempt to supply the theory of resistance implicit in the first volume of *The History of Sexuality*. Indeed, both suggest that Foucault either should (Bersani) or does (Butler) rely upon Freud's theory of sexuality in order to explain how pleasure might resist power.

For instance, Bersani thinks Foucault's skepticism about *scientia sexualis* robs him of an indispensable resource for theorizing resistance. He points out that Freud's was the first major theoretical effort to desexualize pleasure. It was Freud, after all, who first spoke of an unbounded drive and a degenitalized polymorphous perversity that resists any orientation or identity. Bersani states: "The passages in Freud's work that lead to his conclusion that 'the quality of erotogenicity' should be ascribed 'to all parts of the body and to all the internal organs' could be taken as a gloss … Foucault's [call] for a degenitalizing of erotic intensities" (1995: 98). Furthermore, he claims, "For both Freud and Foucault, although in very different ways … the exercise of power produces a resistance to power from within the exercise itself" (ibid.: 100). According to Bersani, in Freud's version of this story the project of mastery can be transformed into a relationship between bodies in which the subject of power is "so obscenely rubbed by the object it anticipates mastering that the very boundaries separating subject from object, boundaries necessary for possession, have been erased" (ibid.). In effect, he argues, Freud approaches a definition of the sexual as "an aptitude for the defeat of power by pleasure" (ibid.). He thinks Foucault should appreciate this aspect of his theory of sexuality.

In fact, Bersani insinuates that Foucault's interest in sadomasochism (SM) as a strategy for producing new, non-sexual (genital) pleasures that exceeds the apparatus of sex-desire is also best explained by an appeal to Freud. Whereas Foucault rejected the idea that SM can be reduced to a mere reproduction of social relationships of domination and subordination, Bersani claims that SM participates in our dominant culture's obsession with power – that it "argues, in spite of itself, for the continuity between political structures of oppression and the body's erotic economy" (ibid.: 90). Furthermore, he suggests, SM is best understood within Freudian terms as aiming at the self-dissolution that accompanies an organism's dysfunctional overriding of the impulse to escape pain. He elaborates: "In this self-shattering the ego renounces its power over the world" (ibid.: 94–5). While the sadist's posture of domination can be a defense against the joys of self-dissolution, the masochist enjoys the thrill of being "temporarily undone" by excessive stimuli (ibid.: 95–100). Bersani links this attraction to self-dissolution to Foucault's call for self-detachment. He dismisses Foucault's lament about the paucity of erotic and relational possibilities and focuses instead on reading his masochistic desires from within a Freudian framework.

Finally, Bersani adds, if desire is mobile, if it resists the fixing of identity by a science of desire, then biological sex need not determine gender. In his view desire becomes an unbounded force that might move us beyond current heterosexist structures of desire.

Alternatively, in *The Psychic Life of Power*, Judith Butler situates herself "between Freud and Foucault" (1997: 83–105). On the one hand, she uses Foucault to render the Lacanian symbolic more dynamic and historically variable. Thus, she rejects Lacan's static conception of the symbolic in favor of a Foucauldian account of power as "productive, malleable, multiple, proliferative, and conflictual" (ibid.: 99). Moreover, she states: "[W]here Lacan restricts the notion of social power to the symbolic domain and delegates resistance to the imaginary, Foucault recasts the symbolic as relations of power and understands resistance as an effect of power" (ibid.: 98–9). She asks why we should assume, with Lacan, that the unconscious is any less structured by relations of power than the symbolic realm in which subjects emerge. For Lacan's account of a resistance rooted in an irretrievable and ultimately ineffectual and ineffable domain outside the symbolic, she substitutes Foucault's view of resistance as involving a reworking and dismantling of the terms of power. In Butler's view, "the symbolic produces the possibility of its own subversions" (ibid.: 99). So far, so good.

On the other hand Butler maintains that Foucault's insights about power, discourse, and subjection require supplementation by a psychoanalytic account of the formation of the psyche. She criticizes Foucault for investing the body "with a psychic meaning that he cannot elaborate within the terms that he uses" (ibid.: 95). In the Lacanian framework that she is revising an individual's entry into the symbolic represents the birth of its subjectivity, i.e., "the linguistic condition of its existence and agency" (ibid.: 11). Insofar as entering the symbolic involves accepting a set of limits on the possibilities for intelligible subjectivity, a set of prohibitions, normative constraints, and ideals provided by others, it comes at a price. The "psyche" for Butler, is that part of the individual that exceeds the conditions that make it possible as a coherent and legible subject. Thus the psyche becomes an unconscious source of resistance to any given set of discursive limitations, norms, and ideals insofar as it represents a part of the individual that is not reducible to its subjectivity – a part of the individual that must be foreclosed if it is to exist as an intelligible, human being. Butler describes it thus: "[T]he psyche, which includes the unconscious, is very different from the subject: the psyche is precisely what exceeds the imprisoning effects of the discursive demand to inhabit a coherent identity, to become a subject" (ibid.: 86). Resistance is secured because the psyche and the subject are distinct. We are not one-dimensional subjects.

Butler wants to preserve the distinction between psyche and subject. She claims that, despite his avoidance of this term, Foucault does too. She criticizes his reduction of the "soul" or "psyche" to an "exterior and imprisoning frame for the body" (ibid.). According to her reading of *Discipline and Punish* he eschews an account of how power relations are interiorized, preferring instead to treat the body as a malleable surface upon which power relations are inscribed. Furthermore, she believes Foucault tacitly appealed to sublimation. She asks: "[I]s there some part of the body which is not preserved in sublimation, some part of the body which remains unsublimated?" (ibid.: 92). In other words, if, in Foucault, the body and the subject are distinct, perhaps Foucault is relying on some notion of a bodily remainder that thwarts normalization. If this is the case, she concludes, Foucault's "body" becomes a stand-in for a psychic process.

Butler's and Bersani's responses to Foucault are both intriguing and provocative. Yet there are reasons to resist their impulses to incorporate his work within a psychoanalytic framework, to provide psychoanalytic explanations of resistance (albeit very different ones!). To be sure, insofar as Foucault regarded discourses as tactically polyvalent, a strategic use of Freud's ideas of polymorphous perversity and the mobility of desire (Bersani's move) was certainly open to him. It is possible that his reluctance to deploy a psychoanalytic theory of sexuality to account for resistance was based merely on his inability to transcend his wariness toward some of its key concepts and the specific historical deployments of it within the practice of psychiatry. In other words, there may be good reasons to challenge his eschewal of the Freudian discourse of desire. After all, the psyche to which Butler is appealing is clearly historically influenced. Yet she construes power as repressive and desire as lack – both moves that Foucault resisted.

There are also good reasons to be wary of such moves, not the least of which is that nowhere in his writings do we find Foucault operating with the notion of an individual psyche except when he is at pains to describe how the psychiatric concept emerged within the apparatus of sexuality. Foucault's aim was to excavate our historical unconscious, not our individual pasts. He did not want to focus on the intractability or impurity of our desires and dependencies, but rather on the possibility of detaching us from ourselves in order to support movement in a different direction. Moreover, *pace* Bersani, in his Collège de France lectures on abnormality he conjectured that the idea of "pleasure not governed by normal sexuality supports the entire series of abnormal, aberrant, instinctive conducts that are capable of being psychiatrized" (Foucault 2003: 287). The idea of an "unbounded [or perverse] pleasure that escapes the heterosexual and exogamous norm" invites efforts to regulate it (ibid.: 75).

A third reason to resist a reconciliation between Foucault and psychoanalytic thought is that he wanted to undermine the assumption that there must be necessary or causal connections between our erotic pursuits of bodily pleasure and our social and political lives. Foucault remarked:

> For centuries we have been convinced that between our ethics, our personal ethics, our everyday life, and the great political and social and economic structures, there were analytical relations – and that we couldn't change anything, for instance in our sex life or our family life, without ruining our economy, our democracy, and so on. I think we have to get rid of this idea of an analytical or necessary link between ethics and other … structures. (Foucault 1997: 350)

Even though identifying such connections could cut both ways, that is, toward consolidating present power structures, or theorizing their subversion, Foucault was understandably reluctant to install a theory of resistance premised on relatively intractable if transformable structures of desire such as the Oedipal triangle, the masochistic desire to be undone by another, and normative heterosexuality. In his conversations with gay activists he lamented the paucity of erotic possibilities and sought to "escape, or help others escape the ready made formulas of the pure sexual encounter and the lover's fusion of identities" (ibid.: 137). As if the only alternative to heteronormativity and the conjugal couple (whether straight or gay) must be anonymous sex.

Psychoanalytic accounts of desire might limit our self-understandings and our sense of erotic possibility. In the end, even if desire is mobile, it tends to operate within an Oedipal frame. It might move us beyond the biological family, but not beyond the tendency to describe all possible relationships in terms of reductive modern categories associated with the nuclear family (for example, mother, father, brother, sister). Hence, Foucault's reluctance to provide a theory of resistance may represent a strategic preference for practice over theory, for experimenting with the limits of our capacities for erotic connection rather than theorizing about them. Finally, given his pre-Stonewall sensibilities concerning homosexuality, Foucault might not have been particularly compelled by accounts of the fluidity of desire. He may have believed that gay identity politics reduces possibilities for gay becoming, that the logic of identity has been oppressive, and still have held open the possibility that homosexual attractions are partly biological. In an interview on sexuality he implied that he was agnostic about the etiology of homosexuality (ibid.: 141–56). This is not incompatible with his critique of the regime of sexuality. In the end, Foucault was not looking for the truth about sex, about power, or about resistance, but merely problematizing current self-understandings and providing resources for experimenting with possibilities for moving beyond them. Nor was it his aim to denaturalize sex. To say that "sex" is a fiction is not to deny that it is bound up in some way with natural phenomena.

The most likely source of Foucault's appeal to pleasure was not Freud, but Nietzsche. Whereas Freud described pleasure as the cessation of tension, Nietzsche understood pleasure as the increased feeling of power that accompanies an activity, a feeling that signals an enhancement of our capacity to act. Foucault appears to have drawn on a version of Nietzsche's distinction between relatively benign and pernicious forms of discipline – those that are life-enhancing and those that are unnecessarily life-denying or spirit-breaking – those that lead to self-overcoming, and those that turn the self against itself or others in ways that diminish its capacity to act – to affect and be affected. Thus, Foucault introduced pleasure as a vehicle that might enable us to sever the capacity enhancing features of the government of individualization from their normalizing functions.

Foucault's Use of Pleasure

Thus far I have suggested that bodies and pleasures might resist normalizing power because they have played a less central role within the modern regime of sexuality than have the concepts of "sex" and "desire." Even though Foucault regarded "sex" as a fiction, the elements it knits together, most importantly pleasures, need not be implicated in its dangerous effects. He left open the possibility of the emergence of other less normalizing ways of knitting such elements together, other possibilities for understanding and living our lives as "sexual" beings that do not regard regulating sexual desire as the bedrock of civilization. If, as Foucault once claimed, "pleasure has no passport," this is not because it is unbounded or ahistorical, but because it is less bound within the modern regime of sexuality than its counterpart, desire-sex (Davidson 2001: 213). It is, in effect, less discursively over-determined.

Moreover, unlike "desire," "pleasures" invite less scrutiny of origins or aims. While pleasure may accompany desires or acts that are morally suspect, the pleasure itself is not typically indicted in such judgments. Hence Foucault remarked:

> The term "pleasure" on the other hand, is free of use, almost devoid of meaning. There is no "pathology" of pleasure, no "abnormal" pleasure. It is an event "outside the subject," or at the limit of the subject, in that something which is neither of the body or the soul, which is neither inside nor outside, in short, a notion not assigned and not assignable. (Foucault 1988b: 32; Davidson 2001: 213)

The scare quotes around "pathology," "abnormal," and "outside the subject" indicate that in this passage Foucault was referring to the role that pleasures play within the discursive apparatus he was rejecting, not making any absolute claim about how they must inevitably function. Even when we distinguish lower from higher pleasures, our judgment tends to be directed at the activity producing pleasure rather than the pleasure itself. That, as Foucault once said, nobody knows what pleasure is may be an indicator of its discursive under-determination by normalizing power.

Therefore, historicizing bodies and pleasures and particular discourses about them does not prevent one from appealing to them as a source of resistance. Presumably, pleasure's power to resist normalization is no less bound up with historically available practices and discourses than is its potential to serve normalizing power relations. Furthermore (*pace* Butler), we can still appeal to pleasures as a natural force. The target of Foucault's critique in our modern regime of sexuality was not the anatomical elements or biological sensations and pleasures themselves, but rather the idea that they are unified by a deep causal principle called "sex." He was curious about the possibility of articulating them within another economy of bodies and pleasures.

The Turn to Ancient Greco-Roman Ethics

It is not until Foucault reframed the history of sexuality project to include a genealogy of ancient Greek and Roman sexual ethics that other such economies of are prefigured. The final two volumes of *History of Sexuality* were partly inspired by the prospect of unearthing alternative practices and discourses of bodily pleasure that might serve as a resource to those struggling against the modern regime of sexuality. He remarked:

> I wonder if our problem nowadays is not, in a way, similar to [the Greeks insofar as they did not relate ethics to science or law] … most of us no longer believe that ethics is founded in religion, nor do we want a legal system to intervene in our moral, personal, private life. Recent liberation movements suffer from the fact that they cannot find any principle on which to base the elaboration of a new ethics. They need an ethics, but cannot find any other ethics than an ethics founded on so-called scientific knowledge of what the self is, what desire is, and so on. (1997: 255–6)

In an interview at Berkeley in 1983, Foucault highlighted the link between sexual ethics and the truth of the self as the central focus of his investigation: "Why do we think it's not possible to have any sexual ethics without the obligation of knowing, deciphering, discovering, disclosing, and telling the truth about ourselves?" (1983a: 19). Maybe sexual ethics should not be a matter of scientific or moral truth about human desire, he conjectured, but a matter of pleasure.

How might turning to Hellenistic ethics and the use of pleasure advance struggles for sexual freedom? First and foremost it opens up the conceptual space for thinking differently, for dislodging dogmas associated with the regime of sexuality. The ancient Greeks did not appear to regard constraints on sexual desire as a central civilizing mechanism. This suggests that civilization can flourish without giving it such primacy. (They did of course police gender very heavily, which suggests that perhaps norms of masculinity were understood as fundamental to civilization. But that is another story.) Moreover, the ethical practices related to the nexus of pleasure-acts-desires, what the ancient Greeks called "aphrodesia," were in effect desexualized insofar as this discourse preceded the emergence of the apparatus of sexuality. Pleasures associated with relations between husbands and wives, even men and boys, were no more or less in need of regulation than those associated with dietary regimens. Foucault explained as follows:

> What seems in fact to have formed the object of moral reflection for the Greeks in matters of sexual conduct was not exactly the act itself (considered in its different modalities), or desire (viewed from the standpoint of its origin or aim), or even pleasure (evaluated according to the different objects or practices that can cause it); it was more the dynamics that joined all three in a circular fashion (the desire that leads to the act, that act that is linked to

pleasure, and the pleasure that occasions desire.) The ethical question that was raised was not: which desires? Which acts? Which pleasures? But rather: with what force is one transported [by them]. (1985: 43)

Thus they were more concerned with the possibility of being enslaved by pleasures than with the act or desire associated with them. As Foucault described him, the ancient Greek aristocratic, male citizen acts "to give to [his] life certain values (reproduce certain examples, leave behind ... an exalted reputation, give the maximum possible brilliance to [his life]" (1997: 271). While this project of self-mastery requires knowledge about desires, acts and pleasures and the impact of particular bodily practices on him, it does not require scrutinizing desires in a "search for their profound nature, their canonical forms, or their secret potential" (1985: 40).

Foucault intimated that ancient ethical schools could provide resources for experimenting in the present. Despite the fact that knowledge of the self plays a central role in these practices, he was intrigued by ancient Greco-Roman ethical schools that subordinated the imperative to "know thyself" to the principle of care for the self. Care for the self, states Foucault, was "one of the main rules for social and personal conduct and for the art of life" (1988a: 226). Along with the French classicist Pierre Hadot, he lamented the eclipse of this broader, existential understanding of philosophy as a "way of life" within post-Cartesian understandings that subordinate concern for the self to the imperative of theoretical and scientific knowledge (Davidson 1998: 195–202). Care of the self (he ultimately privileged a particular form of care or cultivation of the self, namely *askesis*), was a practice that might be resuscitated by homosexuals as part of the project of becoming rather than being homosexual. "To be 'gay,'" Foucault declared, is to try to define and develop a way of life (1997: 138). Thus we might follow the Ancients and treat our bodies and pleasures as the raw materials of creative and aesthetic practices of the self. In effect, we might work on producing an *ars erotica* prefigured at the origins of Western history to counter the pernicious effects of *scientia sexualis*. Rather than presume that sexuality must be sublimated, we could conceive of our bodily practices themselves as works of art (Rajchman 1991).

Perhaps, Foucault imagined, rather than treat homosexuality as a form of desire, we could turn it into something desirable. We might replace our tendency to think about sexuality as something to be discovered with practices of self-creation. Such an approach would entail cultivating our own disciplines to counter those we are resisting and reactivating the ancient understanding of desire as a yearning that follows a pleasurable experience rather than an innate attraction to particular objects. It would break open the idea of any necessary connection between the pleasures one enjoys and one's supposed gender or sexual identity. In this pleasure-based ethics, pleasure becomes a heuristic means of producing new forms of desirable experience, forms of experience that are less bound up with processes of normalization. Cultivating different pleasures could be a means of producing exemplary lives that might become models and supports for others seeking to define a way of life.

To be sure, what distinguishes ancient sexual ethics from their later Christian and modern Western counterparts is not that they were more tolerant. Foucault was quite clear that he did not intend to represent Greco-Roman antiquity as a "golden age" of sexual freedom. He recognized its elitism and sexism. For example, he remarked with disgust that the "Greek ethics of pleasures is linked to a virile society, to dissymmetry, exclusion of the other, an obsession with penetration, and a kind of threat of being dispossessed of your own energy (1983b: 258). Furthermore, he pointed out that in Greek and Roman canon law, acts "contrary to nature" were viewed as especially abominable. Finally, in Greco-Roman antiquity, the Christian Middle Ages, and the modern West, there is significant overlap in prohibitive moral codes insofar as all three contain prohibitions against excessive sexual activity, extra-marital sex, and same-sex relations. Yet the Greco-Roman prohibitions were juridical prohibitions against acts, and did not, for example, involve a medical or moral disqualification of the homosexual as a pathological or inherently immoral type. Thus ancient Greek sexual austerity was connected to a different form of ethical subjectivation from that found in Christianity. How they made themselves into ethical subjects and how and why they made sex into an ethical problem were in fact quite distinct issues from how they are problematized today.

Why Embrace an Ethics of Pleasures?

I have argued that Foucault's appeal to pleasure does not require us to believe that he regarded pleasure as either innocent of power, or as an unbounded force that resists any particular form of desire. Nor did he deny the existence of bodily forces. Instead he appealed to pleasures as historical (and bodily) resources that might be of strategic value in experimenting with new ways of living as erotic beings – ways of living that produce alternatives to subjection within the modern regime of sexuality.

In this scenario individuals are understood as capable of using and regulating pleasures to produce certain styles of embodiment and to undermine the tendency to become entrapped in relatively intractable habits of desiring associated with the intensification of problematic power relations. If they cannot be used as such, then all that one need conclude is that one has reached the limits of present possibilities.

Insofar as Hellenistic understandings of the relationship between desire and pleasure have been eclipsed in the modern regime of sexuality, the potential of pleasures to resist normalizing power has been overlooked. Foucault refocused our attention on this potential. He regarded pleasure as a powerfully compelling, if potentially dangerous, force – one that can be used for good or ill – but also one that is potentially detachable from current understandings of desire. At the very least, to focus on pleasures and bodies rather than desires might work to undo the facile assumptions that gender identity determine sexual orientation, or that the possibilities for erotic connection have been exhausted. It might draw attention to possibilities for bodily pleasure that bear little relationship to one's gender or sexual orientation, still defined as if by one's object choice.

There is much that is compelling in Foucault's effort to rethink strategies for enhancing sexual freedom. Our sexuality does seem burdened with an excess of significance, particularly to those of us who find it difficult to escape being reduced to our sexual identities, who cannot easily escape the shame associated with assumptions typically made about our character, our tendencies toward excess, and our unfitness for citizenship. Many of us who manage to accrue social capital by appearing to have assimilated to heteronormative models – namely, lesbians and gay men in committed, monogamous, relationships with or without children in tow – are aware of the costs to other, less easily assimilated, sexual minorities in this normalizing political strategy. In emphasizing, as Foucault did, the possibility for those of us whose lives represent transgressions of the dominant order to see ourselves as well positioned to create exemplary lives, as pioneers engaged in forming cultural alternatives, and as producing new possibilities for experiencing ourselves and our pleasures, Foucault provides a powerful counter-ideal. He rightly speculated that those of us who have already begun to define ourselves outside of the terms of dominant moral and psychological discourses governing sexuality might be in need of an alternative ethics, a set of self-disciplining practices that enhance our capacities, help us avoid the pursuit of transgression for its own sake, and build character without attaching us more rigidly to the current social order. Rather than embrace disciplines that operate by renouncing passion, Foucault, like Nietzsche before him, wanted to redirect our attention to the possibility for cultivating pleasures that enhance passionate and creative forces, to divorce our pleasures and to divorce us from attachment to harmful and homogenizing ideals. This will not be a risk-free endeavor, but neither is appealing to the discourse of our desires and the compulsion to either acknowledge or eradicate the irrationality and impurities still lurking within them.

What I have said here is by no means sufficient as an argument against those who regard psychoanalytic theory as indispensable for thinking about sex, gender, and power. Nor is it my aim to produce such an argument insofar as I too remain ambivalent about its value for thinking beyond or against the regime of sexuality. After all, it may turn out that we are up against intractable structures of desire – that we do harbor deep desires for self-preservation as well as destruction, for mastery and domination, as well as the loss of control, and, finally, that there is a relative intractability to what we call heterosexuality. We may need an account of ourselves that explores the effects of our profound dependencies on others and our attachments to subordination (Butler 2005).

In the final analysis, I have merely shown that there are good reasons for continuing to be wary of the psychoanalytic discourse of desire. In our efforts to explain what we are and why we do what we do, we limit our sense of who we are. Foucault preferred experimental practice to psychoanalytic theory-building as a strategy for resisting the modern regime of sexuality. He suggested that the cost associated with embracing an ethics of pleasure might be no greater than the risks of continuing to operate within this regime. In the end, he makes a case that at least some of us should embrace an ethics of pleasure and, in so doing, carry on the "undefined work of freedom" that might separate us from the contingencies that currently define who we are.

References

Bersani, L. (1995) *Homos.* Cambridge, MA: Harvard University Press.

Butler, J. (1997) *The Psychic Life of Power: Theories in Subjection.* Stanford, CA: Stanford University Press.

Butler, J. (2005) *Giving an Account of Oneself.* New York: Fordham University Press.

Davidson, A. (1998) *Foucault and His Interlocutors*. Chicago, IL: University of Chicago Press.

Davidson, A. (2001) "Foucault, Psychoanalysis and Pleasure." In *The Emergence of Sexuality: Historical Epistemology and the Formation of Concepts*. Cambridge, MA: Harvard University Press.

Foucault, M. (1978) *The History of Sexuality*, vol. 1: *An Introduction*. New York: Pantheon.

Foucault, M. (1980) "Body/Power." In C. Gordon, ed., *Power/Knowledge: Selected Interviews and Other Writings, 1972–1977*. New York: Pantheon.

Foucault, M. (1983a) Transcript of interview at Berkeley, IMEC.

Foucault, M. (1983b) "The Subject and Power" and "On the Genealogy of Ethics: An Overview of a Work in Progress." In H. Dreyfus and P. Rabinow, eds., *Michel Foucault: Beyond Structuralism and Hermeneutics*, 2nd edn. Chicago, IL: University of Chicago Press.

Foucault, M. (1984) *The Foucault Reader*, ed. Paul Rabinow. London/New York: Penguin.

Foucault, M. (1985) *The History of Sexuality*, vol. 2: *The Use of Pleasure*. New York: Random House.

Foucault, M. (1988a) *Technologies of the Self: A Seminar With Michel Foucault*, ed. L. Martin, H. Gutman, and P. Hutton. Amherst: University of Massachusetts Press.

Foucault, M. (1988b) "Le Gai savoir II." *Mec Magazin* 6 (1): 30–3; repr. in *The Lives of Michel Foucault*, trans. David Macey. New York: Vintage Press, 1993, pp. 364–77.

Foucault, M. (1997) *Ethics, Subjectivity and Truth: The Essential Works of Foucault 1954–1984*, vol. 1, ed. P. Rabinow. New York: The New Press.

Foucault, M. (2000) *Power: Essential Works of Michel Foucault 1954–1984*, vol. 3, ed. J. Faubion. New York: The New Press.

Foucault, M. (2003) *Abnormal: Lectures at the College de France: 1974–1975*. London: Verso.

Gearhart, S. (1995) "Foucault's Response to Freud: Sado-Masochism and the Aestheticization of Power." *Style* 29: 389–403.

Halperin, D. M. (1995) *Saint Foucault: Towards a Gay Hagiography*. Oxford: Oxford University Press.

Halperin, D. M. (2002) *How to Do the History of Homosexuality*. Chicago, IL: University of Chicago Press.

Rajchman, J. (1991) *Truth and Eros: Foucault, Lacan, and the Question of Ethics*. New York: Routledge Press.

Shattuck, R. (2000) "Second Thoughts on a Wooden Horse: Michel Foucault." In *Candor and Perversion: Literature, Education and the Arts*. New York: W. W. Norton & Co.

Warner, M., ed. (1993) "Introduction." In *Fear of a Queer Planet: Queer Politics and Social Theory*. Minneapolis: University of Minnesota Press.

10

Foucault and Normative Political Philosophy: Liberal and Neo-Liberal Governmentality and Public Reason

Paul Patton

One of the features of Foucault's work that most confuses readers is his particular combination of descriptive and normative concerns. On the one hand, he consistently avoids questions of legitimation and justification in favor of a resolutely descriptive approach to the techniques, strategies, and forms of rationality of power. On the other, he makes frequent and explicit normative recommendations, especially in interviews and occasional texts in support of particular causes.[1] His concern to avoid what he described as the classical juridico-discursive way of posing the question of political power is most famously expressed in the recommendation that, in political theory, "we need to cut off the king's head" (1978: 88–9). In a similar vein, the first lecture of his 1978–9 course, *The Birth of Biopolitics*, included a series of methodological comments designed to distinguish his approach to political government from the normative concerns of political philosophy. To that end, he renounced universals such as "the sovereign, sovereignty, the people, subjects, the state and civil society" and instead proposed to begin with the ways in which the practice of government has been theorized and described.

The fact that these lectures focus exclusively on "the rationalization of governmental practice in the exercise of political sovereignty" is enough to put to rest one common misunderstanding of what it means to cut off the king's head, namely that it obliges him to limit his analyses to the forms of micro-power exercised upon individual bodies (Foucault 2008: 2). In his lectures the preceding year, *Society, Territory, Population*, he introduced the concept of governmentality in order to provide an overarching rubric for the study of different ways in which the conduct of individuals and groups could be "conducted." The aim was to show that practices directed at the management of an entire society, its economy, and its population could also be studied in normatively neutral terms as the government of the conduct of others. In particular, the study of governmentality is a means of showing that this kind of analysis of power "is not confined by definition to a precise domain determined by a sector of the scale, but should be considered simply as a point of view, a method of decipherment which may be valid for the whole scale, whatever its size" (ibid.: 186).

However, this methodological rationale for studies of the rationality of different kinds of governmental practice does not explain the attention to liberal and neo-liberal governmentality during the 1978–9 lectures. Seven out of the twelve lectures were devoted to German and then American neo-liberalism. Why this attention to neo-liberalism? As commentators have noted, this was the only time that he devoted lectures to contemporary political history.[2] In the course of these lectures, he offered a number of reasons for his focus on neo-liberalism, ranging from a general rationale for the political efficacy of studying the history of the present to a quite specific "reason of critical morality" for approaching the state and its exercise of sovereign power in this manner (ibid.). In fact, despite the non-normative grid of analysis proposed at the outset, *The Birth of Biopolitics* presents a striking combination of descriptive and normative concerns. As a result, these lectures are especially interesting for exploring the relationship of Foucault's genealogical approach to normative political philosophy. My aim here is to pursue this issue and to ask what political philosophical purposes are served by this kind of empirical study of governmental reason. Rawls's political liberalism provides a helpful framework within which to locate Foucault's analyses of neo-liberal governmentality, in part because it offers a useful characterization of the different kinds of political discourse, including a reflexive account of the discursive space within which political philosophy takes place.

Governmental and Public Reason

In contrast to Foucault's resolutely descriptive approach to the nature of government, Rawls's political liberalism seeks to spell out the normative principles that should inform a just and democratic society. It sets out to describe "how things might be, taking people as a just and well-ordered society would encourage them to be" (Rawls 2005: 213). It provides a clear answer to the question under what conditions the exercise of sovereign power is legitimate, given the equality of citizens and given the existence of a plurality of comprehensive moral, religious, or philosophical views.

A state is legitimate when political power is exercised in accordance with a constitution the essentials of which all citizens as free and equal may reasonably be expected to endorse in the light of principles and ideals acceptable to their common human reason (ibid.: 137, 393). Central to this conception of legitimate government is a concept of public reason that embodies the ideal of respectful and reciprocal relations between citizens who are not assumed to share the same moral commitments and beliefs. Public reason is the manner in which citizens collectively exercise their sovereign political power in drawing up and amending a constitution, and in enacting laws relating to the basic structure of the society or fundamental questions of justice.

Rawls distinguishes the sphere of public reason proper, within which citizens, legislators, judges, and government officials argue about constitutional essentials and matters of basic justice, from the sphere of the background political culture within which citizens argue about all kinds of things related to the political and the public good, including theories of justice and the nature and business of government. The crucial difference between these two spheres is that in the latter citizens are free to argue from the perspective of their respective moral, philosophical, and religious beliefs and commitments, whereas in the former they are constrained by the publicly acceptable conceptions of justice. Citizens in a well-ordered and pluralist society must respect a duty of civility and offer reasons to one another in terms that all can reasonably be expected to endorse. Citizens should appeal only to "beliefs, grounds and political values it is reasonable for others to also acknowledge" (Rawls 2001: 27).

Rawls's conception of public reason is normative in the sense that it expresses an ideal view of the manner in which citizens of a democratic and pluralist polity should relate to one another in debates over constitutional essentials and matters of basic justice: "Understanding how to conduct oneself as a democratic citizen includes understanding an ideal of public reason" (2005: 218). At the same time, to the extent that the content of public reason, the beliefs and political values that make it up in a given society at a given point in its history, will depend upon the available political conceptions of justice, this is a quasi-empirical conception of public reason. The political conceptions that can attract overlapping consensus will ultimately depend on the considered judgments of the society along with the background culture which sustains efforts to systematize and theorize such judgments. Rawls notes that political conceptions of justice may be revised as a result of their interactions with one another or the emergence of new groups and different political problems. The principles, ideals, and standards of argument that make up the content of public reason are those of "a family of reasonable political conceptions of justice and this family changes over time" (ibid.: li). This conception of public reason is therefore normative, but also historical in the sense that, for Foucault, a discursive formation is a historical object that exists in a more or less systematic body of statements or "things said" (*énoncés*).[3]

Rawls does not pay much attention to the ways in which political power can be exercised over and above certain minimal constraints imposed by his theory of justice. Any legitimate sovereign government will have to maintain security, stability, and equality of opportunity, while maximizing the production of primary social goods subject to equal and just distribution of those goods. In Foucault's terms, he does not concern himself with the "how" of power, even though it is clear that he should do so since large swathes of public policy bear directly on questions of basic justice. Rawls notes that "many if not most political questions do not concern fundamental matters" although of course some do: a "full account of public reason" would explain in more detail than he offers in *Political Liberalism* which matters are subject to the restrictions of public reason and to what degree (ibid.: 215). He does occasionally mention, in connection with the questions of basic justice and constitutional essentials that are governed by the requirements of public reason, the "policies" to be adopted. For example, he notes that "on matters of constitutional essentials and basic justice, the basic structure *and its public policies* are to be justifiable to all citizens, as the principle of political legitimacy requires" (ibid.: 224; emphasis added). In the Introduction to the paperback edition of *Political Liberalism*, he suggests that matters of basic justice would include "questions of basic economic and social justice and other things not covered by the constitution" (ibid.: xlviii, n.23).

At this point, Foucault's approach to the forms of governmental reason are an important supplement. His studies of neo-liberal governmentality draw attention to a dimension of political culture that is only marginally present in Rawls's own account, namely conceptions of the nature, purposes, and methods of government, and the ways in which these impact upon the basic structure of society and its public policies. They draw attention to a kind of discourse about the nature and function of government that, while it may not form part of public reason itself, is capable of inspiring a range of contributions to public reason on matters of basic justice. In particular, the lectures on neo-liberalism discuss a range of neo-liberal social policies, such as negative tax alternatives to bureaucratic social security and rational choice approaches to "human capital" and criminality, that clearly fall within the sphere of public reason as Rawls defines it. For this reason, in a variety of ways that I will attempt to identify in what follows, Foucault's approach to liberal and neo-liberal governmentality contributes to a historical understanding of contemporary political normativity.

Governmentality and the State

Although he is not directly concerned with the justice or legitimacy of sovereign government, Foucault's reasons for studying neo-liberal governmentality are no less normative. As I noted above, this work is undertaken partly for what he calls "a reason of critical morality" that has to do with his critical engagement with certain views common among the French extra-parliamentary left during the 1970s. The lectures on neo-liberal governmentality are presented as an explicit challenge to a certain kind of "state phobia" that regards sovereign power as a phenomenon with its own essential characteristics and dynamics. At the heart of this state phobia is an essentialist conception of the state such that administrative, welfare, bureaucratic, fascist, and totalitarian forms of state may all be regarded as expressions of the same underlying form: "[T]here is a kinship, a sort of genetic continuity or evolutionary implication between different forms of state" (Foucault 2008: 187). One does not need to look further than the work of Deleuze and Guattari for an example of this approach. In *A Thousand Plateaus* they propose an abstract definition of the state-form as an apparatus of capture which exists whenever two fundamental conditions are met: the constitution of a milieu of interiority and the establishment of a standard or center of comparison on the basis of which a surplus can be extracted. Less formalized versions of the same approach can be found among a variety of Marxist theories of the state as instrument of class domination, or anarcho-Nietzschean theories of the state as the coldest of all cold monsters. Deleuze and Guattari's concept of the state as an apparatus of capture points to a further element of the state phobia to which Foucault objects, namely the idea that the state possesses its own intrinsic tendency to expand, "an endogenous imperialism constantly pushing it to spread its surface and increase in extent, depth and subtlety to the point that it will come to take over entirely that which is at the same time its other, its outside, its target and its object, namely: civil society" (Foucault 2008: 187).

Foucault's objection to this essentialist conception of the state is, firstly, that it allows its protagonists to deduce a political analysis from first principles and avoid altogether the need for empirical and historical knowledge of contemporary reality. In this sense, he argues that it amounts to a critical discourse the value of which is artificially inflated since it enables its supporters to "avoid paying the price of reality and actuality" (ibid.: 188). On the one hand, it allows the kind of analysis that conflates historically specific institutions and processes as instances of one and the same phenomena so that an analysis of social security ends up referring to concentration camps. On the other hand, the inbuilt dynamism of the state insures that, whatever the context and whatever political process is under discussion, it can always be criticized by reference to the worse that will inevitably follow: "[S]omething like a kinship or danger, something like the great fantasy of the paranoiac and devouring state can always be found" (ibid.). Foucault's analysis of governmentality disqualifies this kind of essentialist conception of the state from the outset. His approach does not seek to extract the essential nature of the modern state but to question it from the outside by "undertaking an investigation of the problem of the state on the basis of practices of governmentality" (ibid.: 78). From this perspective, the institutions and policies of the state are nothing more than the residue or the effects of the ways in which more or less centralized power has sought to govern territories, populations, and economic and social life: they are "the mobile effect of a regime of multiple governmentalities" (ibid.: 77).

A plea for realism about the state and its origins is a constant refrain of Foucault's criticism of state phobia. In this respect, his genealogical sketch of neo-liberal governmentality is but one instance of the broader strategy at work in these lectures. As he describes the aim of his historical analyses at one point: "The problem is to let knowledge of the past to work on the experience of the present" (ibid.: 130). His second objection to state phobia points to its ignorance of the widespread suspicion of the state from within twentieth-century liberalism. In contrast, his analysis of the origins and emergence of German neo-liberalism shows how this kind of critique of the state and its "intrinsic and irrepressible dynamism" was already formulated during the period from 1930 to 1945 in the context of efforts to criticize the whole range of interventionist policies from Keynesianism to National Socialism and Soviet state planning (ibid.: 189). The influence of anti-state liberalism in the postwar period meant that all those on the left who participate in this state phobia are "following the direction of the wind and that in fact, for years and years, an effective reduction of the state has been on the way" (ibid.: 191).

It is at this point in the lectures that Foucault brings his analysis of German neo-liberalism to bear on contemporary French economic and social policy. He makes it clear that the role of "the German model" in his own immediate political context is part of the reason for undertaking these historical analyses: "The German model which is being diffused, debated and forms part of our actuality, structuring it and carving out its real shape, is the model of a possible neo-liberal governmentality" (ibid.: 192). Much of the eighth lecture is devoted to an analysis of the history of French economic and social policy in the postwar period. In the course of the 1970s, under the presidency of Valéry Giscard d'Estaing and the prime ministership of Raymond Barre, France moved toward adopting a neo-liberal economic and social policy heavily influenced by the German model. French economic ministers and advisors considered the abandonment of the postwar policies of full employment and a social security system that functioned on the wartime principle of national solidarity in dealing with the risks faced by individuals, in favor of a neo-liberal system of social security that would avoid imposing additional costs and constraints on the operation of a market economy. An exemplary policy proposal along these lines involved the introduction of a negative tax as a way of insuring a basic level of access to health and other services on the part of those who, for whatever reason, are unable to pay. Foucault's presentation of this neo-liberal approach to social security is not simply critical. His immediate concern is to show that it represents the importation of themes taken directly from the agenda of the German neo-liberals (ibid.: 207). His broader aim is to show that "political actuality" is more complex than is recognized by many proponents of state theory, including those who see no difference between contemporary liberalism and its classic eighteenth- and nineteenth-century forms.

Foucault's critical remarks about state phobia directed at his own intellectual milieu belong to the background culture of politics in which Rawls situates his own political philosophy and that of other normative theorists such as Habermas (Rawls 2005: 382). They are offered from the position of citizen within civil or political society. Similarly, his historical analyses of the policy discourse of public officials and advisors comment upon, rather than engage directly in, public reason. More generally, his account of neo-liberal governmentality shows us some of the elements of contemporary public reason and how these came about in the postwar period. In this sense, he offers a historical account of the terms in which debates about public policy took shape in liberal capitalist democracies. Some of the founding texts of neo-liberal governmentality discussed do not fall within the sphere of public reason narrowly defined, but nor do they fall within the sphere of the background political culture. They occupy an ambivalent place in between background culture and public reason, forming a kind of historically moveable boundary between them. Rawls occasionally refers to this border region as "public political culture," thereby introducing a third dimension along which the boundaries of public reason are subject to change. He distinguishes between background and public political culture. Background culture includes all of the kinds of non-public reasons found in churches, universities, scientific societies, and professional groups (ibid.: 220). It includes the philosophical theories in terms of which philosophers might theorize the political domain, along with the historical, philosophical, and moral theories which inform certain kinds of political party and which, according to Foucault, are one of the ways in which state government has been subverted in the course of the twentieth century (Foucault 2008: 191). By contrast, public political culture refers to the fundamental political ideas current within a given society at a given time. These will include the kinds of ideas about the appropriate functions and techniques of government that Foucault considers under the rubric of governmentality. If the boundaries of public reason are historically mobile by virtue of changes over time in the comprehensive moral beliefs of citizens and to the family of reasonable political conceptions of justice, then Foucault shows us how the boundaries of public reason are also mobile by virtue of changes in public political culture and its impact on policy. His sketches toward a history of liberal and neo-liberal governmentality point to an important vector of change in the boundaries of public reason during the twentieth century. To the extent that neo-liberal ideas have emerged from the pages of academic journals such as *Ordo* and semi-private forums such as the Mont Pelérin Society to become the guiding principles of government throughout the capitalist world, they have progressed from background culture to public reason proper. In directing our attention to ideas such as these, Foucault's analyses of liberal and neo-liberal governmentality enlarge our understanding of the discursive and normative frameworks within which much contemporary sovereign power is effectively exercised.

Liberal and Neo-Liberal Governmentality

I noted earlier that Foucault offers a variety of reasons for devoting time to the analysis of German and American varieties of neo-liberal governmentality. All of these may be subsumed under the general rationale that he offers for undertaking such history, namely that it helps to transform our

experience of the present. In this sense, his analysis of neo-liberal governmentality is an example of the kind of genealogy of the present that he
identifies in "The Subject and Power" (2000: 326–48) as the overriding purpose of all his work. Moreover, to the extent that such genealogy is also a
critical strategy, the aim is to find points of exit from or transformation in
present social reality.

As he points out in lecture six, neo-liberalism had already become "the
program of most governments in capitalist countries" (2008: 149). Since
these lectures were delivered, the "marketization" of national economies
through competition policy and privatization of public services has continued to develop in most Western capitalist countries. In France, the question
of genuine alternatives both to such apparently unrestrained capitalism and
to traditional state communism was also posed in the late 1970s when the
country faced the prospect of a socialist government. Michel Senellart
points out that Foucault's involvement in efforts to rethink the political
orientation and strategies of the French left was among the relevant features of his political activity during the period in which these lectures were
written. In this context, it is noteworthy that he raises the question of socialist governmentality at the end of the fourth lecture: "What would really be
the governmentality appropriate to socialism? Is there a governmentality
appropriate to socialism?" (ibid.: 94). His answer is that if there is such a
thing as socialist governmentality, it remains to be invented.

Part of the interest of neo-liberal governmentality in relation to this
question is that it provides a historical example of the reinvention of liberal
governmentality. Foucault is not uncritical of this type of government,
but neither does he dismiss it out of hand. For example, at one point in his
discussion in lecture nine of the American neo-liberal theory of human
capital, he pauses to ask what is the interest of this theory and his analysis
of it. In response, he suggests that it would be a dangerous mistake to simply brush aside this theory because of its political connotations. Presumably,
he has in mind the treatment of persons as capital and social relations such
as those of parents to their children as forms of investment. To dismiss this
theory out of hand would be a mistake because of the way it enables a new
approach to phenomena that have remained unresolved problems for leftist
economic theory, such as the failure of the rate of profit to fall or the historical question why economic growth takes place in some areas and not
others. Neo-liberalism identifies human capital as an important variable,
moreover one that lies within the capacity of governments to modify. For
this reason, Foucault notes, "we are seeing the economic policies of all the

developed countries, but also their social policies, as well as their cultural and educational policies, being orientated in these terms" (ibid.: 232). He also finds merit in the neo-liberal theory of criminality in which crime is defined as action undertaken by individuals that involves a risk of punishment. This implies a way of understanding and dealing with crime that dispenses entirely with the moral and anthropological theories of criminality that formed part of the carceral apparatus since the nineteenth century. The criminal is simply a person who invests in a course of action where there is an accompanying risk of punishment, nothing more and nothing less. The penal system will therefore no longer seek to reform criminals but will simply seek to reduce the supply of crime by increasing the risk, the likelihood, or the severity of punishment (ibid.: 253).

The tendency to abandon techniques of discipline in favor of purely economic means of producing compliance is a general principle of neo-liberal governmentality that Foucault appears to endorse. For example, in discussing the social and economic policy of the French government during the late 1970s after it had abandoned the objectives of full employment and planned economic growth in favor of a market economy, he points to the consequences with regard to the unemployed and those requiring assistance of a proposal to replace existing social security arrangements with a form of negative taxation. This would imply providing a certain base level of income to insure that no one is completely excluded from the economy and the labor market by poverty. Foucault comments:

> This is a completely different system from that through which eighteenth and nineteenth century capitalism was formed and developed, when it had to deal with a peasant population which was a possible constant reservoir of manpower. When the economy functions as it does now, when the peasant population can no longer ensure that kind of endless fund of manpower, this fund has to be formed in a completely different way. This other way is the assisted population, which is actually assisted in a very liberal and much less bureaucratic and disciplinary way than it is by a system focused on full employment which employs mechanisms like those of social security. Ultimately it is up to people to work if they want or not work if they don't. (Ibid.: 207)

In other words, whatever one's judgment of its merits, neo-liberal social policy is a real and effective alternative to the techniques of discipline. Neo-liberal governmentality involves a conceptual framework quite different from the one that sustained disciplinary government. For this reason,

Foucault's comments on neo-liberal social policy, like those on the economic approach to criminality, help to clarify a remark made two years earlier, at the end of his lecture of January 14, 1976, when he called for a new form of right that would be both anti-disciplinary and emancipated from the principle of sovereignty and that would serve as an effective discursive weapon against disciplinary power (2003: 39–40). Some commentators took him to be suggesting that we need a new universal principle on the basis of which to criticize disciplinary power, while at the same time denying that his work provides any basis for such universal principles of right (Mourad 2003: 453, 456). In contrast, I take his view to be that opposition to disciplinary power should rely upon forms of right that already operate in our present and that are capable of providing effective counter-arguments to the techniques and goals of disciplinary power (Patton 2005: 282). Neo-liberal right satisfies both criteria.

Foucault's analyses of neo-liberal governmentality confirm that he approaches the question of normative bases for critique or resistance to power in terms of actually existing ways of thinking and speaking. This is what neo-liberalism represents in contrast to the earlier techniques of liberal government that required disciplined and obedient subjects of economic processes. For example, the system of social security developed in the aftermath of World War II in France functioned in such a way that it produced and maintained forms of dependency. In contrast, neo-liberal governmentality relies much more on the autonomy and responsibility of citizens and, for that reason, may provide a more effective counter to the techniques of disciplinary power. Foucault is explicit on this in his 1983 interview "The Risks of Security," when he suggests that the rationality that informed the postwar system has reached its limit "as it stumbles against the political, economic and social rationality of modern societies" (Foucault 2000: 366). In response to the "perverse effects" of social security systems that serve to maintain forms of dependency, he acknowledges a legitimate demand for a form of social security that allows for "richer, more numerous, more diverse, and more flexible relationships with others and ourselves, all the while assuring each of us real autonomy" (ibid.).

The implicit principle at work here, and indeed throughout Foucault's critical and genealogical analyses of power, is that resistance to existing forms of government must find support in alternative rationalities of government that are also available in the prevailing political culture. This principle is evident in his analysis of the forms of "counter-conduct" that flourished alongside the institutions and practices of pastoral power in medieval and early modern Europe, as it is in his parallel remarks about the forms of resistance to modern governmentality between the late eighteenth and the early twentieth century. In relation to pastoral power, Foucault argues that the precise mechanisms through which it sought to direct the conduct of individuals provided the basis for forms of counter-conduct through which some dissident subjects sought to conduct themselves differently: asceticism, different forms of community, mysticism, eschatology, and disputes over the proper interpretation of the Scripture (Foucault 2007: 194–216). In relation to the new forms of governmentality that developed in the seventeenth and eighteenth centuries, there were equally a series of counter-conducts based upon the elements of this governmentality: society as opposed to the state, economic truth as opposed to error, universal as opposed to particular interest, freedom as opposed to regulation, and so on (ibid.: 355–7). More generally, he often points to the manner in which resistance to particular ways of being governed is justified by recourse to elements of existing forms of governmental reason. The elements of modern counter-conduct include, but are not confined to, those discursive elements of government that, as societies become more democratic, constitute important components of public reason. However, the general principle remains, namely that resistance on the part of citizens to the ways in which they are governed draws upon the very conceptions of government that inform those practices.

Governmentality and Legitimacy

A further misunderstanding of what it means to cut off the king's head might suppose that normative questions such as the justification for the exercise of sovereign political power have no place in Foucault's analysis. He is relentlessly empiricist in his approach to the nature of liberal and neoliberal governmentality. His goal is to retrace the implicit rationality of these forms of government as expressed in discourse about the nature, functions, and limits of government. However, because these discourses themselves do on occasion raise questions about the justification of political power and the acceptable limits to its exercise, normative questions about the legitimacy and limits of sovereign power do arise in the course of these lectures. A first instance of this kind of oblique consideration of legitimation in his 1978–9 course occurs in the initial lecture, when he compares the manner in which *raison d'état* and modern liberal governmentality set limits to political power.[4] For the former, the only limitation on the domestic exercise of sovereign power was the law and associated notions of right, including the natural rights of individuals. For the latter, the new science of political economy provided a different kind of intrinsic limit to the exercise of political power, namely the question of what it was useful for government to undertake, given its aims and given the self-regulating character of the economic process on which the achievement of those aims depended. Foucault acknowledged that this was a limitation of fact rather than right, "even though at some point the law will have to transcribe it in the form of rules which must not be infringed" (2008: 10).

In the second lecture Foucault returned to the question of how this limitation would be presented in juridical terms. Within the framework of liberal governmental reason defined by political economy, he asks, what is the basis and legitimate extent of public law? (ibid.: 38). He suggests that there were two ways of answering this question in the eighteenth and nineteenth centuries. One approach sought the limits to the legitimate functions of government on the basis of a theory of the natural rights of individuals. This was the path followed by the American Declaration of Independence, Rousseau, and the French revolutionaries. It drew upon the tradition of social contract theories of the nature and limits of sovereign power, which began with a conception of the natural or original rights of the individual and proceeded to define the circumstances in which, and the reasons for which, individuals would consent to cede some of those powers to a sovereign. Typically, this approach also distinguished those rights that individuals would agree to cede and those which they would not. Foucault summarizes this approach as "starting from the rights of man in order to arrive at the limitation of governmentality by way of the constitution of the sovereign" (ibid.: 39). The second approach was that developed by English radicalism at the end of the eighteenth and beginning of the nineteenth century. It began not with the inalienable rights of man but with the question of utility: what it was useful or futile for government to undertake given its objectives, its objects, and its resources. In practice, answers to this question relied upon a calculus of interests, since it was the concept of interest that linked the liberal concern with the self-regulation of markets and the utility of public policy. Government now aimed at increasing both the forces of the state and the well-being of its citizens, and at achieving this through the free operation of the market, thereby insuring that individuals are governed as little as possible. The justification and the limits of government are henceforth understood in terms of a complex interplay of individual and collective interests: "Governmental reason in its modern form, in the forms established at the beginning of the eighteenth century with the fundamental characteristic of a search for the principle of its self-limitation, is a reason that functions in terms of interests" (ibid.: 44).

Foucault suggests that the utilitarian conception has been the stronger tendency within European liberalism (ibid.: 43, fn). However, both the revolutionary theory of human rights and the radical theory of human interests remain active and available forms of limitation and legitimation of government throughout the modern period. Moreover, these correspond to two distinct but interrelated concepts of law and freedom: law conceived as the expression of collective will versus law conceived as the result of "a transaction that separates the sphere of intervention of public authorities from that of the individual's independence" (ibid.: 41); a juridical concept of freedom based on the imprescriptible rights of individuals versus a utilitarian concept of freedom as simply "the independence of the governed with regard to government" (ibid.: 42). This characterization of the two conceptions of freedom corresponds in many respects to the freedom of the moderns that Benjamin Constant sought to contrast with the freedom of the Ancients. Whereas the latter consisted in active participation in the collective power of the people concerned, the former consisted above all in the independence of the citizen in the pursuit of his private life, an independence made all the more necessary and valuable by the development of commerce (Constant 1988).

Foucault's brief sketch of the two forms of limitation of the powers of governments effectively identifies one of the central concepts within modern political normativity. He points to the two ways in which this modern concept of freedom has been defended, but also to the predominance of the utilitarian version and the manner in which it leaves the way open to a more comprehensive conception of individual interests. The underlying principle of a transaction between individual and governmental interests leaves open the possibility that the freedom of individuals might be extended to take into account a broader range of individual interests, of the kind addressed in Marshall's third-generation citizenship rights or the second principle of Rawls's conception of justice. Rawls's difference principle expresses the idea that all citizens have an interest in maximizing their access to primary social goods, insofar as this is consistent with preservation of the fundamental juridical and political rights of all citizens. The Rawlsian citizen is ultimately a subject of interest, endowed with a capacity to form a conception of the good and a life plan "designed to permit the harmonious satisfaction of his interests" (Rawls 1999: 80). Foucault's comments on the different forms of limitation of state power that accompany different conceptions of government point to the role of these conceptions in producing modern liberal democracy and its public political culture. He provides a historical perspective on the elements, tensions, and developments within the kind of normative structure that Rawls and other liberal theorists seek to defend.

A second example of indirect engagement with the question of legitimacy occurs in Foucault's discussion of the neo-liberal governmentality that informed the policies and institutions of the German Federal Republic in the postwar period. He refers to a speech in April 1948 by Ludwig Erhard, who was responsible for the economic administration of the Anglo-American zone, calling for the removal of state interference and arguing for reliance on the market as the primary mechanism of economic governance. He points to Erhard's remark that "only a State which established at once the liberties and the responsibility of its citizens can legitimately speak in the name of the people" as evidence that what was at stake here was nothing less than "the legitimacy of the state" (2008: 81). Foucault takes Erhard's speech and the postwar German state to provide a historical case in which the conception of the nature and tasks of government effectively changes the normative bases of sovereign power. It is perhaps not the only historical example of a radically economic state: he mentions Venice and the United Provinces in the sixteenth century as other possible instances (ibid.: 86). In this case, the invocation of economic freedom as a basis of political right was also a solution to the particular historical problem of legitimizing a new German state not yet established that would be institutionally and juridically discontinuous with the Nazi state that preceded it. However, it is also a striking contemporary example of a state in which there is "a permanent genesis, a permanent genealogy of the state from the economic institution" (ibid.: 84).

Fully aware that he is adding a layer of implicit meaning to the text, Foucault takes Erhard's speech to express a new form of legitimation of state power. Its sovereignty is justified not on the basis of its juridical institutions, but on the basis of its guarantee of economic freedom. It is not simply that economic growth is the basis for a political consensus that sustains the postwar German state, although he does claim that there was such a consensus, but also that the economic institutions could serve as the basis for legal and political sovereignty. This form of justification of state authority challenges political philosophical views of legitimacy grounded in the basic legal and political rights of citizens. In contrast to liberal criteria of legitimacy that rely upon an implicit contract to insure protection of fundamental rights or maximal satisfaction of fundamental interests, this neo-liberal conception of legitimacy relied upon a contract implicitly entered into by any free participant in the economic system. To the extent that economic freedom and responsibility were guaranteed by the state, exercise of that freedom and responsibility implied allegiance to the state and its institutions (ibid.: 83).

In the final lectures of this course, Foucault returns to the question of the justification for and limits to state power raised at the outset. He points to the problem posed for liberal governmentality from its inception by the emergence of the market and *homo oeconomicus*. At the heart of this problem was the incompatibility of the juridical subject of right and the economic subject of interest: how was government to be exercised, limited, and justified in relation to economic as well as juridical subjects? He points to the different ways of resolving this conflict that have been proposed since the eighteenth and nineteenth centuries, beginning with the concept of civil society. Neo-liberalism represents a novel solution to this problem. It amounts to a real transformation in liberal governmentality that effectively reversed the relationship hitherto maintained between the state and the market. Its novelty lay in the primacy accorded to the market as the institution and idea that the state had to express and maintain. His analysis of German neo-liberal governmentality implied that the legitimacy of the postwar German state was underwritten by the market and economic growth so that, even up to the present, "the economy, economic development and economic growth produces sovereignty; it produces political sovereignty through the institution and institutional game that, precisely, makes this economy work. The economy produces legitimacy for the state that is its guarantor" (ibid.: 84).

If this analysis is correct, it provides further evidence of the contribution that the historical analysis of governmentality can make to our understanding of the normative frameworks of modern liberal public reason. It shows not only how different conceptions of the purposes, methods, and objects of government have succeeded one another in the European tradition, but also how these concepts affect contemporary ways of understanding the limits and the legitimacy of the exercise of state power. His analysis of neo-liberalism and the emergence of new kinds of governmental reason associated with the market state raises questions about the adequacy of normative political philosophies that remain grounded in juridical reason.

Notes

1   For example, in a 1977 interview on the extradition of Klaus Croissant, lawyer
    for the Red Army Faction, Foucault referred to the "rights of the governed,"
    including the right to be properly defended in a court of law, and described these
    as "more precise, more historically determined than the rights of man" (1994:
    362). In a 1982 interview on the issue of gay rights, he advocated the creation of
    new forms of relational right that would recognize same-sex relationships (1997:
    157–62). In a 1983 interview on "The Risks of Security," he endorsed the idea of
    a right to the "means of health" and also a right to suicide (2000: 365–81). Finally,
    in a 1984 speech in support of non-governmental organizations attempting to
    protect Vietnamese refugees being attacked by pirates in the Gulf of Thailand, he
    spoke of the right of international citizens to intervene in matters of interna-
    tional policy hitherto reserved for governments (2000: 474–5). For argument
    that there is no tension between Foucault's conception of social relations as
    power relations and his appeals to notions of right, see Patton 2004 and 2005.

2   The editor of these lectures, Michel Senellart, comments that the study of
    German neo-liberalism and American anarcho-liberalism "is Foucault's sole
    incursion into the field of contemporary history throughout his teaching at the
    Collège de France (Foucault 2007: 385). Francesco Guala describes the lectures
    in 1979 as his one and only "diversion into contemporary political philosophy"
    (2006: 429).

3   Discursive formations are also normative in the sense that they involve rules
    that determine what can be said in a particular domain. For this understanding
    of Rawls's public reason as a discursive formation in Foucault's sense I am
    indebted to Sandra Field and discussions relating to her MA thesis on "Political
    Liberalism and Political Change," University of New South Wales, 2006.

4   An earlier example arises in his discussion of the emergence during the eight-
    eenth century of the new art of government that brought apparatuses of secur-
    ity to bear on populations. Foucault notes that this change in the understanding
    of government only rendered more acute the problem of the legal basis and
    institutional form of sovereign state power (2007: 106–7).

References

Constant, B. (1988) "The Liberty of The Ancients Compared with that of The
    Moderns" (1819). In B. Fontana, ed. and trans., *Political Writings*. Cambridge:
    Cambridge University Press, pp. 309–28.
Foucault, M. (1978) *The History of Sexuality*, vol. 1: *An Introduction* (1976), trans.
    R. Hurley. London: Allen Lane/Penguin.

Foucault, M. (1994) *Dits et écrits 1954-1988*, vol. 3: *1976–1979*. Paris: Éditions Gallimard.

Foucault, M. (1997) *Essential Works of Foucault 1954–1984*, vol. 1: *Ethics*, ed. P. Rabinow, trans. R. Hurley et al. New York: New Press.

Foucault, M. (2000) *Essential Works of Foucault 1954–1984*, vol. 3: *Power*, ed. J. D. Faubion, trans. R. Hurley et al. New York: New Press.

Foucault, M. (2003) *"Society Must Be Defended": Lectures at the Collège de France 1975–1976*, ed. M. Bertani and A. Fontana, trans. D. Macey. New York: Picador.

Foucault, M. (2007) *"Security, Territory, Population": Lectures at the Collège de France 1977–1978*, ed. M. Senellart, trans. G. Burchell. Houndmills, Basingstoke, and New York: Palgrave Macmillan.

Foucault, M. (2008) *"The Birth of Biopolitics": Lectures at the Collège de France 1978–1979*, ed. M. Senellart, trans. G. Burchell. Houndmills, Basingstoke, and New York: Palgrave Macmillan.

Guala, F. (2006) "Critical Notice: *Naissance de la biopolitique. Cours au Collège de France, 1978–1979*, Michel Foucault, ed. M. Senellart. Seuil/Gallimard, 2004." *Economics and Philosophy* 22: 429–39.

Mourad, R. (2003) "After Foucault: A New Form of Right." *Philosophy and Social Criticism* 29 (4): 451–81.

Patton, P. (2004) "Power and Right in Nietzsche and Foucault." *International Studies in Philosophy* XXXVI (3): 43–61.

Patton, P. (2005) "Foucault, Critique and Rights." *Critical Horizons* 6 (1) December: 267–87.

Rawls, J. (1999) *A Theory of Justice*, rev. edn. Cambridge, MA: Harvard University Press.

Rawls, J. (2001) *Justice as Fairness: A Restatement*. Cambridge, MA: Harvard University Press.

Rawls, J. (2005) *Political Liberalism: Expanded Edition*. New York: Columbia University Press.

11

Foucault, Philosopher of Dialogue

Christopher Falzon

One fundamental point of agreement that emerged between Foucault and Habermas is that both rejected the Kantian paradigm of critique grounded in the notion of a transcendental subject (see Kelly 1994: 3–4, 11). For Foucault, genealogy is a form of history that can account for the constitution of knowledge, discourses, etc. without reference to a constitutive subject; while central to Habermas's approach is his rejection of the "philosophy of the subject" in favor of the "intersubjectivist paradigm of communicative action" (McCarthy 1984: x). For Foucault, the end of "man," a foundational subject providing ultimate normative yardsticks, is not the creation of a deficiency but "the unfolding of a space in which it is once again possible to think" (1970: 342). His critical work seeks "to know to what extent it is possible to think differently, rather than legitimating what is already known" (1985: 9); to promote new forms of self, thought, and action, and to give impetus to the "undefined work of freedom" (1997: 316). Yet without direction, doesn't this amount to an unrestricted notion of autonomy? Influenced perhaps by Nietzsche, Foucault calls on us to "create ourselves as a work of art" (ibid.: 262), but without guidance for self-creation, aren't we left only with arbitrary choices, an "aesthetic decisionism," in which one has to take "irrationalist leaps" to affirm anything? (Wolin 1986).

As Paul Healy notes in his insightful discussion, the problem here for many critics is Foucault's overly self-oriented stance, a Nietzschean self-assertion which lacks acknowledgment of an intersubjectivity to which our choices might be accountable, serving as a check on their arbitrary exercise. In this respect, he might be thought to fall *behind* Kant, who recognizes that the proper, non-arbitrary exercise of autonomy requires connectedness to intersubjectivity, since his autonomous subject is constrained to accept only those norms that could be agreed to by all rational beings (Healy 2005: 68). This is notwithstanding Kant's own moral solipsism, in which a solitary, self-sufficient Kantian subject is reconciled with the universality of ethical principles only through a kind of pre-established synchronization of the reflection of all rational beings. One reading of Habermas is as making the intersubjective dimension of Kant's account explicit, transposing reflection on the universalizability of norms from solitary moral consciousness to a community of speaking subjects in dialogue (see McCarthy 1978: 326). So Foucault might be taken to have fallen behind both Kant and Habermas in this respect. My aim here, first of all, is to bring out the counter-claim, explored by Healy and others (e.g. Coles 1992; Falzon 1998; Thompson 1999), that far from turning to arbitrary subjectivism, Foucault's thinking is in fact amenable to a dialogical interpretation, offering an understanding of subjects as immersed in inherently reciprocal intersubjective relations.

As Healy goes on to argue, a dialogical reading of Foucault goes some way toward providing the desired intersubjective accountability. The development of new forms of thought and action takes place within reciprocal forums of intersubjectivity, in which the encounter with difference can make us aware of concealed presuppositions that limit our thinking, and of new possibilities for thinking and acting that have informed others, the recognition of which can challenge and lead to a transformation of our own way of thinking. But he questions whether this is enough, as Foucault provides no ground rules for evaluating the relative merits of competing positions, advancing transformation by principled means, and rendering change rationally motivated (see Healy 2005: 76–9). My second aim, however, is to suggest that rather than a Foucauldian dialogue falling short of providing full accountability, it is limits to accountability that open the way to a conception of ourselves as immersed in dialogue. On this reading, dialogue provides the larger context for the emergence of the forms in terms of which we account for what we think and do, the normative arrangements in the social world. A dialogical reading also makes it possible to situate freedom as self-creation, the production of new forms, and the critical reflection that gives this freedom impetus. And understood in these terms, Foucault's account can be differentiated not only from an arbitrary subjectivism but also from Habermas's version of dialogue.

Sartre and Unconditioned Autonomy

To begin with, Foucault's picture can be contrasted with the kind of account in which abandoning ultimate grounds is indeed seen as robbing us of all normative standards and leading to arbitrary subjectivism. The claim that Foucault embraces Nietzschean self-assertion implies that this trajectory is in Nietzsche, and Nietzsche certainly envisages a solitary reinvention of the self. But whether or not this reinvention can be identified with unconditioned self-assertion, there are aspects of his thinking that seem at odds with subjectivism, and which Foucault claims as influences. In particular there is Nietzsche's genealogical concern to understand the processes beyond ourselves through which we become subjects; and the "theme of the overman who would be completely different from man," which Foucault says pointed him beyond phenomenology and existentialism "which maintained the primacy of the subject and its fundamental value" (2000: 248). A more straightforward candidate for the turn to an unconditioned subjectivism would indeed be Sartre in his existentialist phase. The criticism would then be that Foucault's self-creation is akin to Sartre's existentialist conception of self-making. This is something that Foucault explicitly denies (1997: 262), and a useful way of situating his position is to contrast it with the existentialist one. Both Foucault and the existentialists start with the renunciation of religion and metaphysics as grounds for moral action and social bonds (Dreyfus and Rabinow 1986: 112), but there is a large difference in their understanding of what flows from this.

For Sartre, the consequence of there being no ultimate, particularly religious, justification for action, is that there are no normative standards we can appeal to for guidance, rendering our existence meaningless and absurd. Having been "abandoned" by God, our lives have no pre-given point or purpose (Sartre 1956: 201–2). Thus Sartre's protagonist in *Nausea* finds that not only his own existence but everything around him seems arbitrary, "superfluous," and contingent (1963: 182–3). At the same time, for Sartre, the judgment that life lacks justification, that we are adrift in a meaningless world, is not merely negative. It opens the way to the positive position of *Being and Nothingness*, the vision of radical self-assertion in which the heroic human subject takes center stage as the creator of purpose and meaning (see Manser 1966: 18). Guiding norms or justifications for action become something we ourselves generate, giving direction to our existence through choices that are themselves unjustifiable, arbitrary. Questions can be raised about the tenability of this radically free subject, but the prior question is whether having no ultimate ground for what we think and do means we no longer have any normative standards we can appeal to.

Indeed, in "The Absurd," Nagel makes the point against existentialism that even if justifications run out, this does not rob us of reasons for acting. Chains of justification repeatedly come to an end in life, yet no larger context is required to give what we do a point. Many things we do are self-justifying;

and even if we did want to provide a further justification for pursuing things commonly thought self-justifying, that justification would have to end somewhere too. If nothing can justify unless it is justified in terms of something outside of itself, there is an infinite regress, and no chain of justification can be complete. Thus, to require that everything we do is justified, completely "reasonable," is an impossibly high demand. If all reasons that come to an end are deemed inadequate, it becomes impossible to supply adequate reasons (Nagel 1979: 12–13). The implication here is that any ultimate ground we might claim to be required to justify what we do is also going to be inadequate, since it is itself going to lack justification. Indeed, to insist on an ultimate ground in the name of justification is to make the paradoxical demand that everything must be grounded, except that which grounds. So we need to abandon both the idea that an ultimate foundation is required for us to have orienting norms and the corresponding claim that without it we will fall into irrationality and arbitrariness. The real alternative to both foundationalism and existentialism is to give up their shared idea that only ultimate grounds will provide us with a meaningful, principled existence, and accept that we can have reasons or grounds for what we think and do even if these justifications are limited, coming to an end at a certain point.

Nagel himself explores this alternative. Even if justifications run out, he argues, we cannot help living in a principled way. There is an "unavoidable seriousness" to our lives. We are committed to being a certain sort of person, living a certain sort of life, and this involves adhering to a framework of "justification and criticism, which controls the choices that we make and supports our claims to rationality" (1979: 15). Taylor similarly speaks of a set of commitments and values that are central to who we are, an "identity" providing a horizon of evaluation in terms of which we reflect and weigh up the choices and actions we undertake (1985: 34–5). This is necessary if we are to be agents; without it we would be crippled, unable to choose and act. Given this, Sartre's positive ideal, the subject free of all orienting norms, wholly choosing itself, becomes problematic. It would not be radically free but incapable of choosing (ibid.: 34). In Nagel's terms a Sartrean subject would lack all "seriousness." Sartre himself condemns what he calls the "spirit of seriousness" – the view that there are values given to us, and that moral choice is a kind of deduction from necessary grounds – as serving to conceal the extent to which we are choosing our values and actions. But it would seem that without some seriousness, some framework of values to which we are committed and in terms of which we can make choices, we cannot function as agents.

It remains the case, however, that beyond a certain point we cannot justify what we think and do. This is Nagel's second point, that while we live our lives seriously, we can also step back to find that the "whole system of justification and criticism, which controls our choices and supports our claims to rationality," stands on responses and habits "that we should not know how to defend without circularity, and to which we shall continue to adhere even after they are called into question" (1979: 15). Yet even if from our "external" reflective viewpoint we can recognize the contingency and specificity of our aims, this does not rob us of meaning and purpose. For Nagel, our situation is absurd, but not in the Sartrean sense of lacking meaning. Rather, it is the opposition between the reflective view of ourselves and the serious lives we nonetheless continue to lead that gives rise to the sense of absurdity. Even if we were to invoke some higher concern from which it is impossible to step back – be it "service to society, the state, the revolution, the progress of history, the advance of science, or religion and the glory of God," the kind of ultimate justification that Sartre does not think available to us – that would merely defer the issue, since it can be put into doubt the same way the aims of an individual life can (ibid.: 16–17). What we need to do is recognize the intrinsic absurdity of our situation, our reliance on norms that are themselves ultimately unjustified.

What Nagel suggests then is that even if there is no ultimate justification for what we think and do, this does not rob us of all normative direction, requiring us to become heroic Sartrean creators of our existence. We continue to have a standpoint from which to think and act, but what is highlighted is the *finite* character of this standpoint, the "immanent, limited nature of an enterprise like a human life" (ibid.: 22). This finitude becomes apparent when we reflect on ourselves. Absorbed in our lives, we do not have a sense of the limitedness of what we do; this only becomes apparent when we stand back and reflect on the activities we are engaged in. When we "see ourselves from outside" or "transcend ourselves in thought," we are able to grasp the limits of our existence, the "contingency and specificity of our aims and pursuits" (ibid.: 14, 23).

Foucault: The History Behind the Self

Foucault similarly departs from the existentialist trajectory, though his account also goes beyond Nagel's in crucial ways. He shares the existentialist renunciation of religion and metaphysics as grounds for moral and social action, in his case particularly the human being as foundational self from which are to be deduced norms of thought and action. He also rejects the kind of rationality that accompanies this self, an "absolute" rationality that provides the standards for evaluating existing historical forms and practices (see Foucault 2000: 229–30; Smart 1985: 139). But he does not think that abandoning a foundational rational subject means the end of all normative justification. He rejects the "blackmail" that says either you are for a foundational rationality, or you fall into irrationality (Foucault 1997: 313; 1998: 441; 2000: 299, 328, 358). Instead, he insists, our practices don't exist without "a certain regime of rationality," forms of rationality which are not merely corrupted rationalizations or ideological mystifications, but play a necessary organizational role. An absolute rationality thus gives way to rationalities that have an instrumental role relative to practices, to multiple "forms of rationality [that] inscribe themselves in practices" (2000: 228, 230). These are specific rational schemas, enmeshed with practices, which provide calculated, reasoned prescriptions, rules, and procedures, serving to organize institutions, arrange spaces, and regulate behaviors. Emerging in the context of the management and administration of various parts of the social body, these "programmes of conduct" inform individual behavior, inducing rational, rule-governed, principled conduct in individuals (see Foucault 2000: 229–31; 1998: 450, 451; 1997: 317).

So Foucault, like Nagel, does not see the absence of ultimate grounds as depriving us of normative direction and guidance. We cannot exist except as determinate kinds of subject, formed, principled beings (Foucault 1997: 290; Patton 1989: 267). We always proceed in terms of a background of norms, values, a certain rationality that is nonetheless finite, contingent, and specific. But Foucault also goes beyond Nagel, for whom recognition of our finitude is only the negative recognition that beyond a certain point we cannot rationally justify the normative standards we rely on. Absent here is any historical context for that normative framework. Foucault fills this gap by pointing to a larger social and historical context in terms of which the emergence of our orienting norms, the conditions of possibility for subjectivity, can be understood. Indeed, we can say that the lack of justification beyond a certain point makes it possible for us to exist as rational subjects. If we had to provide complete justification for what we think and do, we would be condemned to an impossible task. To be able to function as agents, we need to rely on principles that are accepted without question, taken on faith, imposed from outside (even if we come to question them later). In Foucault's terms, we can only have an orienting framework because we are finite, limited in what we can justify, the beneficiary of external influences, the nurturing, training, and investments of others, the larger history that shapes us. Our finitude, then, has a positive significance in this context. By the same token, Foucault's historicizing reflection, his strategy of historical "decentering," has a positive role to play. Rather than effacing the self, history gives it a place to stand, its "historical a priori" (Foucault 1972: 128). In reflecting historically on ourselves, we apprehend the principles that we depend on in their historical emergence. These principles are still revealed to be non-necessary, unjustified, and contingent; but now, this is historical contingency.

As such, with the abandonment of a foundational self, the self itself as finite becomes the object of historical reflection. Hence Foucault's characterization of his genealogical approach as a form of history that dispenses with the subject, that can account for "the constitution of the subject, knowledges, domains of objects etc without having to make reference to a subject which is either transcendental in relation to the field of events, or runs in its empty sameness throughout the course of history" (2000: 118). It is precisely such a history that is excluded if we posit a foundational self, a further problem for the self so understood. Not only does it involve proposing, in the name of the need for justification, a foundation that is itself ungrounded. Since it excludes history, no account can be given of how this founding self might emerge. Hence also Foucault's questioning of the false historicization of the self, of history construed in Hegelian terms as the continuous, necessary unfolding of an underlying rational self that "runs in its empty sameness throughout the course of history." Not only does this foundational self remain problematically ahistorical in the last analysis; a history subordinated to it amounts to an unhistorical conception of history. Genuine historical reflection needs to get rid of the foundational self, to "evade metaphysics" rather than be "bent to a suprahistorical perspective" (Foucault 1998: 379).

The Self Behind History

Foucault's abandonment of ultimate grounds thus leads him not to an irrational Sartrean subjectivism, but to a finite rational subject, whose finitude is manifested in the limits to what we can rationally justify in our existence; or more positively, the self's character as historically situated and shaped. However, Foucault does not want to bring the "whole weight of history down on our shoulders" (2000: 458). To say we are historically formed is not to say that we are simply reducible to a function of history, passively shaped by forces that impose forms upon us. Indeed, if history were all-embracing in this way, we could not account for the emergence of these forms themselves. They would simply be reproduced in our practices. There would be nothing beyond those forms that could figure in any account of how they might arise or be transformed.

This is arguably the problem for Foucault's own historicizing account in its earlier archaeological form. Here the human being is decentered as foundational subject of knowledge, the conditions of knowledge being found in an anonymous system of discourse which governs the truth or falsity of statements uttered within it, in which human beings can assume various speaking positions. We are thus subject to a historically emergent discursive system that is itself unjustified, contingent. But the subject is also reduced to an element within this discursive field. There may be something "other," but this amounts to a "sublime alterity" (Thompson 1999: 197), as in the early treatment of madness as a radical escape from the constraints of reason. And while archaeology offers a non-Hegelian history in which there are shifts from one self-contained episteme to another, it can offer no explanation as to why these shifts occur. The shift from archaeology to the genealogical form of historical analysis involves not only moving from an exclusive concern with knowledge to consider also normative rules, or from a focus on discourse to one where discursive practices of organization and classification are seen as bound up with non-discursive practices of power. There is also a shift to a more dynamic picture in which the interplay of power and resistance makes it possible to account for the emergence and transformation of social forms. Now the subject is neither merely constructed by external circumstances, nor a sublime alterity. It enters into the historical process, both shaped by and also resisting prevailing forms. The self is now fundamentally involved in a reciprocal interplay with power, an interplay that is constitutive of history.

Here, to be wholly shaped by historical circumstances is equivalent to being in a state of domination. In this context, forms of conduct are entirely imparted to individuals by external forces, processes of training that shape bodily forces or capacities for action, turning bodies into certain kinds of subject, beings who conform in their behavior to particular norms. They are thereby rendered "docile," able to be strategically deployed in various ways (and to participate in the training and utilization of others). Certainly, in middle period works like *Discipline and Punish* and the first volume of

History of Sexuality, as Foucault himself recognizes, there is a focus on domination, disciplinary systems, and the subject as a product of power (see Foucault 1997: 177). Yet even here domination is not the primary state. Forces are always imposed on other forces, and there is always the possibility of resistance, of reversal. Foucault emphasizes the essentially relational nature of power, with resistance as indispensable to its operation, coextensive with it, its limit, underside, or counter-stroke. Hence the characterization of the social field as a "network of relations, constantly in tension, in activity," with "innumerable points of confrontation, focuses of instability" (1977: 26, 27). It is a multiplicity of mobile, reversible force-relations, of "opposing strategies," "offensives and counter-offensives," of forces in reciprocal interplay (1980: 61; 1979: 95).

It is true that here, the subject is viewed primarily in terms of its role as a product or instrument of social regulation, with resistance identified rather obscurely with the body (see e.g. Foucault 1979: 157). However, a striking feature of the later writings is that the subject also comes to be identified with resistance. It is now "the subject of action through which the real is transformed," and through such transformative revolt "subjectivity ... is brought into history" (Foucault 2000: 236, 452). So it not only perpetuates but also resists power and challenges what is currently legitimate, which is not merely to refuse the existing situation but to go beyond the limits it imposes, to create "new forms of life" (Foucault 1997: 164, 168). Hence also the importance of one's relation to oneself in the later writing. Resistance now involves not only challenging social regulation, but also breaking from oneself insofar as one is the product of subjectifying social regulation. The dimension of self-relation is present in the middle period works, but only as perpetuating domination (by internalizing the panoptic gaze, or embracing a constraining identity in the course of confession). Later, how we relate to ourselves also comes to play a key role in resistance, as the breaking from oneself at the heart of resistance to subjectifying regulation.

With the incorporation of resistance into the notion of the subject, Foucault can also speak of the "free subject," where freedom is the capacity not only to act but to behave differently, to resist. A key part of this is freedom in relation to oneself, the capacity to transgress imposed limits that constitute who we are, and engage in acts of self-creation, develop "new forms of subjectivity" (2000: 336). Here, "the relationships we have to have with ourselves are not ones of identity, rather they must be relationships of differentiation, of creation, of innovation (1997: 166). We have to "create ourselves as a work of art," in the sense of relating to ourselves and our lives not simply as given, but as able to be creatively formed and transformed (1997: 262; see also Oksala 2007: 98). The power relation itself is now formulated in terms of free subjects. The exercise of power is "a mode of action on the actions of others," in which "each subject tries to direct the other's conduct" (Foucault 2000: 341). Unlike violence exercised over a wholly passive other, in power relationships those over whom power is exercised must be maintained as free subjects, always capable of resisting, turning the tables, reversing the relationship (ibid.: 340, 342, 346; 1997: 167, 292). The power relation is now characterized as an "agonism," as "at the same time reciprocal incitation and struggle … a permanent provocation" (2000: 342). It is a "strategic game" between liberties, "in which some try to control the conduct of others, who in turn try to avoid allowing their conduct to be controlled or try to control the conduct of the others" (1997: 299).

Dialogue

In this way, although Foucault himself does not use the term, we arrive at a recognizably dialogical conception of social relations, of social relations as characterized by reciprocity – an interplay of forces, an agonistic relationship between subjects, a strategic game between liberties. On this basis, Foucault explicitly rejects any attempt to find a fundamental, determining factor underlying social developments: "[n]othing is fundamental … There are only reciprocal relations" (2000: 356). It is in terms of the reciprocal interplay of forces, constitutive of the social field, that forms of social organization can be accounted for, to the degree that this interplay is arrested and some forces are able to direct others in a relatively constant manner. Thus in the first volume of *The History of Sexuality*, force relations are said to "constitute their own organisation" (Foucault 1979: 92). Power "insofar as it is permanent, repetitious, inert and self-reproducing, is simply the overall effect that emerges from all these mobilities, the concatenation that rests on them and seeks in turn to arrest their movement" (ibid.: 93). Later, power is distinguished from domination in these terms. What characterizes power "is the fact that it is a strategic relation that has been stabilized through institutions … So the mobility in power relations is limited" (1997: 169). There is inequality but still some mobility and the possibility of influencing "the behaviour or non-behaviour of the other" (ibid.: 167). At the extreme, no longer a power relation, is domination, when an individual or group "succeed in blocking a field of power relations, immobilizing them and preventing any reversibility of movement by economic, political or military means," and relations become "blocked and frozen" (ibid.: 283, 285; see also ibid.: 292; 2000: 346–7).

Forms of social organization, including states of domination, are thus understood to be derivative in relation to the dialogue of forces. In this context individuals can be regarded as having an active role in the formation of social forms, without those forms being reducible to the dictates of sovereign agents. Social forms are not determined by an all-powerful agency, or the responsibility of any particular individual or group. They arise "anonymously" (Foucault 1979: 95), which is not to say that no agents are involved, that it is a mindless mechanical process, but that they emerge piecemeal through a collective historical dialogue, a series of encounters, struggles, offensives and counter-offensives, combats and transformations (see Foucault 1980: 61; 2000: 226–7). Equally, these social forms cannot be said to have been established through a rational process, which is not to say that they are irrational, but that they arise out of the larger interplay of forces. The multiple conflicts, debates, and negotiations between different groups give rise not to a rationally ordained order but to "functionally expedient and provisional forms of social organisation" (Olssen 2002: 496). These developments are not "absurd" in the sense of being incoherent and inexplicable, but intelligible in terms of "the intelligibility of struggles, of strategies and tactics," the "logic of opposed strategies" (Foucault 2000: 116; see also 1980: 61).

In turn, these social forms shape and sustain kinds of individual agency, without individuals being reduced to functions of impersonal structures. Relatively enduring forms of social order emerge, making various "personages," kinds of agency, possible (see Foucault 1980: 62). But these forms remain derivative, emerging out of the interplay of power and resistance; and they can always be changed through renewed resistance. Social forms and individuals are thus involved in an open-ended interplay, a dialogue, in which the forms that govern and condition individuals are continually being renegotiated and transformed by the individuals who rely on them. Forms of rationality are themselves elements in this dynamic. Insofar as they are bound up with the ordering of practices, playing an organizational and justificatory role therein, they also arise through this larger dialogue; and resistance to forms of life includes challenging the rationalities bound up with them (see Foucault 2000: 324–5). Thus Foucault is able to say that reason has a history, undergoing a series of transformations interwoven with changes in forms of practice, that establish what counts as rational in a particular context and time (see 1998: 442–3, 448–9, 450, 451). This is not to say that the forms of rationality are irrational, but that they "reside on a base of human practice and human history" (1998: 450), and can thus emerge and change.

The idea of dialogue here thus incorporates both aspects of Foucault's account – the emphasis on the self as historically formed, and the concern with freedom, the capacity to resist prevailing forms – in the dynamic interplay between ourselves and our circumstances. In this dynamic, resistance is never simply unconditioned freedom, nor is it simply negated by power. It remains tied to its social context, always relying on "the situation against which it struggles," yet there can be no power without resistance, and so resistance "comes first … in this dynamic" (1997: 168, 167). We cannot escape from power relations, and are inevitably influenced by our circumstances, but to be in a power relation means that there is always the possibility of resisting and changing our situation. More broadly, we may be products of a larger history, conditioned by historically emergent social forms; but resistance also enters into that history, participating in the dialogical interplay of forces out of which those forms emerge; so that, as Foucault puts it, it is only because of such resisting voices that we can be said to have a history at all (2000: 452). And resistance in the present may be a breaking from historically emergent social forms, but it also remains within history understood as the dialogical interplay of forces through which social forms also come to be transformed.

Dialogue so understood also brings together two kinds of finitude: the finitude of the self insofar as it is the product of external forces, of imposed forms, and the finitude of the forces that inform and determine it, in the face of its resistance to external determination. That is, we are situated, but insofar as we are more than the product of our circumstances, the social forms that define us are rendered finite in their turn. They emerge and come to be transformed through the dialogue between ourselves and our circumstances. In both cases, dialogue involves a movement to overcome finitude. Resistance aims to go beyond the forms that constrain it, to develop new forms of action; while power is the movement to overcome resistance, to delimit possibilities, and to impose a specific direction on forces. But in both cases finitude also has a necessary, positive role to play. On the one hand, our being finite, limited in what we can justify about our thought and action, means that it is possible for us to emerge, to be formed out of a larger history, and to acquire a normative standpoint that we could not acquire otherwise; and transformation is not a matter of unconditioned transcendence, escaping all constraints, but expanding the social space of possibilities for action. On the other hand, resistance, going beyond the limits of what is legitimate, challenging prevailing forms and their justifications, provides the necessary "outside" that makes it possible for these orienting forms to emerge and also to be transformed, through the ongoing historical interplay of power and resistance.

Social forms can be said to depend on resistance in the further sense that resistance imposes limits or constraints on the sorts of forms that can be imposed on the social body. Even if there is no higher rational justification or necessity for the particular social forms that happen to arise out of the interplay of forces (in terms of a foundational self or human nature), this does not mean that any form can be implemented, that the social world simply yields to whatever is envisaged. That would render social forms entirely arbitrary, and the emergence of any particular form unintelligible. In practice, organizing schemes have to be put to the test of reality, to establish how effectively elements of the social body can be organized in practice. Thus rational schemes, programs, ideals of complete social organization, may be envisaged, as in the eighteenth-century visions of a disciplined society or a perfectly functioning panoptic regime discussed in *Discipline and Punish*, but they are not effortlessly imposed on a passive populace. Rather, they confront and have to overcome resistance; and resistance continues to manifest itself in the face of power, requiring in turn the modification of programs and the development of new strategies if power is to maintain its sway. Resistance thus serves as the "reality principle" that power must conform to even as it seeks to overcome it.

Similarly, resistance depends on social constraints in the further sense that they impose limits on the sorts of transformation that are possible. That is, even if there is no higher justification or necessity for the forms of resistance and change pursued (once again in terms of a foundational self or human nature), not just any change can be brought about. That would make the forms of life generated, the particular changes brought about, entirely arbitrary and unintelligible. Rather, if freedom is to be more than an "empty dream," it has to be put to the "test of reality" (Foucault 1997: 316), to determine in practice what changes are possible. There are constraints on resistance precisely insofar as it does not lead effortlessly to the transformation of prevailing forms. It has to confront and overcome power; and power continues to affect us in that any changes resistance brings about can always be transformed in turn, calling for new forms of resistance (see Foucault 1980: 56–7; 1997: 166–7). This is the reality principle that resistance has to conform to even as it seeks to bring about change, the "real" that confronts the subject of action (Foucault 2000: 326); and the ongoing confrontation with forms of power means that resistance continually needs to modify itself and develop new strategies of its own if it is to be effective in bringing about change.

So, understood in this way, Foucault's renunciation of ultimate grounds, of the foundational subject, leads not to an arbitrary subjectivism but to a subject enmeshed in dialogue. Dialogue's fundamental character is reflected in the derivative character of social forms which emerge to the degree that dialogue is arrested. This amounts to an inversion of the foundationalist picture. Rather than the forms that structure our existence being provided by a timeless foundational subject, they are "historically a priori," arising out of dialogue. Nor, to characterize Foucault's non-Hegelian conception of history more fully, is this a dialogue secretly dominated by the foundational subject, a dialectical process moving necessarily toward the subject's self-realization. It is an open dialogue, not "programmed" in advance, or imbued with rational necessity, and the historical forms emerging from it are contingent and unjustified. For Foucault "'dialectic' is a way of evading the open and always hazardous reality of conflict by reducing it to a Hegelian skeleton" (2000: 116). But even if this interplay proceeds without an underlying foundational subject, rational necessity, or overarching rules, there are nonetheless constraints on the moves that can be made within it, arising from the dialogue situation itself. Power is constrained by resistance, and vice versa. It is because of this that historical dialogue, while not meaningful in terms of an overarching telos, is not absurd in the sense of being incoherent. It is intelligible, in terms of the pragmatic logic of strategy, of what works in practice (see Foucault 2000: 116).

Communion and Critique

It might nonetheless be argued that this dialogically interpreted Foucault falls short of being properly dialogical. Genuine dialogue requires communion or consensus, coming together, as well as difference. From this standpoint the problem for Foucault is that he emphasizes difference, conflict, and lacks any sense of a common ground, a horizon of shared values and practices, in which the resisting subject could be located. Hence also the issue raised by Coles, that though we may want to move away from subjugative practices, we cannot move away from some sense of shared practices and values. Resistance alone is not sufficient for a social order. There needs to be a way to belong to our present which is not merely that of getting free of it (Coles 1992: 93). At its strongest, this becomes the charge that Foucault lacks a genuine notion of intersubjectivity, offering merely encounters between competing, self-assertive atoms which can only relate to others by reducing them to instruments for the realization of their own purposes (see Thompson 1999: 198). This claim also informs criticism that Foucault has no basis for social critique, in the sense of an ideal of harmonious intersubjective existence.

This brings us back to Habermas, who might seem to offer a fuller notion of dialogue. Communion and consensus are very much to the fore in his account. He understands language to be fundamentally oriented toward reaching unforced, collective agreement about the proper norms to govern social life. These will be generalizable norms, that all who participate in the dialogue can agree upon, a shared value horizon that will have been established purely through the "force of better argument." Every time we speak, we "necessarily anticipate" this life of unlimited communication, of rational discussion free from power and coercion, of collective self-determination (see Habermas 1974: 314; 1983: 245). As McCarthy notes, Habermas can be read as transposing Kant's foundationalist ethics from solitary reflecting moral consciousness to a community of speaking subjects in dialogue (see McCarthy 1978: 325–6). Kant's principle of principles, the rational justification of moral norms in terms of their universalizability, becomes their validation in terms of rational consensus through collective dialogue. With this, Habermas can also be said to have fully articulated the idea implicit in Kant, that the proper exercise of freedom presupposes relatedness to intersubjectivity. Autonomous subjects are now constrained to embrace only those maxims that could be agreed to by all rational beings engaged in open dialogue.

Habermasian dialogue, then, emphasizes what is common, common procedures of argumentation required of those who participate, and agreed-upon norms toward which genuine discourse must move. By the same token, a frequent criticism of Habermas is that he neglects differences between individuals. Given the primary concern with what is common to all, it is difficult to incorporate that which locates and particularizes within discourse. Habermas, though not unconcerned with difference, tends to subordinate it to the universalizable. For example, he distances himself from Kant's view that moral reflection requires the exclusion of irredeemably particular desires and interests from consideration in order to establish the universal norms acceptable to all thinking beings. He insists that individual desires and interests cannot be excluded from dialogue about the proper ends of life, for it is precisely about them that agreement is sought. However, these can only be taken into account to the extent that they are common to all. The aim of dialogue is to come to a consensus as to which desires and interests can be generalized, and hence able to be the basis of universal norms of behavior (see McCarthy 1978: 325–8). There is no room here for particular perspectives reflecting particular desires and interests, or for ongoing conflicts between them.

At the same time, it is not clear that rejecting the idea of dialogue as a community of speaking subjects, collectively determining norms through rational consensus, necessarily leaves us with a multiplicity of atomized, competing individuals bent on subjugating one another, reducing one another to mere instruments for their purposes. As a characterization of Foucault's view of social relations, this is a reappearance of the idea that Foucault, in abandoning foundations, turns to heroic self-assertion; and once more, this is arguably closer to Sartre than Foucault. Sartre wants to situate his radically self-determining subject while also preserving its unconditioned freedom. As such, situatedness represents a pure threat to freedom, and the self is only situated insofar as it escapes its situation and reduces it to a function of its choices, determining its significance in the light of its freely chosen goals. This simultaneous turn toward and flight from situatedness extends to Sartre's treatment of relations with others. The self is also located in a world of others, but insofar as we encounter the other, it is purely as that which threatens to rob us of our freedom, to reduce us to an instrument of its goals; and to remain free we have to overcome the other's freedom, reducing it in turn to an instrument of our goals. Social relations become the endless war of competing selves, each seeking to pre-serve its freedom by subordinating the other.

Once again it is necessary to refer to the different path that Foucault takes, toward a self that is inherently relational, both situated and more than a product of its circumstances. Here situation is not simply a threat to the subject, and the self is not only that which escapes its circumstances. The self is necessarily dependent on a prior history, on social forms and those who perpetuate them, through which it acquires the norms it cannot provide for itself, and which enable it to function as an agent. In reproducing these norms through our actions, we also share them with others, and are part of a social order amounting to a community of shared norms and practices. Certainly, the middle period writings emphasize the role of subjugation in establishing communal identity. The identity of communities derives not from consensus or contract but from practices of subjugation (see Foucault 1977: 169; Simons 1995: 53, 56). But it remains the case that it is not domination but the interplay of power and resistance that is fundamental here. The subject is not in the first instance a mere product or instrument of power. While subjects are shaped by their circumstances, power relations only exist to the extent that the individual remains a subject in the further sense of being capable of resisting, affecting that which affects it. Only through resistance, and the interplay of power and resistance, are forms of community able to arise, and to continue to emerge.

So Foucault's account, while emphasizing resistance and struggle, remains dialogical in the sense of making reciprocal interplay central; and here, resistance is not simply opposed to community. We continue to depend on our community even as we resist subjugation and challenge its limits; and struggles to transgress communal forms are necessary for their emergence and transformation. The interplay of power and resistance, constitutive of the social field, is the forum in which prevailing communal forms are challenged, fought over, and come to be transformed. This is not the idealized Habermasian dialogue where we rise above the fray, putting out of play all factors except better argument in order to reflect on norms presupposed in ordinary life, determine proper norms and evaluate existing ones. Not only does the ideal community of rational speaking subjects seem remote from ordinary human interaction. As Hoy notes, this account makes critical evaluation of existing forms dependent on an ideal perspective – that which all ideal judges would agree to – that is itself empty and contextless (Hoy and McCarthy 1994: 268). In contrast, Foucault's dialogue remains part of ordinary interaction, as the encounters and struggles between situated perspectives, bound up with power and resistance, through which historically specific social forms emerge and change. Prevailing, taken-for-granted norms and patterns of action are called into question through the concrete encounter with that which resists, with different forms of thinking and ways of life. This dialogical encounter also provides the context in which Foucault's form of critique may be understood.

Here, lack of a transcendent ideal does not condemn us to conformity to existing circumstances. Resistance is inherent in the social field. Critique presupposes resistance, as an "instrument for those who fight," an indirect means of challenging social reality (Foucault 2000: 235–6). Insofar as the self not only resists but is also implicated in power and the curtailment of resistance (both internalizing power and imposing it on others), resistance can also take the indirect form of adopting a different, non-dominating attitude toward that which resists; with critical implications for forms of power we are implicated in. As such, critique can be construed as proceeding immanently, within the dialogical social field. As Hoy argues, what opens assertions or viewpoints to critical scrutiny are empirical encounters with conflicting evidence or someone who disagrees (Hoy and McCarthy 1994: 268). But also required here is that what disagrees is not simply denied, or read so as to confirm the original standpoint.[1] That would be to perpetuate domination. A different attitude is required, a non-dominating openness to that which is different, which in turn opens the prevailing standpoint to critical scrutiny. It can no longer simply be taken for granted, or accepted as the only possible way of thinking. Its universality or self-evidence is called into question. This does not amount to its denial but its problematization. It is revealed as a particular, finite viewpoint, which also means one can consider what costs there might be in thinking this way, what possibilities of living it might blind us to or keep us from (see Foucault 2000: 358).

Arguably, Foucault's critical-historical investigation, his genealogical inquiry, can be seen as an extended form of this critical attitude, and thus as similarly framed by the dialogical context. Here one apprehends prevailing forms of thought and life in the light not only of current forms of resistance, but of a whole history of encounters and struggles out of which present forms have emerged. This is not the kind of history that serves merely to confirm present ways of thinking, reading the past as a function of our present standpoint, progressing necessarily toward it. Rather, it is a critical "history of the present," a historical reflection that is open to that which stands outside a narrative of progress, calling attention to the ways schemes of social ordering have failed to achieve their intended results, looking to liberate the "divergence and marginal elements" in history (Foucault 1977: 31; 1998: 379). It thereby serves to establish a "historical memory of the struggles," to reveal the "connections, encounters, supports, blockages, plays of force, strategies and so on that at a given moment establish what subsequently counts as being self-evident, universal and necessary" (Foucault 1980: 86; 2000: 226–7). Once again, critique does not simply deny present forms of thinking. It is not a "gesture of rejection" but goes beyond the "inside–outside alternative" to be at the "frontiers" (Foucault 1997: 315). It throws forms of life that appear self-evident, universal, and necessary into relief as specific, finite forms of life which have emerged contingently out of a history of struggles.

Foucault contrasts this form of critique with Kant's foundationalist form, in a manner entirely intelligible given this dialogical interpretation. As noted, the dialogical account itself effectively inverts the foundationalist picture in that the forms structuring our existence are not universal forms grounded in a transcendental self, but emerge from "below," out of historical dialogue. And genealogical critique, which comprehends the historical dialogue out of which the present emerges, also represents an inversion. Whereas Kantian reflection looks to establish universal, necessary conditions for thought and action, reflection now asks: "in what is given to us as universal, necessary, obligatory, what place is occupied by whatever is singular, contingent, and the product of arbitrary constraints" (Foucault 1997: 315). Rather than grounding what we think and do, it points to their specificity, contingency, and finitude. It thereby serves to unsettle habitual, taken for granted ways of thinking and acting, to undermine their self-evidence, to call into question their apparent necessity (see Foucault 1988b: 265; 1997: 139, 315; 2000: 226, 456). They are rendered strange and unfamiliar, "absurd" in a specifically Foucauldian sense. It is not that we no longer have any justifications for what we do, but the framework that we rely on for justification is shown to have emerged out of a history that itself has no underlying necessity or foregone conclusion.

The dialogical account not only locates present forms as emerging historically out of the interplay of power and resistance, but also as subject to transformation through ongoing resistance and dialogue. This is mirrored in genealogical critique, where to apprehend the forms that define us as finite, historically emergent, contingent, is also to open the possibility that they might be different, and thus promote resistance and the continuation of historical dialogue. Again, Foucault presents critique as an inverted form of Kantian reflection, where the concern is to establish the limits we must renounce transgressing. Now, reflection separates out "from the contingency that has made us what we are, the possibility of no longer being, doing, thinking what we are, do or think" (Foucault 1997: 315–16). Critique "is at one and the same time the historical analysis of the limits imposed on us and an experiment with the possibility of going beyond them" (ibid.: 320). In this manner, critical reflection will "give new impetus to the undefined work of freedom" (ibid.: 316), the transformation of self and the social forms shaping it. It will open up "the space of freedom understood as a space of concrete freedom, that is, of possible transformation" (Foucault 1998: 449–50; see also 1988a: 11). This is the spirit that Foucault identifies as animating his own critical studies: a commitment to knowing how far it is possible to think differently, rather than legitimating what is already known (1985: 9).

Conclusion

On the basis of the preceding, we can see that this work of freedom, his effort to think differently, is far from an unrestricted Sartrean autonomy. In the absence of ultimate grounds, we emerge as finite beings who, beyond a certain point, cannot justify the norms governing us, a finitude that is not merely a lack, a deficiency, but points to our immersion in a larger dialogue. In this dialogue we are shaped historically, as we must be in order to acquire orienting norms, and, through resistance, we affect our circumstances in turn, as we must for there to be the historical dialogue through which the norms governing us emerge in the first place. Critical reflection in the light of resistance calls attention to the finitude of the forms that govern us, their ungroundedness and specificity, but again this is not merely a negative apprehension. It involves recognizing both that these forms have arisen historically, and that it is possible for them to be transformed; a recognition that assists forms of resistance and, more broadly, facilitates the larger dialogue.

Foucault certainly provides no ground rules for assessing alternative positions that emerge in this dialogue. However, the argument here is that, rather than Foucault's dialogical account failing to provide full accountability, it is the actual limits to rational accountability that open the way to the dialogical reading of Foucault. Historical dialogue is a process that exceeds what can be rationally determined by its participants. Frameworks of rational justification themselves emerge within it. In this dialogical context, critique can take the negative form of calling attention to the finitude of existing forms, but with positive consequences. It is motivated by a situation in which prevailing ways of doing things have become contested in practice, and serves to facilitate that contestation. It is not critique itself but the larger contestation it promotes that will determine what changes ultimately come about. Hence critique is an instrument for those who fight; its use "should be in processes of conflict and confrontation"; what is to be done has to be determined not by critics but by those who resist; and if reality is transformed it will be when all those involved have been through conflicts and confrontations, when critique has been "played out in the real" (see Foucault 1988b: 265; 2000: 235, 236).

So Foucault does not simply fail to provide ground rules for change; his not doing so is deliberate and is consistent with a dialogical reading. At the same time, he is not proposing unconditioned change. He insists that the aim of critique is not the complete overcoming of existing forms of life, liberation from all constraints, the wholesale transformation of contemporary culture (see 2000: 234; 1997: 316). It is, rather, the modification of the forms that shape one, the continuation of dialogue. And while dialogue is not itself a normative ideal that critique serves to realize, but is already constitutive of social reality, it nonetheless provides a *raison d'être* for critique. Critique finds justification as a means of facilitating ongoing dialogue in the face of domination, promoting the free and unimpeded interaction of competing viewpoints. More broadly, social relations conceived dialogically implicitly include what Simons calls a "regulative ideal" (1995: 86) for the assessment of political regimes, namely a society open enough to permit dialogue and the possibility of transformation. The ideal is not the overcoming of all constraints but the continuation of dialogue. As Foucault puts it, the important question is "not whether a culture without constraints is possible or even desirable but whether the system of constraints in which a society functions leaves individuals the ability to transform the system" (1997: 147–8). Here Foucault also sets himself against Habermas's ideal of an unlimited discourse. The problem for him is not one of trying to dissolve power in the "utopia of a perfectly transparent communication," but, rather, establishing the conditions "that will allow us to play these games of power with as little domination as possible" (1997: 298).

This regulative ideal amounts to a "principle of principles," not in the Kantian sense of a formula for determining moral norms in terms of their universalizability, or Habermas's criterion of rational consensus, but the vision of an open dialogue out of which norms can emerge and be transformed. This ideal also provides a sense in which some forms of social life are better than others. The measure of social progress is not how closely society approaches a higher, more perfect form, one governed by wholly rational norms, but the extent to which it moves away from dominative forms of life in which the possibilities of engaging in dialogue, of going beyond and modifying constraints, are limited. Foucault's "optimism" with regard to social progress relates to the prospects for such transgression and modification, and consists in the recognition that "[s]o many things can be changed, being fragile as they are, tied more to contingencies than to necessities, more to what is arbitrary than to what is rationally established, more to complex but transitory historical contingencies than to inevitable anthropological constants" (2000: 458).

To sum up, the argument here has been that Foucault does not turn from a foundational self to a subjective decisionism, in which one entirely creates one's own forms through radical choices, but to a normatively governed yet finite self, which both depends on and participates in a larger historical dialogue. This dialogue provides the conditions for the forms of life, the orienting norms that structure individual existence, the context for their emergence and transformation. Here, far from a dialogical account failing to provide rules for rationally motivated transformation, it is limits to accountability that open the way to a conception of ourselves as immersed in dialogue. Critical reflection no longer proceeds in the name of a higher rational self that provides ultimate grounds for forms of life, but calls attention to the limitedness, the finitude, of forms of life, and in so doing facilitates the larger dialogue. Understood in these terms, Foucault may be seen as contributing both to a philosophy of dialogue and to the possibility of dialogue in practice.

Note

1   An attitude echoed in Foucault's "polemicist," who, by construing the other merely as a threat, abolishes them from any possible dialogue, and insures the "triumph of the just cause he has been manifestly upholding from the beginning" (1997: 112).

References

Coles, R. (1992) *Self/Power/Other: Political Theory and Dialogical Ethics.* New York: Cornell University Press.

Dreyfus, H. and P. Rabinow (1986) "What is Maturity? Habermas and Foucault on 'What is Enlightenment.'" In D. Hoy, ed., *Foucault: A Critical Reader.* London: Blackwell.

Falzon, C. (1988) *Foucault and Social Dialogue.* London and New York: Routledge.

Foucault, M. (1970) *The Order of Things: An Archaeology of the Human Sciences,* trans. A. M. Sheridan Smith. New York: Pantheon; London: Tavistock.

Foucault, M. (1972) *The Archaeology of Knowledge,* trans. A. M. Sheridan Smith. New York: Pantheon.

Foucault, M. (1977) *Discipline and Punish: The Birth of the Prison*, trans. A. Sheridan. London: Allen Lane, Penguin.

Foucault, M. (1979) *The History of Sexuality*, vol. 1: *An Introduction*, trans. R. Hurley. London: Allen Lane, Penguin.

Foucault, M. (1980) *Power/Knowledge: Selected Interviews and Other Writings, (1972–1977)*, ed. C. Gordon. New York: Pantheon.

Foucault, M. (1985) *The History of Sexuality*, vol. 2: *The Use of Pleasure*, trans. R. Hurley. New York: Random House.

Foucault, M. (1988a) "Truth, Power, Self: An Interview with Michel Foucault." In L. H. Martin et al., eds., *Technologies of the Self: A Seminar with Michel Foucault.* Amherst, MA: University of Massachusetts Press.

Foucault, M. (1988b) "The Concern for Truth." In L. Kritzman, ed., *Michel Foucault, Politics, Philosophy, Culture: Interviews and Other Writings*, trans. A. Sheridan. London and New York: Routledge.

Foucault, M. (1997) *Essential Works of Foucault, 1945–1984*, vol. 1: *Ethics: Subjectivity and Truth*, ed. P. Rabinow. New York: The New Press.

Foucault, M. (1998) *Essential Works of Foucault, 1945–1984*, vol. 2: *Aesthetics, Method, and Epistemology*, ed. J. Faubion. New York: The New Press.

Foucault, M. (2000) *Essential Works of Foucault, 1945–1984*, vol. 3: *Power*, ed. C. Gordon. New York: The New Press.

Habermas, J. (1974) "Postscript." In *Knowledge and Human Interests*, 2nd edn., trans. J. Shapiro. London: Heinemann.

Habermas, J. (1983) *Philosophical-Political Profiles*, trans. F. Lawrence. Cambridge, MA: MIT Press.

Healy, P. (2005) *Rationality, Hermeneutics and Dialogue: Towards a Viable Postfoundationalist Account of Rationality*. Aldershot: Ashgate.

Hoy, D. and T. McCarthy (1994) *Critical Theory*. Oxford and Cambridge, MA: Blackwell.

Kelly, M. (1994) "Introduction." In *Critique and Power: Recasting the Foucault/Habermas Debate*. Oxford and Cambridge, MA: Blackwell.

Manser, A. (1966) *Sartre: A Philosophic Study*. London: Athlone Press.

McCarthy, T. (1978) *The Critical Theory of Jürgen Habermas*. Cambridge: Polity.

McCarthy, T. (1984) "Translator's Introduction." In Jürgen Habermas, *Reason and the Rationalization of Society*, vol. 1 of *The Theory of Communicative Action*, trans. T. McCarthy. Boston, MA: Beacon Press.

Nagel, T. (1979) "The Absurd." In *Mortal Questions*. Cambridge: Cambridge University Press.

Oksala, J. (2007) *How to Read Foucault*. London: Granta Books.

Olssen, M. (2002) "Michel Foucault as 'Thin' Communitarian: Difference, Community, Democracy." *Cultural Studies Critical Methodologies* 2 (4): 483–513.

Patton, P. (1989) "Taylor and Foucault on Power and Freedom." *Political Studies* 37: 260–76.

Sartre, J.-P. (1956) "Existentialism is a Humanism." In W. Kaufman, ed., *Existentialism from Dostoevsky to Sartre*, trans. W. Kaufmann. Cleveland, OH: World Pub. Co.

Sartre, J.-P. (1963) *Nausea*, trans. R. Baldick. Harmondsworth: Penguin.

Simons, J. (1995) *Foucault and the Political*. London and New York: Routledge.

Smart, B. (1985) *Michel Foucault*. Tavistock: Ellis Horwood.

Taylor, C. (1985) "What is Human Agency?" In *Philosophical Papers*, vol. 1. Cambridge: Cambridge University Press.

Thompson, S. (1999) "The Agony and the Ecstasy: Foucault, Habermas and the Problem of Recognition." In *Foucault contra Habermas: Recasting the Dialogue between Genealogy and Critical Theory*. London: Sage.

Wolin, R. (1986) "Foucault's Ethical Decisionism." *Telos* 67: 71–86.

Index

absence d'oeuvre 61, 75
absolute knowledge 22, 24–7
absolute truth 18
absolutization 72
abstraction 108
abstraction of nothingness 23
"Absurd" 224, 232
academic syllabus 29
accountability 223, 241
actualitas 64
actus purus 65
adaequato intellectus et rei 63
adolescence 84
aesthetic decisionism 222
agent-neutral criteria for autonomy 91
agonism 1, 10, 94, 231
alarm clocks 150–1
Alcoff, Linda 191
Aldrovandi, Ulisse 133
alètheia 64, 68
alienated soul 18
alms-giving 180
alterations 27–8, 30
Althusser, Louis 18, 118–19, 131
amazement 1
ambiguity 103, 105, 126, 134
ambivalence 132
American Declaration of
    Independence 216
American neo-liberalism 212

American Pragmatism 12, 143, 157
analytic of man 128–9, 132, 134
anarcho-Nietzschean theories 208
Anglo-American philosophy 11
anonymity 232
anthropological sleep 129
Anthropology (Kant) 123–4
anthropology 19, 21, 123, 133
anti-Cartesian conception of
    subject 109
anti-humanism 11, 78, 118–42
anti-identity politics 13
anti-Nietzschean theories 36
antiphilosophy 25–6
anxiety of influence 169
aphrodesia 198
Aphrodite 173
apodictic claims 132–3
aporia 120
appropriate chagrin 11
arbitrary constraints 26
arbitrary discourse 155
arbitrary subjectivism 223, 225
archaeological territory 148–9
Archaeology of Knowledge
    (Foucault) 3, 30, 36–7,
    43, 49, 143, 145, 152
"Archaeology and the Sciences"
    143, 147
argumentation 236

Aristotle 1–2, 64, 109, 113, 124
ars erotica 199
art of life 71
artifacts 159
ascesis 3
asceticism 48, 51, 215
askesis 199
assertoric 133
assujettissement (subjugation)138
assumed knowledge relationship 69
asymmetrical coercion 86
asymmetry 84
Augustinian confidence 139
austerity 108
authoritarianism 10, 95
authority 84
autonomy 27, 33, 78–85, 102, 119, 138,
    223–6, 241
  inhibiting influences 90
  post-conventional 83–4
  unconditioned 223–6

Bacon, Francis 1
Badiou, Alain 25
Barbin, Herculine 178, 181
Barre, Raymond 210
Bataille, Georges 29, 167–8
Baudelaire, Charles 2, 6, 26
beginning again 95
being gay 199
being knowledge 154
Being and Nothingness (Sartre)
    121, 224
Being and Time 19, 63, 148
"being-in-the-world" 148
Bergson, Henri 25, 27
Bersani, Leo 13, 187, 191–4
bi-directional interpretation 106
Birth of Biopolitics (Foucault) 14,
    204–5
Birth of the Prison (Foucault):
    see Discipline and Punish

Birth of Tragedy (Nietzsche) 44–5
blackmail 87, 227
Blanchot, Maurice 29, 118, 168
blindness 67
Blumenberg, Hans 139
bodily pleasures 173
Borges, Jorge Luis 30
brainwashing 90
Braudel, Ferdinand 118–19
breeding to autonomy 86
Brunschvicg, Léon 25
brute physical resistance 105
Buffon, Georges-Louis Leclerc 133
Butler, Judith 13, 84–5, 94, 187,
    191–4, 202

Camus, Albert 128
Canguilhem, Georges 169
capitalism 212
carceral apparatus 213
care for self 2, 70–1
"Care of the Self as a Practice of
    Freedom" (Foucault) 138
Cartesian moment 65, 73, 109, 199
Cartesianism 119
Cassian, John 154
causality 37
certain consciousness of
    criminality 181
chagrin 11
characterization of "man" 11
characterization of transcendental 130
charity 107
Chinese encyclopedia 30
Chomsky, Noam 155
Christianity 7, 18, 40, 65, 72–3, 200
Cicero 122
citizenship rights 217
classical experience of madness
    165–7, 181
classicism 74
cogito 73

Coles, Romand 235–6
collective rational discourse 14
Collège de France 4, 6–8, 18, 25, 61, 65,
    67, 70, 169–70, 176, 194
colonization 68, 82
coming to terms with Hegel 27
common awareness 110
communality 138
communion 235–41
community of action 179
complete history of morals 41
complexes of dispositional states 114
concealment 63–4
concepts of experience 165–9
conceptualization 110
concrete existence 125
concrete singularity 21
configuration of finitude 122
connaissance 12, 68, 73, 144–6, 151,
    153–4, 156, 171
Constant, Benjamin 217
constraints 26, 61, 91, 157–8
constructivist sense of truth 104–5
consumer capitalism 1
contemplative disinterest 152
contingent conditions for
    subjectivity 81, 87
continual free self-transformation 34
continuous recommencement 27
contradictions 20, 24, 31
conversion to self 71
Cooper, David 181
Copernican turn 123–4, 130, 132,
    135, 137
correlativity 138, 170
counter-conduct 212, 223
criminality 171, 181, 186
criterial sense of truth 104
critical history of thought 6
critical morality 208
critical ontology of self 6
critical reflexivity 85

critical theory 78–98
critique 6, 235–41
Critiques (Kant) 6, 65, 124, 127,
    130–2
cryptonormativism 79
cultural relativism 104
curiosity 1–3, 15
Cynics 6–8

dandyism 139
danger 188
Darwin, Charles 148
Dasein 23, 63–4, 75, 148
Davidson, Arnold 80, 191
Davidson, Donald 11, 99–117
    and Foucault 99–117
    on interpretation 106–8
    misperception 101–6
    proposal 108–15
de Chardin, Teilhard 128
de Gaulle, Charles 28
de Saussure, Ferdinand 155
de-subjectivation 169–70
Dean, Timothy 187
"death of man" 19, 118–42
decentering 228
decisionism 222
degenitalizing erotic intensity 192
Deleuze, Gilles 1, 5, 18, 27, 34,
    53, 189, 208
Delphi 68, 70
democratization of truth 67
demonstrative truth 67–8
Derrida, Jacques 18, 27, 74, 127
Descartes, René 25, 65, 70, 73–4,
    123–4, 146
descent 38–42
    vs. origin 38–42
desire 185–203
d'Estaing, Valéry Giscard 210
destining 63
Detienne, Marcel 68

Dewey, John 12, 111, 113, 157, 162, 166
diachronic development of thought 31
diagnosis of what we are 61
dialectic 21, 23–4, 28–30
dialogue 14, 222–45
  conception of social relations 231–5
  philosophy of 222–45
Diderot, Denis 148
dignity of man 128
Diogenes 8
Dionysian revival 61
disciplinary subjection 86
discipline 86
Discipline and Punish (Foucault) 9–10,
    31, 45, 67, 70, 81, 109, 177–8,
    190, 194, 229–30, 234
disclosedness 63
discourse 100–1
  of desire 185–203
  of sex-desire 188–90
discriminations 93
discursive practice 143, 146, 148–51
disentangling power from validity 83
displacement of humanist
    concepts 134
dispositif (apparatus) 172, 191
docility 229
  of domestic subjectivity 150
dogmatic doze 30
dominion 44
double impasse 135
doubling 11, 18
Dream of D'Alembert (Diderot) 148
Dreyfus, Hubert 60–1, 100, 102, 105,
    108–9, 143, 224
drugs 88
dumbness of reality 103
dynamism 209

École des Annales 118, 131
École Normale 4, 25
Edelman, Lee 187

effectiveness 158–9
effects of power 102
eidos 64
elitism 200
elusiveness 3
emancipatory force 136
embracing ethics of pleasure 185–203
empirical finitude 125–8, 133
empirical generalization 31
empirico-transcendental double 11,
    122–4, 128, 132, 134, 137
empty dream 234
endorsement of structural account of
    autonomy 92
energeia 64
English moralism 43, 50
enigmatic treasure of things 147
Enlightenment 6–7, 17, 26, 28, 78,
    86–8, 119–21
énoncé (statement) 143, 155–6, 207
entailment 129–30
entanglement of power and
    validity 78–98
  conclusion 93–5
  genetic fallacy 85–93
  subjection and autonomy 79–85
Entbergen 148
Entdecken 63
enunciative facts 37
epimeleia heautou ("care for self") 70
  see also care for self
Epimetheus 139
epistemē 30–2, 46, 122–3, 133–5, 139,
    147–8
epistemic determination 127–8, 134
epistemologization 149, 153–4, 158
equality of opportunity 207
Erfahrung 162
Erhard, Ludwig 218
Erlebnis 162
erotic intensity 192
erudition 39

escaping Hegel 25
Essential Works (Foucault) 60
essentialism 130, 139
eternal damnation 73
ethical self-cultivation 69
ethico-political intervention 88
ethics 79–81, 185–203
    of pleasure 185–203
ethnography 133
ethological ethics 50
etiology of homosexuality 196
evading metaphysics 228
événementielle ("eventful") human
    history 119
event-atomism 43
everyday experience 166, 169–70, 173
everyday speech acts 108
exact relations between Nietzsche and
    Foucault 56–8
excitement 8
exclusion 168
exegesis 50
exercise of power 66–7
existence of God 124
existentialism 4, 18, 20–1, 24–5, 28–9,
    33, 60, 118, 128, 224
experience 162–85
experiential sense of truth 104–5
explanation *see* introduction of
    meaning
extemporization 62
externalism 90–2

fabrication 174
factuality 105
Faith and Knowledge (Hegel) 21
fallacy of the genetic fallacy 85–93
Falzon, Christopher 14
Faust 22
feminist Foucauldianism 87–8
Fichte, Johann Gottlieb 27, 130
Finas, Lucette 52–4

finitude 122–5, 240
first pass at history of truth 65–9
Fontana, Alessandro 37
forgetting truth of being 63–4, 69, 73
formation of subject 109
Foucault/Habermas debate 78–9, 89
Foucault's use of pleasure 196–7
foundational subjectivity 146
foyers of experience 170–2
Franco-Prussian war 17, 44
Frankfurt School 7
Fraser, Nancy 81–2, 85–6, 88–93, 120
freedom 14, 19, 33, 58, 61, 81
Freemasonry 39
French Society of Philosophy 4
Freud, Sigmund 33, 83–4, 187, 192–3
Future of Human Nature
    (Habermas) 84

Gadamer, Hans-Georg 100, 162, 166
game of strategy 80
Garaudy, Roger 11, 120–3, 128
"gavagai" 110
gay activism 195–6
gay press 186
Gay Science 50
Gearhart, Suzanne 191
genealogy 3–6, 37–43, 56–8, 80, 88–94
    of ethics 3–6
Genealogy of Morals (Nietzsche) 38–41,
    43–5, 49–51
generality 84
Genesis 122
*Genesis and Structure of Hegel's
    Phenomenology of Spirit*
    (Hyppolite) 18–21, 23
genetic fallacy 41, 78, 85–93
German Federal Republic 218
German neo-liberalism 209–11, 219
Geschick 63
gesture of rejection 239
global skepticism 32

gnōthi seauton 70
"God is dead" 157
Goethe, Johann Wolfgang con
    22, 148
"golden age" 200
governance 125
government of individualization 189
governmental reason 205–8
governmentality 208–11, 215–19
   and legitimacy 215–19
   and the state 208–11
governmentalization 7, 55–6
grand narrative 31–2
gravitational pull of Greek
    city-state 1
Great Confinement 167
Greco-Roman ethics 69–75, 186,
    197–200
   sexuality 69–75, 173
grounding 146–7
Group for Information on Prisons 5
Guattari, Felix 189, 208
Gutting, Gary 8–9, 168–9, 181

Habermas, Jürgen 10, 14, 78–85, 119,
    136, 210, 222–3, 236–8
   contra Foucault 79–85
habit formation 111–12
habit-inculcating interpretative
    success 114
habits 111
Hacking, Ian 143–4
Hadot, Pierre 199
Halperin, David 189
Han, Béatrice 30–3, 172–3
happenstance 109
Healy, Paul 222–3
Hegel, Georg Wilhelm Friedrich 4,
    7–9, 17–35, 119, 122, 131, 146,
    228–9, 235
   and Foucault 17–35
Hegelian history 119

Heidegger, Martin 5, 10, 18–19,
    30, 36, 48, 60–77, 118–42, 148
   and Foucault 60–77
   Foucault and history of truth: first
     pass 65–9
   Foucault and history of truth:
     second pass 69–75
   and history of truth 62–5
Hellenistic understandings 201
Herkunft 38–9
hermeneutics 37, 49–51, 60, 70, 73, 129
Hermeneutics of the Subject
    (Foucault) 70
heterosexist understanding 187
heterosexuality 195
Heyes, Cressida 87–8
hieroglyphic script of man's moral
    past 40
histoire sérielle 131
historical change 38
historical facts 24
historical materialism 131
historicity of experience 175, 180
historiography 80
history 42–8, 226–31
   behind self 226–8
   self behind 228–31
   vs. politics 42–8
history of being 69
History of Madness (Foucault) 4, 12,
    30–1, 60, 149, 167–71, 181
history of morals 40–1
History of Sexuality (Foucault) 2, 5–7,
    10, 12–13, 32, 40, 45, 48, 52, 56,
    81, 109, 169–70, 173–4, 177,
    186–92, 197, 230–1
history of subjectivity 136
history in traditional sense 42
history of truth 60–77
   and Foucault: first pass 65–9
   and Foucault: second pass 69–75
   and Heidegger 62–5

holistic description of the world 104
homo oeconomicus 219
homosexuality 186–7, 189, 195–9
Honneth, Alex 81–2
Hoy, David Couzens 238–40
human capital 208
human consciousness 24
humanism 11, 23, 33, 118–42
humanitates 122
Husserl, Edmund 19, 70, 119,
    127, 130, 146
hybrid European 47
hypothesis-mongering 39
Hyppolite, Jean 8, 18–27

*Idea for a History from a Cosmopolitan
    Point of View* (Kant) 131
ideal point 137
idealism 17–18, 20, 101, 105
identity politics 187
idiosyncratic success 107
ignorance 67
illusion of substantial unity 112
immorality 186
individualistic subjectivism 14
individuation 80, 83, 85–6
ineffability 21–2, 30
infinite understanding 125
insidious ruse of power 94
intellectual hygiene 100
intellectual intuition 126
intellectual panorama 28
intellectual synchronicity 111
intelligibility of struggle 232
intent 113–15
internalism 90–2
internalization 83
interpretation 48–56, 99–117
    Davidson on 106–8
interpretive inclinations 110
intersubjective accountability 223, 236
intra-familial relations 53–4

intrinsic value 121
introduction of meaning 51
introduction to Foucault's
    philosophy 1–16
    philosophical curiosity 1–3
    philosophical trajectory 3–8
    reading Foucault's
        philosophy 8–15
intuitus originarius 125
irrationalist leaps 222, 225, 227
irrealism 101–2, 105
irreducible anteriority 126–7
irreductibility of thought 175–6
irrepressible dynamism 209
isolating mechanisms of causality 37

Jacobi, Carl Gustav Jacob 21
James, William 12, 18, 157
Joyce, James 162
Judeo-Christian morality 44

kairos 6
Kant, Immanuel 4–7, 9–10, 17, 26, 30,
    33, 65, 73–4, 87, 92, 121–5,
    128–30, 222–3, 240
Keynesianism 209
Kierkegaard, Søren 17, 27
"know yourself" 70, 199
knowledge-practices 151
"knowledge-that" 151
Koyré, Alexandre 19

"La verité et les formes juridiques"
    (Foucault) 137
Lacan, Jacques 118, 193
Lachelier, Jules 17
Laing, R.D. 181
Las Meninas 99–100
law-making 54
Lawler, Leonard 24–5
LBGT groups *see* lesbian, bisexual, gay,
    transsexual groups

Le Malheur de conscience dans la philosophie de Hegel (Wahl) 17
le vécu 168–70, 173, 178
legitimacy 204, 215–19
    of the state 218
lesbian, bisexual, gay, transsexual groups 187
lèthe 64
Letter on Humanism (Heidegger) 118
lettres de cachet 178
Lévi-Strauss, Claude 118–19
Levinas, Emmanuel 19
liberal governmentality 204–21
Lichtung 63
life-affirming forces 94
lifeworld 81–2
lightning flash of infinite understanding 125
limit-experiences 29–30, 105, 165–7
linguistic idealism 101–2, 105, 108
lived experience 12, 29, 168–9, 178
living body 2
locus of dissociated self 112
locus of truth 65
Logic and Existence (Hyppolite) 20, 25
Logos 23–4
long-term nonintentional capacity 113
looking otherwise 2
lost knowledge 154

McWhorter, Ladelle 87–8
madness 4, 12, 30–1, 61
malaise 178
malice 44
Malleus Maleficarum 144, 154
Marcel, Gabriel 18
marketization 212
Marshall, Thomas Humphrey 217
Marx, Karl 7, 27, 31–2, 120–2, 131, 208
masquerade 46
master race 44
matrix of experience 169–74

Mead, Margaret 83
mechanisms of causality 37
mediation 21–2
medicalization 54
medicine of madness 149
medievalism 73
Meditations (Descartes) 65, 74
megalomania 45
Mental Illness and Psychology (Foucault) 60
"mere things" 121
Merleau-Ponty, Maurice 28
metaphysical error 75
metaphysical mystery 152
metaphysical supposition 158
metaphysics 65, 226–8
    renunciation of 226–7
micro-physics of power 32
Mirandola, Pico Della 122, 139
misperception 101–6
modern regime of sexuality 198
modern sexuality 3
modernity 26, 62, 72–4, 79–81, 90–1
modes of existence 171
Mont Pélérin Society 211
Montaigne, Michel de 122
moral consciousness 236
morality 38–40
morals 38–9
muteness 159
mysticism 215

Nagel, Thomas 225–7
National Socialism 209
natural language 23
nature of power 32
Nausea (Sartre) 224
Nazism 28–9, 218
nefarious consequences 128
nefarious nature of autonomous subjectivity 86
Nehamas, Alexander 104

neo-Kantianism 17, 153–5
neo-liberal governmentality 204–21
new forms of life 230
new genealogy of morals 37
new valuations 42
"Nice Derangement of
        Epitaphs" 100, 106
Nicomachean Ethics (Aristotle) 109
Nietzsche, Friedrich 1, 5, 7, 9, 29,
        36–59, 65–8, 87, 93, 104, 131, 143,
        146, 151–3, 157, 165–8, 196, 222–4
    conclusion 56–8
    interpretation 48–56
    origin vs. descent 38–42
    politics vs. history 42–8
"Nietzsche, Genealogy, History" 9,
        37–8, 42–8, 51
nihilism 78, 133, 157
"nobody is perfect" 4
non-discursive practice 148–51
non-forgetting 68
non-metaphysical content 136
nonhumanism 131
nonintentional capacity 113–14
nonlinguistic brutality 103, 105
normalization 13–14, 170, 172, 191
normative political philosophy 14,
        204–21
    governmental and public
        reason 205–8
    governmentality and
        legitimacy 215–19
    governmentality and state 208–11
    liberal and neo-liberal
        governmentality 211–15
not-knowledge 154
nothingness 23
notion of sex 188
nuclear family 195

objectivity 137, 173, 180–1
obstructive skepticism 107

Ockham 139
Oedipal frame 187, 190, 195
Oedipus Rex (Sophocles) 66–7
omega of knowledge 130
"On Truth and Lies in a Nonmoral
        Sense" 40
"On Use and Abuse of History" 43–4
ontology 6, 19, 24, 62, 71, 75, 112–14,
        148–50
optimism 44, 242
oracle 68
Oratio (Mirandola) 139
Order of Things (Foucault) 6, 11–12,
        28–31, 33, 37, 45–6, 74, 99,
        121–3, 128–33, 168
Ordo 211
origin 38–42
    of morality 38
    vs. descent 38–42
origin of morality 38
oscillation 179
"other" 229, 234
"outside" 234
overarching telos 235
overcoming finitude 233

pairing of sentences 105
panatragicism 19
panopticized society 86, 230
paralysis 178
parrhesia 7–8
partial history of morals 40
passing theories 106–7, 111, 113
pathological effects 82
Patton, Paul 14
pearls in Babylon 146
peril of anthropology 132
permanent provocation 231
perspectivist sense of truth 104–5, 186
perversity 192, 194, 212
phenomenology 4, 19, 23–5,
        28–9, 46, 119, 127, 168–9, 173

philosopher *malgré lui* 5
philosophical curiosity 1–3, 15
Philosophical Discourse of Modernity
(Habermas) 79, 81, 93
philosophical intensity 165
philosophical militancy 8
philosophical trajectory 3–8
philosophy of dialogue 14, 222–45
communion and critique 235–41
conclusion 241–3
dialogue 231–5
history behind the self 226–8
Sartre and unconditioned
autonomy 223–6
self behind history 228–31
Pico Della Mirandola, Giovanni
122, 139
plasticity of human self-creation 138
Plato 6–7, 33, 64–7, 70–1, 73,
75, 145, 157–8
Platonic–Christian assumptions 157
pleasure 190–7
Foucault's use of 196–7
and power 190–1
reading Foucault on 191–6
pleasure of analysis 191
plebeian heroes 67
pluralistic society 206
political actuality 210
Political Liberalism (Rawls) 207
political sovereignty 204
politicization 54
politics 42–8
vs. history 42–8
politics of transformation 13
polymorphous perversity 194
Portrait of the Artist as a Young Man
(Joyce) 162
positivity 49, 125–6, 130, 149
possibilities of use 146
post-archaeology 11
post-conventional autonomy 83–4, 89

post-Nietzschean moment 48
postmodern Pragmatism 12, 157–8
postwar enthusiasm for
existentialism 118
power 78–98, 190–1
entanglement with validity 78–98
as game of strategy 80–1
and pleasure 190–1
power relations 52–5, 80, 180
power-produced truth 103–4
Power/Knowledge (Foucault) 152, 154
power–knowledge regimes 81
practice-inculcated nonintentional
capacity 113–14
pragmatism 143
pre-ontological understanding of the
world 63
pre-Stonewall sensibilities 19
presentism 79–81
prestigious discourse 155
primitivity 127
primordial lack 188
principle of charity 107
prior theories 106–7, 111, 113
prison of the body 190
privacy 163–4
problematization 7, 87, 138, 176–9
progressivism 119
proposal 108–15
provocative experience 105
psyche 84–5, 193–4
psychiatry 60, 178
Psychic Life of Power (Butler) 193
psychoanalysis 1, 185, 187–90, 195, 202
psychosexual development 189
public political culture 211
public reason 204–21
Putnam, Hilary 157–8

quasi-empirical conception of public
reason 206
quasi-transcendental finitude 127, 135

queer theory 13, 185–203
  discourse of sex-desire 188–90
  Foucault's use of pleasure 196–7
  introduction 185–8
  power and pleasures 190–1
  reading Foucault on pleasures 191–6
  turn to Ancient Greco-Roman ethics 197–200
  why embrace ethics of pleasures? 200–2
questioning the taken-for-granted 4
Quine, W. V. O. 110

Rabelais, François 122
Rabinow, Paul 100, 102, 105, 108–9, 143, 224
radical translation 109–10, 112
rapprochement 11, 136, 139
rationalism 122–3, 204, 226–8, 234
Rawls, John 14, 119, 205–8, 210–11, 217–18, 220
re-elaboration of theory of power 52
re-making experience 179–82
reactivation 131
reading Foucault on pleasures 191–6
reading Foucault's philosophy 8–15
real history of morals 39
realism 102, 107, 209
reality of experience 162–3
reciprocity 231
reconciliation 195
reconstruction 132
redeploying pleasure 190
Reé, Paul 43–4, 50
reflexivity 90
Reformation 7
regime of truth 101
regulative ideal 242
reign of man 130
reinvention of self 224
relation of entailment 129–30

relativism 79, 101–2
relativization of truth 102
Renaissance 122, 139, 165
renunciation of religion 226–7
repetition 27
representation 66, 158
repressive hypothesis 191
reproblematization 177, 179, 181
reproduction of life 80
resemblance of things 122
resistance 56, 105, 194, 230, 233–5, 238–9, 241
responsibility 39
rethinking experience 162–84
  matrix of experience 169–74
  re-making experience 179–82
  two concepts of experience 165–9
  work of thought 175–9
return of language 134
return of morality 36
return of the subject 137
"Risks of Security" (Foucault) 214
ritual of discourse 150
ritualized act 66–7
Rivière, Pierre 178, 181
rootedness 87
Rorty, Richard 103, 105, 143, 157–8
Roussel, Raymond 178, 216
rules 155–6
rupture 66–7

sadomasochism 88, 192
salvation 73
sapere aude 7
Sartre, Jean-Paul 11, 14, 18–19, 28, 33, 120–3, 128–33, 146, 223–8, 237
  subjectivism 14
savoir 12, 144–6, 151, 153–4, 156, 171
Sawicki, Jana 13
scientia sexualis 189, 191, 199
scientific domain 148–9
scientific rationalism 44

scientific-representational truth 68
Searle, John 99–100, 103, 108, 112–14
second pass at history of truth 69–75
self behind history 228–31
self-assertion 139, 224
self-beratement 189
self-consciousness 20, 23–4, 27
self-creation 12, 120, 138–9, 199,
    222–3, 230
self-cultivation 69, 71
self-deprecation 4
self-disciplining practices 201
self-dissolution 192
self-justification 224–5
self-knowledge 18, 21, 70–5, 153
self-mastery 71, 199
self-negation 19
self-reflective knowledge 75
self-representation 65
self-reproduction 231
self-sufficient Kantian subject 223
self-transformation 9, 34, 55, 87, 188
Sellars, Wilfrid 103
Senellart, Michel 212
sens 133
sensation 21, 167
senses of truth 104–5
sensibility 127, 167–8
serious speech 143–4
sex-desire 188–90
sexism 200
sexual normalization 186
sexuality 69–75, 165, 173, 202
    as experience 165
    as political apparatus 52
Shakespearian tragedies 19
sharpened sense of reality 2
significations 29
silent philosophical laughter 129
"simply Nietzschean" 36–59
singularity 21–2, 27, 112, 170
Sisyphean philosophy 27

situatedness 237
skepticism 18, 20, 22–3, 32, 49, 107–10,
    123, 139, 158, 192
slave-morality 41, 44, 51
SM *see* sadomasochism
social norms 180
socialization 80, 83–5, 89, 93, 112
Society Must be Defended
    (Foucault) 45
Society, Territory, Population
    (Foucault) 204
Socrates 1, 7–8, 44, 64, 66, 71
sodomy 189
solipsism 136
sophistication 7
Sophocles 66–7
souci de soi 2
    see also care of self
space of reasons 84
speaker utterances 110
specific conditions of possibility for
    subjectivity 81, 87
specificity 6, 240
speech activity 99
speech transaction 106–8
Spinoza, Baruch 1
spirit of seriousness 225
spirit of the times 31
state and governmentality 208–11
state phobia 208–9
state-based interpretative
    dispositions 114
statistics 153
Stoics 6–8
strategic action 82
stratification of supervenient
    interpretations 56
structuralism 4, 102, 118, 134, 155
subject formation 112–13
"Subject and Power" (Foucault)
    55, 212
subjection 10–11, 79–86, 95

subjectivism 14, 223, 228
subjectivity 61–2, 65–6, 70, 73, 81, 86, 114, 120, 129–30, 136–8, 169–74, 181, 230, 236
"Subjectivity and Truth" (Foucault) 70
subjugated knowledge 94, 154
subjugation 138, 237–8
sublation 22
sublimation 194
sublime alterity 229
subordination 85
substance 71, 148–9
subsumption of bodies 80
subversion 193, 195
supervenience 56
supremacy 71
surface of history 134
surging from negation 121
surreptitious appropriation of rules 49
synoptic form of knowledge 123
synthesis 22, 27
synthesizing the manifold 126
systematically distorted communication 82–3

taken-for-granted norms 238
techné 61, 72, 145
techné tou biou 71–2
technologies of self 71, 80
ten commandments 41
test of reality 234–5
testing of the limit 167
thaumazdein 1
the taken-for-granted 4
theoretical authoritarianism 10, 95
Theory of Communicative Action (Habermas) 81–2
theory of knowledge 143–61
theory of systems 28
there-being 63
    see also Dasein
thought 175–9

"Thought of the Outside" (Foucault) 61
Thousand Plateaus 208
totality 27, 148
    of relations 148
traffic rules 54–5
Träger 119
trajectories 3–8, 48
transcendence 94, 133, 233–4
    of the ego 133
    unconditioned 233–4
"Transcendental Aesthetic" (Foucault) 127
transcendental apperception 124
transcendental consciousness 46
transcendental ego 33
transcendental finitude 125–7, 130–4
transformation 13, 55, 162, 166, 169–70, 181, 192, 223, 233–4, 240–3
transgression 165, 167, 202, 240
Trombadori, Duccio 28
true life 8
truth of being 60, 63
truth is currency 101
truth of man 130
truth-candidacy 144, 154, 156
truth-events 68
truth-games 70
truth-making 106
truth-telling 7, 88–9
truth-value 144, 152, 154–5
truthfulness 153
Tully, James 79
turn to Ancient Greco-Roman ethics 197–200
two concepts of experience 165–9

ubiquity of power relations 52
unavoidable seriousness 225
unbroken intelligibility 28
unconcealment 63–4

unconditioned autonomy 223–6
unconditioned transcendence 233–4
undefined work of freedom 222
unhappy consciousness 18–20, 25, 28
universal norms 236–7
universal structures 176
unrealization 47
unreasonableness 79
unrestricted Sartrean autonomy 241–3
Untimely Meditations (Nietzsche) 43
Ursprung 38–9
use of pleasure 70, 196–7
Use of Pleasure (Foucault) 70, 188
user expectation 106
utilitarian ethics 50, 217
utopia 242

validity 78–98
    basis of speech 82–3
    to power 93–4
valorization 2
Velasquez 99–100
Venice and the United Provinces 218
veritable culture of self 72
Vers le concret (Wahl) 18
very grave fault 137

vice 2
vicissitudes of human history 27
violence 38, 49, 138
voluntary inservitude 7

Wagner, Richard 44
Wahl, Jean 17–20
Warner, Michael 176
Weber, Max 152, 154
"What is Enlightenment?"
        (Foucault) 6, 17, 26
Whitebook, Joel 191
Whitehead, Alfred North 18
why embrace ethics of pleasure? 200–2
"Will to Know" (Foucault) 5
Will to Power (Nietzsche) 45
will-to-power 38, 57
wirkliche Historie 42–3
wisdom 152
witchcraft 144
wonder 1–2
work of thought 175–9
World War II 17, 28, 174, 214
"Wow!" effect 53

zero degree 167

Printed and bound by CPI Group (UK) Ltd, Croydon, CR0 4YY

07/07/2026

14916221-0001